Mary Sharp Smith
(Mrs. Philip Smith)
233 Saegler Blvd
May 7, 1973   Abilene
                        Tex -

David Wade's Magic Kitchen

I dedicate
this book
to my
beautiful
Becky.
She may
not be
the most
outstanding
cook but
she is,
indeed, the
world's most
wonderful
wife.

Introduction

I have been one of the privileged few to actually visit with David Wade in his Magic Kitchen. He may not be able to fry chicken or make gravy as well as I can, but believe the colonel, all of his magic recipes are tongue-licking good.

One of my interests is collecting cookbooks from all over the world and there is a special place in my library for all of David Wade's publications. I have known David for many years and have appeared with him on television from New York to San Francisco. He is a most personable, delightful individual to know but when he enters a kitchen, it is like Toscanini conducting a great symphony orchestra. I thoroughly recommend this new cookbook, David Wade's Magic Kitchen, to all my friends and, using the slogan that David is so widely known by, good living and bon appetit'.

Colonel Harland Sanders

Table of Contents

Recipes
From Television Shows

This section has many of the most popular recipes presented on "The Gourmet". Mr. Wade's wide-spread reputation in the food field has been enhanced by his television program even though he is involved in many other phases of the food industry.

Vegetables

Perhaps the most underrated and unplanned part of any menu is the vegetable course. This section provides imaginative recipes which will brighten the taste buds and create new appreciation for our important but usually forgotten vegetables. Do not overcook them as they will lose much of their nutritional value as well as flavor and color.

Asparagus Tulips

2 pounds fresh asparagus

1/2 cup salad oil

2 tablespoons lemon juice

1 teaspoon salt

1 teaspoon minced fresh onion

1/8 teaspoon pepper

6 hard-cooked eggs

Paprika (optional)

Cook asparagus in covered saucepan in small amount boiling, salted water over low heat until just tender. Drain and place in pie pan. Cool. Combine salad oil, lemon juice, salt, minced onion and pepper and pour over asparagus. Cover and chill at least 2 hours. Cut hard-cooked eggs in half, crosswise. Remove yolks and prepare for deviled eggs according to favorite recipe. Fill whites with yolk mixture using pastry tube. Sprinkle filling with paprika, if desired.

Just before serving, place asparagus on large platter to form stems of bouquet. Arrange egg halves at top of asparagus stalks to form blossoms.

Makes 4 to 6 servings.

Artichoke Parmesan Custard

2 packages (9 ozs. each) frozen artichoke hearts

1/2 cup canned tomatoes, drained

1 teaspoon salt

1/4 teaspoon pepper

1/4 teaspoon garlic salt

2 teaspoons chopped parsley

1/2 cup grated Parmesan cheese

3/4 cup water

1/4 cup olive oil

6 eggs

Place artichoke hearts on bottom of greased 2-quart casserole. Coarsely chop tomatoes and spread over artichokes, then sprinkle with salt, pepper, garlic salt, parsley and grated Parmesan cheese. Add water and olive oil, cover, and bake in moderate oven (350 degrees) 1 hour or until artichokes are tender. Remove cover. Beat eggs until light and fluffy and pour over artichokes. Continue baking, uncovered, 15 to 20 minutes or until eggs are set. Makes 8 servings.

Belgian Smothered Potatoes

6 large potatoes

1/2 cup butter

3 tablespoons dry white wine

1 teaspoon onion powder

3/4 teaspoon salt

1/4 teaspoon coarse ground black pepper

1 tablespoon freeze-dried chives

Peel and quarter potatoes. In a heavy skillet melt butter. Add potatoes and remaining ingredients except chives. Cover tightly. Cook over low heat for 45 minutes; remove cover; add chives. If any cooking liquid remains, turn heat high so that moisture evaporates.

Makes 6 servngs.

Broccoli and Rice Casserole

3 tablespoons butter or margarine

1/4 cup chopped green pepper

1/4 cup chopped onion

1/2 cup chopped celery

2 cups cooked rice

2 packages frozen chopped broccoli, cooked

1 can (10 1/2 ozs.) condensed cream of chicken soup

1/2 cup milk

1 jar (8 ozs.) pasteurized process cheese

Heat butter or margarine in skillet over medium heat, add chopped green pepper, onion and celery and saute. Mix sauteed vegetables with cooked rice and cooked broccoli in 2-quart casserole.

Mix cream of chicken soup and milk together and pour over above mixture. Spread pasteurized process cheese over top. Bake in moderate oven (350 degrees) for 30 to 40 minutes.

Makes 6 servings.

Note: If desired, cubed cooked ham or chicken may be added to rice-broccoli mixture.

Broccoli Bouquet

1 bunch fresh broccoli (about 1 1/2 lbs.)

2 medium tomatoes

1/2 teaspoon salt

1/4 teaspoon sugar

1/8 teaspoon pepper

2 tablespoons melted butter or margarine

Cook broccoli in covered saucepan in small amount boiling, salted water over low heat until just tender. Remove stem ends from tomatoes and cut each tomato into 6 wedges. Sprinkle with salt, sugar and pepper. Saute tomato wedges over medium heat in melted butter or margarine for 3 minutes. Arrange drained broccoli on 12-inch round platter to resemble "bouquet." Place tomato wedges around base of broccoli. Pour tomato drippings over broccoli.

Makes approximately 4 servings.

Cabbage A La Bretonne

2 cups beef stock

1 medium head cabbage, cut into 8 wedges

2 eggs, well beaten

3/4 cup light cream

1/2 teaspoon salt

Freshly ground pepper

Nutmeg

3 tablespoons olive oil

3 tablespoons tarragon vinegar

2 teaspoons sugar

Paprika

Place beef stock and cabbage wedges in saucepan and cook over low heat until cabbage is tender. Drain and keep warm. Mix beaten eggs, light cream, salt, freshly ground pepper and nutmeg to taste together in mixing bowl.

Bring olive oil, tarragon vinegar and sugar to boil in saucepan over low heat. Add this mixture to egg mixture, stirring. Return to saucepan and cook over very low heat until thickened, stirring constantly. Remove core from cabbage and place in warm bowl. Pour sauce over cabbage. Sprinkle with paprika. Let stand few minutes before serving.

Makes 4 servings.

Cauliflower With Cheese Sauce

1 large head cauliflower, separated into flowerlets

3 tablespoons butter or margarine

1 medium onion, chopped

1 small green pepper, seeded and chopped

1 can (2 ozs.) mushroom stems and pieces

1 cup shredded sharp Cheddar cheese

2 cans (10 1/2 ozs. each) white sauce

2 tablespoons toasted sesame seeds

Cook cauliflower in covered saucepan in small amount boiling salted water 10 minutes or until barely tender. Melt butter or margarine in skillet over medium heat and saute onion, green pepper and mushroom pieces until onion is clear.

Place in alternate layers in greased 2-quart casserole, drained, cooked cauliflower, sauteed vegetables, shredded Cheddar cheese and white sauce. Sprinkle with toasted sesame seeds and bake in moderate oven (350 degrees) 30 minutes or until bubbly.

Makes 8 servings.

Celery Oriental

1/4 cup butter or margarine

4 cups sliced celery, 1/2-inch thick

1/3 cup soy sauce

1 teaspoon sugar

1/4 teaspoon ground ginger

1/8 teaspoon pepper

Salt to taste

Melt butter or margarine in saucepan over medium heat. Add sliced celery and stir while cooking 3 to 4 minutes. Add soy sauce, sugar, ground ginger and pepper. Cook 2 minutes, stirring. Add salt to taste.

Makes 6 servings.

Cheese Puffed Potato Casserole

4 egg yolks

4 cups well-seasoned mashed potatoes

1 cup shredded sharp Cheddar cheese

4 teaspoons finely chopped onion

4 teaspoons finely chopped green pepper

1 teaspoon celery salt

1 teaspoon David Wade Worcestershire Powder

Salt and pepper to taste

4 egg whites

Paprika

The day before serving beat together egg yolks, and mashed potatoes until well mixed. Stir in shredded Cheddar cheese, onion, green pepper, celery salt, Worcestershire Powder and salt and pepper to taste. Refrigerate until ready to bake.

Just before serving, beat egg whites until soft peaks form and fold into potato mixture. Spoon lightly into greased 7 x 13-inch baking dish. Sprinkle with paprika. Bake in moderate oven (375 degrees) 25 minutes.

Makes 6 servings.

Company Potato Casserole

6 medium potatoes, peeled

1 cup sour cream

1 can (10 1/2 ozs.) condensed cream of chicken soup, undiluted

1 teaspoon salt

1/4 teaspoon pepper

1/4 teaspoon curry powder

4 hard-cooked eggs, sliced

1/2 cup soft bread crumbs

1/2 cup shredded sharp Cheddar cheese

Cook potatoes in covered saucepan in small amount of boiling, salted water over low heat until tender. Drain and cut in 1/4-inch thick slices. Combine sour cream, cream of chicken soup, salt, pepper and curry powder. Place in 2-quart casserole in alternate layers, in order given, using 1/3 of quantity for each layer the sliced potatoes, sliced hard-cooked eggs and cream mixture. Combine bread crumbs and shredded Cheddar cheese and sprinkle over top.

Bake in moderate oven (350 degrees) 30 minutes or until thoroughly hot and brown on top.

Makes 6 servings.

Corn-Zucchini

2 tablespoons butter or margarine	1 teaspoon salt
6 small zucchini, thinly sliced (3 cups)	1/8 teaspoon liquid pepper seasoning
1 tablespoon butter or margarine	1 can (1 lb.) tomatoes
1 small onion, chopped (1/4 cup)	1 teaspoon David Wade Worcestershire Powder
1 tablespoon flour	2 cups uncooked whole kernel corn
1/2 teaspoon rosemary	1/2 cup coarse bread crumbs
	2 tablespoons grated cheese

Melt butter or margarine in large skillet over medium heat, add sliced zucchini and saute 5 minutes. Remove zucchini from pan and set aside. In same skillet melt butter or margarine and add chopped onion, saute 5 minutes or until just tender. Remove from heat. Blend in flour, rosemary, salt and liquid pepper seasoning, then stir in tomatoes and Worcestershire Powder and bring to boil over low heat for 1 minute, stirring constantly.

In 1 1/2-quart baking dish, arrange zucchini, tomato sauce and uncooked corn in alternate layers. Combine bread crumbs and grated cheese and sprinkle over top. Bake in moderate oven (350 degrees) 40 minutes or until crumbs are golden brown.

Makes 6 servings.

Green Beans
With Mushrooms

2 pkgs. (10-oz. size) frozen French-style green beans

2 tablespoons finely chopped onion

2 tablespoons olive or salad oil

3 pimientos, cut in strips

1 tablespoon finely chopped parsley

1/2 teaspoon salt

1/4 teaspoon pepper

1 teaspoon David Wade Worcestershire Powder

1 can (3-oz.) sliced mushrooms drained

Cook the beans as directed on package labels and drain. In a large skillet, saute onion in hot oil until tender — about 3 minutes. Add beans and remaining ingredients and heat thoroughly.

Makes 4 servings.

Creamed Celery Amandine

2 cups celery, sliced crosswise

Salt and freshly ground pepper to taste

2 tablespoons butter or margarine

1 tablespoon chopped onion or 1/2 teaspoon chopped chives

2 teaspoons flour

1/2 cup cream

1/4 cup chicken broth

1/4 cup toasted almonds

Place sliced celery, salt and freshly ground pepper and butter or margarine in saucepan with tight-fitting cover. Cover and cook over low heat until celery is almost tender, about 15 minutes, shaking pan frequently. Add chopped onion or chives and continue cooking until tender. If lid is not tight-fitting, add small amount water, if necessary. Celery should be almost dry at end of cooking time.

Blend in flour, then gradually add cream and chicken broth. Bring to boil and cook until thickened, stirring. Add toasted almonds.

Makes 4 servings.

Cream Cheese And Squash Casserole

4 1/2 to 5 pounds yellow banana squash, thinly sliced

1 large onion, chopped

1 teaspoon sugar

1 cup water

Salt and pepper to taste

3 packages (8 ozs. each) cream cheese

4 tablespoons butter or margarine

Salt and pepper to taste

Buttered bread crumbs

Combine sliced squash, chopped onion, sugar, water and salt and pepper to taste in saucepan. Cover and cook over low heat until squash is tender enough to mash with potato masher. (Do not overcook). **Drain, reserving liquid. Mash squash.**

Combine squash liquid and cream cheese in saucepan and cook over very low heat until blended, add butter or margarine and salt and pepper to taste.

Place squash in 4-quart casserole. Cover with cheese mixture and mix lightly with fork. Cover with buttered bread crumbs. Bake in moderate oven (350 degrees) 30 minutes or until crumbs are browned.

Makes 12 servings.

Egg-and-Green Bean Casserole

1 pkg. (9-oz.) frozen French-style green beans

1/4 cup butter or margarine

1/4 cup finely chopped onion

1/4 cup unsifted all-purpose flour

2 cups milk

2 teaspoons salt

1/8 teaspoon pepper

Dash dried thyme leaves

Dash savory

2 teaspoons David Wade Worcestershire Powder

1 tablespoon chopped parsley

6 hard-cooked eggs, sliced ·

1/4 cup fine bread crumbs

1/2 cup grated Swiss cheese

Cook beans as directed on package then drain and set aside. Preheat oven to 375 degrees.

Melt butter in medium saucepan and saute onion until tender — about 3 minutes. Remove from heat and blend in flour, then milk. Add seasonings and parsley. Bring mixture to a boil, stirring and then simmer for 2 minutes.

Layer beans, eggs and sauce in 1 1/2 quart casserole. Combine crumbs and cheese; sprinkle over top. Bake 20 minutes.

Makes 4 servings.

Fresh Broccoli, Sicilian Style

2 tablespoons olive oil

1 medium onion, thinly sliced

1 clove garlic, sliced

1 1/2 tablespoons flour

1 cup chicken stock or chicken bouillon cube dissolved in 1 cup boiling water

4 anchovies, chopped

1/2 cup sliced black olives

1/8 teaspoon pepper

2 cups shredded Mozzarella or American cheese

1 3/4 pounds fresh broccoli, cooked and drained

Heat olive oil in 1-quart saucepan over medium heat. Add sliced onion and sliced garlic and saute 1 to 2 minutes or until limp. Blend in flour, then add chicken stock or bouillon cube dissolved in cup of boiling water. Cook and stir 5 to 6 minutes or until mixture is of medium thickness. Add chopped anchovies, sliced black olives, pepper and shredded Mozzarella or American cheese. Mix well then pour over cooked, drained broccoli. Serve immediately.

Makes 6 servings.

Glazed Broccoli With Almonds

2 pounds fresh broccoli or

2 packages (10 ozs. each) frozen broccoli

1/4 cup butter or margarine

1/4 cup flour

1 cup light cream

1 bouillon cube dissolved in 3/4 cup hot water

2 tablespoons sherry

2 tablespoons lemon juice

Pepper to taste

1/2 teaspoon monosodium glutamate

1/4 cup grated Parmesan cheese or 1/2 cup shredded Cheddar cheese

1/4 cup slivered, toasted almonds

Cook broccoli in covered saucepan in small amount boiling salted water over low heat until just tender. Drain and place in shallow

8 x 12-inch baking dish. Melt butter or margarine in saucepan over very low heat and blend in flour. Gradually add light cream, bouillon cube dissolved in hot water and cook until thickened, stirring. Add sherry, lemon juice, pepper and monosodium glutamate and pour over broccoli. Sprinkle with grated Parmesan cheese or shredded Cheddar and slivered almonds. Bake in moderate oven (375 degrees) 20 minutes.

Makes 6 servings.

Golden Squash Puff

3 cups mashed cooked
    acorn squash

1/2 cup dark molasses

3 tablespoons whole wheat
    flour

1 1/4 teaspoons salt

1/4 teaspoon nutmeg

1/4 teaspoon ginger

3 egg yolks

3 egg whites

1/4 cup finely chopped pecans

Blend cooked squash, molasses, flour, salt, nutmeg, ginger and egg yolks together. Beat egg whites until stiff but not dry. Fold egg whites into squash mixture. Turn into greased 1 1/2-quart round baking dish. Sprinkle chopped pecans around edge. Bake in moderate oven (350 degrees) 1 hour or until top is golden brown and slightly crusty.

Makes 6 to 8 servings.

Note: All-purpose flour may be substituted for whole wheat flour.

Holiday Baked Eggplant

1 medium eggplant

2 cups cubed dry white bread

1 can (6 ozs.) evaporated milk

3 tablespoons butter or margarine

1/4 cup finely chopped onion

1/4 cup finely chopped celery

1/4 cup finely chopped green pepper

1 egg

1 tablespoon chopped pimiento

1 teaspoon David Wade Worcestershire Powder

1/2 teaspoon salt

Dash pepper

Pinch sage, if desired

1 medium tomato

1/2 cup grated Cheddar cheese

Peel eggplant and cut into quarters, soak in salted water overnight. Drain and dice. Cook in covered saucepan in 1/2-inch boiling water over low heat 20 minutes or until almost done. Soak cubed bread in evaporated milk. Melt butter or margarine in saucepan over medium heat. Add chopped onion, chopped celery and chopped green pepper and saute 15 minutes or until golden brown.

Combine bread, eggplant and sauteed vegetables. Add egg, pimiento, Worcestershire Powder, salt, pepper and sage and mix well. Pour half of mixture into 1 1/2-quart baking dish. Slice tomato thin and arrange half of slices over eggplant mixture. Repeat with remaining eggplant mixture and tomato. Top with grated Cheddar cheese. Bake in moderate oven (375 degrees) 20 minutes. Serve hot.

Makes 4 servings.

Green Pea Casserole

4 eggs, beaten

1 cup milk

3/4 teaspoon salt

1/4 teaspoon pepper

1 cup canned green peas, drained

1/4 cup chopped celery

1 cup cheese-flavored puffs

4 slices crisp-cooked bacon, minced

1/2 cup cheese-flavored puffs

Combine beaten eggs, milk, salt, pepper, green peas, chopped celery, 1 cup cheese puffs and minced bacon in mixing bowl. Pour into greased 1 1/2-quart casserole. Top with remaining 1/2 cup cheese-flavored puffs and bake in moderate oven (350 degrees) 40 minutes.

Makes 4 servings.

Italian Spinach

2 pounds spinach, washed and trimmed

3 tablespoons butter

3 tablespoons olive oil

1 clove garlic, finely chopped

Salt to taste

1/4 teaspoon cayenne

Coarsely grated Parmesan cheese

Melted butter

Cut spinach into coarse shreds. Plunge into boiling, salted water and parboil 30 seconds. Drain well and place in flame-proof baking dish. Heat butter and olive oil in skillet over low heat. Add chopped garlic, salt and cayenne and cook 5 minutes. Mix oil mixture with spinach. Sprinkle with grated Parmesan cheese and melted butter. Broil 3 inches from full heat until brown.

Makes 6 servings.

Kentucky Bean Chowder

3/4 cup diced, peeled carrots

2 tablespoons butter or margarine

2 tablespoons minced onion

2 tablespoons minced green pepper

2 tablespoons flour

1 1/2 teaspoons salt

1/8 teaspoon pepper

1 cup milk

1 can (1 lb.) baked beans, in tomato sauce

3 frankfurters, grated (1 cup)

Cook carrots in covered saucepan in 1-inch boiling, salted water over low heat until tender. Drain, reserving liquid. Melt butter or margarine in saucepan over medium heat. Add minced onion and minced green pepper and saute until golden. Reduce heat to very low, then stir in flour, salt and pepper. Combine carrot liquid plus enough water to make 1 cup and milk and gradually add milk mixture to flour mixture and cook until thickened, stirring constantly. Add cooked carrots, baked beans and grated frankfurters. Heat to serving temperature.

Makes 4 servings.

Luncheon Asparagus Riviera

4 tablespoons butter or margarine

2 tablespoons flour

2 cups milk

1 can (6 ozs.) salmon

Salt and pepper to taste

1 package (10 ozs.) frozen asparagus spears

1/2 cup grated Parmesan cheese

Melt butter or margarine in saucepan over very low heat and blend in flour. Gradually add milk and cook until mixture begins to thicken, stirring constantly. Drain salmon, remove skin and bones and break into small pieces, then add to sauce mixture. Add salt and pepper.

Prepare frozen asparagus spears according to package directions, remove from heat and drain. Place asparagus in baking dish. Pour salmon mixture over asparagus and sprinkle with grated Parmesan cheese. Bake in moderate oven (350 degrees) 15 minutes or until cheese is melted.

Makes 4 servings.

Mushrooms And Pepper Roma

1 pound fresh mushrooms
(about 5 cups sliced)

2 large green peppers

1/4 cup olive oil

1 medium onion, sliced

2 large tomatoes, peeled
and sliced

3/4 teaspoon salt

1/8 teaspoon black pepper

1/8 teaspoon oregano leaves

1/8 teaspoon basil leaves

1/16 teaspoon garlic powder

2 teaspoons David Wade
Worcestershire Powder

Rinse mushrooms, dry and slice. Slice green peppers into 1/2-inch strips. Heat olive oil in large skillet over medium heat, add mushrooms, pepper strips and sliced onion and saute until mushrooms are golden. Add tomatoes, salt, black pepper, oregano leaves, basil leaves, garlic powder and Worcestershire Powder, stirring gently. Reduce heat to low. Cover and simmer 20 minutes, stirring occasionally. Serve with meat or eggs.

Makes 6 to 8 servings.

Patio Potatoes

2 1/2 pounds potatoes, cooked

3 cups medium cream sauce

2 cups shredded mild
Cheddar cheese

1 can (4 ozs.) peeled green
chilies, rinsed and cut in
pieces

2 teaspoons salt

2 cloves garlic, pureed

Buttered bread crumbs

Peel, slice or cube cooked potatoes and place in 1 1/2-quart baking dish. Combine cream sauce, shredded Cheddar cheese, green chili pieces, salt and pureed garlic in saucepan. Cook over very low heat until cheese is melted. Pour cheese mixture over potatoes. Sprinkle buttered crumbs over top. Bake in moderate oven (350 degrees) until thoroughly hot and crumbs are brown.

Makes 6 to 8 servings.

Quadrettini Spinach

1/4 cup olive oil

1/3 cup minced onion

3 cloves garlic, crushed

1/2 cup diced carrots

3 stalks celery, diced

1 pound ground round steak

1/2 cup sherry

1 can (6 ozs.) tomato paste

1 can (1 lb. 4 ozs.) tomatoes

1 tablespoon salt

1/2 teaspoon pepper

4 ounces medium noodles

1 package (10 ozs.) frozen chopped spinach

1/2 cup buttered fresh bread squares

1/2 cup grated process Cheddar cheese

Grated Parmesan cheese

On the day before or early in the day of serving, heat olive oil in large skillet over medium heat, add onion, garlic, carrots and celery and saute until lightly browned. Add ground round steak and cook until red color has disappeared. Add sherry and simmer over low heat few minutes, stir in tomato paste, tomatoes, salt and pepper and simmer 2 to 2 1/2 hours. Refrigerate sauce until 45 minutes before serving.

Cook noodles according to package directions. Cook frozen spinach according to package directions, then drain both well. Add to sauce. Pour into 1 1/2-quart casserole. Sprinkle with buttered bread squares and grated Cheddar cheese. Bake in moderate oven (350 degrees) 30 minutes or until browned. Serve with grated Parmesan cheese.

Makes 6 to 8 servings.

Peas European

2 tablespoons butter or margarine

1 cup sliced fresh or canned mushrooms

1/4 cup minced onion

1/4 teaspoon salt

Dash pepper

1/4 teaspoon nutmeg

1/8 teaspoon dried marjoram

2 tablespoons sherry (optional)

2 cups drained, hot, cooked or canned peas

Melt butter or margarine in skillet over medium heat. Add mushrooms and minced onion and saute 5 minutes or until tender. Add salt, pepper, nutmeg, marjoram and sherry. Add peas and mix well.

Makes 4 servings.

Springtime Potato Salad

1 1/2 pounds new potatoes

1 clove garlic, split

1/2 cup thinly sliced celery

1/4 cup chopped scallions

1 teaspoon salt

1/8 teaspoon pepper

2 tablespoons lemon juice

1/2 cup mayonnaise

1 large green pepper

Stuffed olives

Cook new potatoes in covered saucepan in small amount boiling, salted water over low heat until just tender. While potatoes are cooking, rub wooden bowl with split garlic clove. Combine thinly sliced celery, chopped scallions, salt and pepper in wooden bowl and let stand at room temperature. Peel cooked potatoes and cut in half, lengthwise, then slice crosswise in 1/4-inch thick slices. Place in mixing bowl. Sprinkle with lemon juice and toss lightly, then chill.

One hour before serving time, place potatoes in wooden bowl with celery and scallions. Spoon mayonnaise evenly over potatoes. Toss lightly and chill. Halve green pepper lengthwise and remove seeds. Cut 6 strips from pepper and cut remaining pepper into leaf shapes. To serve salad, place ice cream scoop of salad on 6 individual salad plates. Press pimiento-stuffed olive into center of each serving. Arrange green pepper strips for stems and add green pepper leaves.

Makes 6 servings.

Sauteed Julienne Snap Beans

1 tablespoon instant
   minced onion

1 tablespoon water

2 tablespoons salad oil

4 cups fresh snap beans, cut
   in julienne strips

2 tablespoons chili sauce

1 teaspoon David Wade
   Worcestershire Powder

3/4 teaspoon salt

1/4 teaspoon pepper

1/16 teaspoon garlic salt

Soften minced onion in water. Heat salad oil in 9-inch skillet over medium heat and add softened onion and snap beans. Cover and cook 8 to 10 minutes. Add chili sauce, Worcestershire Powder, salt, pepper and garlic salt and continue cooking 5 to 7 minutes or until beans are crisp tender. (If necessary, add 1 to 2 tablespoons hot water.)

Makes 6 servings.

Squashatash

1/4 green bell pepper

1 cup water

1 teaspoon salt

1/3 cup corn oil

5 medium crook-neck
   squash, sliced

1/2 medium onion, thinly
   sliced

2 tablespoons butter or
   margarine

1/2 teaspoon salt

1/4 teaspoon pepper

Dash garlic salt

1 ear fresh or frozen cooked
   corn, kernels cut from ear

Place bell pepper, water and salt in saucepan and boil over low heat 3 to 4 minutes. Remove from heat. Remove pepper and allow liquid to cool slightly. Heat corn oil in skillet over medium heat and add squash and onion and saute until tender, stirring. Add butter or margarine, salt, pepper and garlic salt and cook until blended. Then add cooked corn and bell pepper cooking liquid and cover, simmering over low heat 10 minutes or until liquid is reduced to one half.

Makes 4 servings.

Turnips In Sour Cream

6 white turnips

1 tablespoon caraway seed

1/4 cup sour cream

1/2 teaspoon dried basil

Paprika

Lemon juice

Cook turnips and caraway seed in covered saucepan in boiling, salted water over low heat 10 minutes. Drain and cool. Peel and slice turnips. Place in greased 1 1/2 quart casserole. Add sour cream and dried basil. Cover and bake in moderate oven (350 degrees) 25 minutes or until tender. Sprinkle with paprika and small amount lemon juice. Serve hot.

Makes approximately 6 servings.

Zesty Green Beans

1 can (1 lb.) whole or cut green beans

1 tablespoon salad oil

2 tablespoons slivered almonds

1/2 cup coarsely chopped celery

2 teaspoons dry chicken stock base

1 teaspoon soy sauce

1 teaspoon sugar

1 teaspoon white vinegar

1 teaspoon David Wade Worcestershire Powder

Salt to taste

1 tablespoon water

2 tablespoons cornstarch

6 slices crisp-fried bacon, crumbled

Drain and reserve liquid from green beans. Heat salad oil in skillet over medium heat, add slivered almonds and fry. Add chopped celery and cook 3 minutes. Add bean liquid (1/2 cup approximately), chicken stock base, soy sauce, sugar, white vinegar and Worcestershire Powder. Cover and simmer over low heat 3 to 5 minutes. Add drained beans and heat thoroughly. Add salt to taste. Blend water and cornstarch together and add to bean mixture. Continue cooking until sauce is thickened. Sprinkle crumbled bacon over top.

Makes 4 to 6 servings.

Meats

Alsatian Chicken

1/4 cup butter or margarine

2 broiler-fryers, cut in serving pieces

6 shallots or green onions, chopped

1/2 pound mushrooms, sliced

1 teaspoon salt

Pepper to taste

1 cup Riesling or Traminer wine

Herb bouquet (parsley, bay and thyme)

2 egg yolks

1/2 cup light cream

Melt butter or margarine in skillet over medium heat. Add chicken pieces and cook until lightly browned. Add shallots or green onions, mushrooms, salt and pepper and cook 4 to 5 minutes. Add Riesling or Traminer wine and herb bouquet and cover, simmering over low heat 30 minutes or until chicken is tender. Remove chicken from pan and place on serving platter. Keep warm. Remove herb bouquet. Continue cooking until mixture in pan is reduced to half.

Beat egg yolks and light cream together and add small amount of hot mixture to cream mixture, stirring constantly. Gradually stir this mixture into hot mixture and continue cooking 1 or 2 minutes or until slightly thickened, stirring constantly. Do not boil.

Pour mixture over chicken.

Makes 6 to 8 servings.

American Family Baked Spaghetti

6 slices bacon

1 1/2 pounds ground lean beef

Salt

Pepper

1 large onion, diced

1 medium-sized green bell pepper, diced

1 large can sliced mushrooms, drained

1 tooth garlic, crushed

1 tablespoon David Wade Worcestershire Powder

5 drops tabasco sauce

1/2 teaspoon basil

1/2 teaspoon oregano

1/2 teaspoon dehydrated parsley flakes

1 can (1 lb. 1 oz.) peeled tomatoes

1 can (8 oz.) tomato sauce

1 can (6 oz.) tomato paste

1 pound package spaghetti

Grated parmesan cheese

Fry bacon in large metal skillet or Dutch oven until brown and remove bacon from container. Place ground beef into the bacon fat and lightly brown, stirring constantly. Salt and pepper meat to taste. Add onion, green bell pepper, drained mushrooms and crushed garlic. Continue to cook slowly, stirring until onion and green bell pepper become soft. Add Worcestershire Powder, tabasco sauce, basil, oregano and parsley flakes. Add tomatoes, tomato sauce and tomato paste. Lower heat to simmer and continue stirring and cooking slowly for 15 minutes. Cook spaghetti according to directions on package, place in colander and thoroughly wash away starch. Combine spaghetti with meat sauce in a large ovenware baking dish. Place lid on dish and into pre-heated 350 degree oven and bake for 45 minutes. Remove from oven and let stand for 15 minutes before serving. Top with parmesan cheese if desired. Recipe serves 8.

Baked Chicken Breasts Tuscan

6 chicken breasts, about 12 ounces each

2 cups sour cream

1/4 cup lemon juice

1 tablespoon David Wade Worcestershire Powder

4 teaspoons celery salt

2 teaspoons paprika

4 cloves garlic, finely chopped

4 teaspoons salt

1/2 teaspoon pepper

1 3/4 cups packaged dry bread crumbs

1/2 cup butter or margarine

1/2 cup shortening

Cut chicken breasts in half and wipe well with damp paper towels. Combine sour cream, lemon juice, Worcestershire Powder, celery salt, paprika, garlic, salt and pepper in large mixing bowl. Place chicken in sour cream mixture, coating each piece well. Cover and let stand in refrigerator overnight. Remove chicken from sour cream mixture and roll in bread crumbs.

Place in shallow baking dish. Melt butter or margarine and shortening in small saucepan over low heat. Spoon half of melted shortening-butter mixture over chicken. Bake in moderate oven (350 degrees) 45 minutes. Spoon remaining shortening-butter mixture over chicken. Bake 10 to 15 minutes longer or until chicken is tender and browned.

Makes 12 servings.

Baked Turkey Thermidor

1 package (10 ozs.)
frozen green peas

2 cups chopped cooked
turkey

1 cup diced celery

1 can (5 ozs.) water chestnuts,
drained and thinly sliced

1/2 cup sliced toasted almonds

2 tablespoons chopped
green pepper

1 tablespoon grated onion

2 tablespoons chopped
pimiento

2 tablespoons white wine

1 tablespoon lemon juice

1/2 teaspoon salt

1 can (10 1/2 ozs.)
condensed cream of chicken
soup, undiluted

1/2 cup milk

2 slices white bread, cubed

1 cup grated sharp
Cheddar cheese

Cook green peas according to package directions, then drain. Combine cooked peas, cooked turkey, diced celery, water chestnuts, almonds, green pepper, grated onion and chopped pimiento in 2-quart casserole. Sprinkle with white wine, lemon juice and salt. Toss gently until well mixed.

Combine cream of chicken soup and milk in small saucepan, stirring until smooth. Bring to boil over low heat stirring constantly. Add to turkey mixture, mixing well. Sprinkle with bread cubes. Bake in moderate oven (375 degrees) 20 minutes or until bread cubes are toasted. Sprinkle with grated Cheddar cheese. Return to oven and continue baking until cheese is melted.

Makes 6 to 8 servings.

Beef-Macaroni Loaf

1 package (8 ozs.) elbow macaroni

2 tablespoons butter or margarine

2 tablespoons flour

1 teaspoon salt

1/4 teaspoon pepper

1 egg, beaten

2 cups milk

1/2 cup grated Parmesan cheese

1/4 cup onion, chopped

1 tablespoon butter or margarine

1 1/2 pounds ground beef

1 egg, beaten

1/2 can (10 1/2 ozs.) condensed tomato soup

1 teaspoon salt

1/4 teaspoon pepper

Steamed red and green pepper rings (optional)

Cook macaroni according to package directions; drain and return to pan. Stir in butter or margarine. Add flour, salt and pepper, tossing until well mixed. Combine beaten egg and milk and pour over macaroni. Cook over medium heat until thickened, stirring constantly. Remove from heat. Stir in Parmesan cheese.

Saute chopped onion in butter or margarine over medium heat until soft. Add ground beef and cook until brown, breaking up with fork as it cooks. Combine beaten egg, tomato soup, salt and pepper and stir into meat mixture. Remove from heat. Line greased 9 x 5 x 3-inch pan with double thickness of foil, leaving 1-inch overhang. Grease foil. Place half of macaroni mixture in pan, top with meat mixture. Cover with remaining macaroni mixture. Bake in moderate oven (350 degrees) 1 hour or until top is browned. Remove from oven and let cool in pan 10 minutes. Loosen sides with knife and lift from pan with foil. Place on serving dish and slip foil from under loaf. Garnish with steamed red and green pepper rings, if desired. Slice and serve with Tomato Sauce.

Makes 6 to 8 servings.

Tomato Sauce

1/2 can (10 1/2 ozs.) condensed tomato soup

1 can (8 ozs.) tomato sauce

1 teaspoon sugar

1/4 teaspoon basil

2 teaspoons David Wade Worcestershire Powder

Combine all ingredients in saucepan and bring to boil over low heat, then simmer 2 to 3 minutes. Serve hot over Beef-Macaroni Loaf.

Boeuf En Daube

3 pounds lean round of beef

1/4 cup flour

1 teaspoon seasoned salt

1/2 teaspoon seasoned pepper

6 strips bacon

2 cloves garlic, finely minced

1 ounce (2 tablespoons) warm brandy

12 small mushrooms

1 can (10 1/2 ozs.) condensed beef bouillon

1 cup red table wine

12 very small white onions, peeled

12 small carrots, sliced

6 peppercorns, slightly bruised

4 whole cloves

1 bay leaf, crumbled

2 tablespoons chopped fresh parsley

1/4 teaspoon dried marjoram

1/4 teaspoon dried thyme

1 teaspoon David Wade Worcestershire Powder

1/2 teaspoon salt

1/2 cup red table wine

Cut beef into 1-inch cubes. Combine flour, salt and pepper in paper sack and shake beef cubes in mixture. Fry bacon in heavy skillet over medium heat until brown but not crisp. Remove bacon from skillet and cut into 1-inch pieces, then place in 2-quart casserole. Add minced garlic and beef cubes to fat in skillet and cook over medium heat until browned, turning frequently.

Pour brandy into skillet and light with match. When flames die down remove meat and place in casserole with bacon. Add mushrooms to drippings and cook over medium heat until lightly browned. Remove mushrooms and place in casserole with meat. Add beef bouillon and 1 cup table wine to drippings and bring to boil, stirring to loosen bits of food from bottom of skillet. Pour liquid into casserole. Add onions, carrots, peppercorns, cloves, bay leaf, parsley, marjoram, thyme, Worcestershire Powder and salt. Pour 1/2 cup red table wine over all and cover tightly. Bake in low oven (300 degrees) 3 hours. Serve with tossed salad and French bread.

Makes 5 to 6 servings.

Braised Venison Roast

2 medium onions, thinly sliced

1 carrot, peeled and thinly sliced

2 shallots, minced (optional)

2 stalks celery

1 clove garlic

1 teaspoon salt

1/4 teaspoon dried thyme

2 bay leaves

12 black peppercorns

2 whole cloves

2 cups red or white wine

1/2 cup salad oil

3 to 6 pound venison roast

Salt and pepper

3/4 cup cooking oil

1/4 teaspoon powdered thyme

1/4 teaspoon basil leaves

1/2 teaspoon garlic powder

1/8 teaspoon rosemary

1 medium bay leaf

1 cup rich beef broth

1 tablespoon David Wade Worcestershire Powder

3/4 cup red or white wine

3 tablespoons dehydrated parsley flakes

4 medium white onions, peeled and quartered

4 cups stock

1/4 cup sifted flour

3 cups milk

Mix sliced onion, sliced carrot, minced shallot, celery, garlic, salt, thyme, bay leaves, peppercorns, cloves, wine and salad oil together and pour over venison roast. Let stand in refrigerator 24 hours. Drain marinade from roast.

Season roast with salt and pepper. Heat cooking oil in heavy Dutch oven over medium heat, add roast and cook until brown on all sides. Reduce heat to low. Add thyme, basil leaves, garlic powder, rosemary, bay leaf, beef broth, Worcestershire Powder and wine to roast. Sprinkle dehydrated parsley flakes over surface of roast. Cover tightly and simmer 2 hours. Add onion and continue simmering 1 hour.

When roast is tender, pour 4 cups stock off into saucepan and heat slowly over low heat. Blend in flour, then milk. Continue cooking until mixture is slightly thickened, stirring constantly. Pour sauce over venison roast and serve.

Makes 8 servings.

Chicken A La King

1/4 cup butter or margarine

1/4 pound fresh mushrooms, sliced

1/2 green pepper, chopped

2 pimientos, chopped

3 tablespoons flour

1/2 teaspoon salt

1 cup chicken broth or bouillon

1/2 cup milk

Dash pepper

1/4 teaspoon turmeric

1 teaspoon sugar

1/2 cup heavy cream

2 egg yolks, slightly beaten

2 cups cubed, cooked chicken

Melt butter or margarine in saucepan over medium heat; add sliced mushrooms, chopped green pepper and chopped pimiento and saute 5 minutes or until mushrooms are tender. Remove from heat. Stir in flour and salt, then blend in chicken broth or bouillon and milk and cook over low heat until mixture thickens and boils, stirring constantly. Stir in pepper, turmeric and sugar.

Blend heavy cream and slightly beaten egg yolks together and stir into sauce. Add cubed chicken and continue cooking until hot. Serve on toast triangles or biscuits.

Makes 4 servings.

Chicken in Orange-Almond Sauce

1 3/4 pound broiler-fryer, cut in serving pieces

1/4 teaspoon salt

1/4 cup butter or margarine

2 tablespoons flour

1/4 teaspoon salt

1/8 teaspoon cinnamon

Dash ginger

1 1/2 cups orange juice

1/2 cup slivered, blanched almonds

1/2 cup seedless raisins

1 cup orange sections

4 cups cooked rice

Wash chicken pieces in cold water and pat dry. Sprinkle with salt. Heat butter or margarine in large skillet over medium heat; add chicken and fry until lightly browned. Remove chicken from pan. Combine flour, salt, cinnamon and ginger and blend into pan drippings to make smooth paste. Add orange juice and cook, stirring constantly, until sauce bubbles and thickens. Return chicken pieces to skillet. Add slivered almonds and raisins, reduce heat to low.

Cover and cook 45 minutes or until chicken is tender. Add orange sections and cook until heated through. Serve chicken and some of sauce on bed of cooked rice. Pass remaining sauce.

Makes 4 servings.

Chicken Santa Fe

2 broiler-fryers (2 1/2 to 3 lbs. each) cut in serving pieces

6 tablespoons butter or margarine

2 medium onions, sliced

1/2 pound mushrooms, sliced

1 cup dark or light raisins

1 1/4 cups water

4 teaspoons salt

1/4 cup lemon juice

2 teaspoons monosodium glutamate

1/2 teaspoon ground cloves

1/2 teaspoon allspice

1/2 teaspoon ginger

1/4 cup brown sugar

1 cup walnut halves

4 teaspoons cornstarch

1/2 cup water

2 cups seedless grapes

2 cups orange sections

12 maraschino cherries, washed

Saute chicken pieces in butter or margarine in heavy Dutch oven over medium heat until golden. Add onion, mushrooms, raisins, water, salt, lemon juice, monosodium glutamate, ground cloves, allspice, ginger and brown sugar, cover and simmer over low heat 40 minutes or until tender, turning occasionally. Add walnut halves. Push chicken pieces to one side of pan.

Blend cornstarch and water and add to liquid in pan. Cook until liquid is thickened and smooth. Add grapes, orange sections and maraschino cherries and cook 2 minutes. Serve at once.

Makes 8 servings .

Chili-Spaghetti

1 package (8 ozs.) spaghetti

1/2 cup margarine or shortening

1 pound ground beef chuck

3 medium onions, chopped

1/2 cup canned or cooked whole kernel corn

1 can (10 1/2 ozs.) condensed tomato soup

1 can (17 ozs.) tomatoes

1 can (3 or 4 ozs.) sliced or button mushrooms and liquid

1 can (4 ozs.) pimientos, slivered

1 to 2 tablespoons chili powder

1 tablespoon salt

1/4 teaspoon pepper

1 teaspoon sugar

Cook spaghetti according to package directions, reducing cooking time to 3 minutes. Drain and set aside. Melt margarine or shortening in Dutch oven or heavy saucepan over medium heat. Add ground beef and chopped onion and saute until meat loses red color. Add spaghetti, corn, tomato soup, tomatoes, sliced mushrooms and liquid, pimientos, chili powder, salt, pepper and sugar and mix well. Cover and cook over very low heat 1 hour. Turn off heat and let stand 30 minutes. Heat to serving temperature, if necessary.

Makes approximately 8 servings.

Chinese Pepper Steak

1 1/2 pounds sirloin steak, 1-inch thick

1/4 cup fat or vegetable oil

1 clove garlic, crushed

1 teaspoon salt

1 teaspoon ground ginger

1/2 teaspoon pepper

3 large green peppers, seeded and sliced

2 large onions, thinly sliced

1/4 cup soy sauce

1/2 teaspoon sugar

1/2 cup beef bouillon

1 can (6 ozs.) water chestnuts, drained and sliced

4 green onions, cut in 1-inch pieces

1 tablespoon cornstarch

1/4 cup water

Cooked hot rice

Freeze sirloin steak for 1 hour, then remove from freezer and cut into

1/8-inch thick slices. Heat fat or vegetable oil in skillet over medium heat, add crushed garlic, salt, ground ginger and pepper and saute until garlic is golden. Add steak slices and brown lightly for 2 minutes. Remove meat from pan. Add sliced green pepper and sliced onion and cook 3 minutes. Return meat to pan. Add soy sauce, sugar, bouillon, water chestnuts and green onion. Mix cornstarch and water together and stir into mixture. Simmer over low heat 2 minutes or until sauce is thickened. Serve over hot rice.

Makes 6 to 8 servings.

Cocktail Meat Balls

1 pound ground beef	1 cup Dr Pepper
1 egg, beaten	1/4 teaspoon dry mustard
1/2 cup fine dry bread crumbs	2 tablespoons catsup
1 teaspoon salt	1/8 teaspoon pepper
Dash pepper	1 tablespoon vinegar
1 tablespoon salad oil	1 tablespoon soy sauce
1 clove garlic, cut in 4 pieces	

Combine ground beef, beaten egg, bread crumbs, salt and pepper and shape into bite-size balls. Fry in small amount of hot fat in skillet over medium heat until browned. Heat salad oil in saucepan over very low heat and saute garlic pieces being careful not to brown. Remove garlic. Add Dr Pepper, mustard, catsup, pepper, vinegar and soy sauce and bring to boil over medium heat. Add meat balls to sauce and reduce heat to very low. Cook until meat balls have absorbed most of sauce. Serve hot.

Makes approximately 4 dozen.

Country Chicken Balls

1 egg, slightly beaten

3/4 cup milk

1/4 cup packaged dry bread crumbs

1/4 cup finely chopped toasted blanched almonds

1 teaspoon salt

1/2 teaspoon hickory-smoked salt

1/8 teaspoon pepper

3 cans (5 oz. size) boned chicken, ground (4 cups)

1 tablespoon flour

5 tablespoons butter or margarine

1/2 cup sliced onion

1/2 cup sliced celery

1/2 cup sliced green pepper

1 1/2 cups chicken bouillon

1/2 teaspoon monosodium glutamate

1 tablespoon sugar

1 tablespoon cornstarch

1 tablespoon lemon juice

1/2 cup seedless green grapes

4 1/2 cups cooked white rice

In large bowl, combine egg, milk, bread crumbs, almonds, 1/2 teaspoon salt, hickory-smoked salt, and pepper; mix well. Add chicken, tossing lightly. Using 2 level tablespoons for each, shape chicken mixture into 24 balls. Roll balls lightly in flour, coating completely. In 4 tablespoons hot butter in large skillet, saute chicken balls until browned on all sides. Remove from heat; keep warm.

In blazer pan of chafing dish, heat remaining butter over direct heat. When hot, saute onion, celery, and green pepper about 5 minutes, or until vegetables are tender. Add bouillon, monosodium glutamate, sugar and remaining salt; cook, stirring occasionally, until mixture starts to simmer (about 15 minutes.) Combine cornstarch with lemon juice until smooth. Stir into mixture in chafing dish; continue to simmer, stirring constantly, until mixture is thickened and translucent (about 5 minutes). Add chicken balls and grapes; simmer 5 minutes longer. Place over boiling water in water pan, to keep warm. Serve over hot rice.

Makes 6 servings.

Creole Beef Casserole

1 1/2 pounds ground beef

1/4 teaspoon liquid red pepper seasoning

1 teaspoon salt

1/4 teaspoon dry mustard

1/2 teaspoon thyme leaves

1 tablespoon minced parsley

2 tablespoons butter or margarine

2 medium onions, chopped

1 clove garlic, peeled

1 can (1 lb.) seasoned stewed tomatoes

1 can (6 ozs.) tomato paste

1/4 teaspoon liquid red pepper seasoning

1 teaspoon salt

2 teaspoons David Wade Worcestershire Powder

1 package (10 ozs.) frozen lima beans, thawed

Mix ground beef, red pepper seasoning, salt, mustard, thyme leaves and minced parsley together lightly. Melt butter or margarine over medium heat, add seasoned meat, chopped onions and garlic and saute until meat is browned. Remove garlic. Turn at least half of meat mixture into 1 1/2-quart casserole. Combine stewed tomatoes, tomato paste, red pepper seasoning, salt and Worcestershire Powder and pour over meat. Sprinkle with lima beans.

Place remaining meat mixture in center of beans. Cover and bake in moderate oven (350 degrees) 45 minutes.

Makes 6 servings.

Creole Chicken

Fat from 1/2 pound of cooked bacon

2 medium onions, diced fine

1 green bell pepper, diced fine

1 large can of mushrooms

1 small can tomato paste

1 small can tomato sauce

1 No. 2 can of peeled tomatoes

1 tablespoon garlic salt

Dash of pepper

Dash of Tabasco

1 tablespoon David Wade Worcestershire Powder

1/4 cup white wine

1 4-pound baking chicken

Salt and pepper

1 large supermarket paper bag

cotton string

Place the bacon fat into a skillet. (Do not use the bacon.) In this bacon fat saute onions, green bell pepper and mushrooms until soft. Then add tomato paste, tomato sauce, peeled tomatoes, garlic salt, pepper, Tabasco, Worcestershire Powder and wine. Simmer for 12 minutes with the cover on the skillet.

Make sure baking size hen is a few degrees below room temperature. Lightly salt and pepper hen to taste. Place 1/2 of the sauce in the cavity and cover the chicken with the other half. Carefully place chicken inside paper bag and close the open end securely. Tie this end tightly with string then place paper bag containing the chicken and sauce into a lower section of a shallow roasting pan. Place roasting pan into a preheated 350 degree oven and cook for one hour and thirty minutes. Remove from oven and very carefully tear a hole in the top of the paper bag permitting live steam to escape then rip away paper. Serve the Creole Chicken on a platter of fluffy white rice.

Recipe serves 6.

Danish Meat Balls

2 pounds chopped lean beef

3/4 cup instant minced onion

2 teaspoons salt

1/2 teaspoon nutmeg

1/4 teaspoon pepper

2 eggs, beaten

2/3 cup flour

1/4 teaspoon salt

1/16 teaspoon pepper

2 teaspoons David Wade Worcestershire Powder

1/4 cup shortening

1 cup bouillon or water

1 bay leaf

1 1/2 cups water

Combine chopped beef, minced onion, salt, nutmeg, pepper and beaten eggs and shape into 2-inch balls. Combine flour, salt, pepper and Worcestershire Powder. Roll meat balls in flour mixture. Heat shortening in skillet over medium heat, add meat balls and cook until brown on all sides. Add bouillon or water and bay leaf. Cover and cook over low heat 20 to 30 minutes or until meatballs are done. Remove meatballs. Blend 3 tablespoons of remaining flour mixture into drippings left in pan. Cook until flour is browned. Stir in water and continue cooking until thickened, stirring constantly. Serve meatballs and gravy with fluffy mashed potatoes.

Makes 5 to 6 servings.

Delta Pork Chop Casserole

4 loin pork chops, 3/4-inch thick

Seasoned salt

1/2 cup uncooked regular or processed white rice

1 can (10 3/4 ozs.) beef gravy (1 1/4 cups)

Dash liquid red pepper seasoning

1/4 cup water

1 teaspoon salt

Dash pepper

4 medium onions

2 large carrots, cut diagonally into 1-inch slices

Trim some fat from pork chops and heat fat in skillet over medium heat. Sprinkle chops with seasoned salt and fry in hot skillet until well browned on both sides, then remove chops to 2-quart casserole. Add white rice to drippings in skillet and cook until browned, stirring. Stir in beef gravy, red pepper seasoning, water, salt and pepper. Arrange onions and carrot slices on top of chops. Pour gravy mixture over all. Bake, uncovered, in moderate oven (350 degrees) 1 hour or until chops and vegetables are tender.

Makes 4 servings.

Dixie Fried Chicken

2 (2 1/2 lbs. each) broiler-fryers	1/4 teaspoon white pepper
1 cup corn meal	2 teaspoons parsley flakes
1 cup pancake mix	2 teaspoons David Wade Worcestershire Powder
2 teaspoons instant minced onion	2 slightly beaten eggs
2 1/2 teaspoons salt	Shortening

Cut fryers into serving pieces. Combine corn meal, pancake mix, minced onion, salt, white pepper, parsley flakes and Worcestershire Powder in mixing bowl. Dip chicken pieces in slightly beaten eggs then dip in corn meal mixture. Fry in heavy skillet in 1/2-inch hot shortening over medium heat until brown on all sides. Place browned chicken in shallow baking pan. Bake in moderate oven (350 degrees) 1 hour or until tender.

Makes 6 servings.

English Roast Beef Pie

2 tablespoons butter or margarine

1 small onion, minced

1 can (16 ozs.) carrots

1 can (16 ozs.) peas

1/2 teaspoon liquid red pepper seasoning

1 can (13 ozs.) roast beef and gravy

1 can (4 ozs.) refrigerated biscuits

Melt butter or margarine in skillet over medium heat, add minced onion and saute. Remove from heat. Add carrots, peas and red pepper seasoning and mix well. Add this mixture to roast beef and gravy and pour into deep 1 1/2-quart casserole. Separate biscuits pulling each in half. Place one inch apart on top of mixture in casserole. Bake in hot oven (400 degrees) 15 to 20 minutes or until biscuits are golden brown.

Makes 4 servings.

German Braised Steak

3 pounds round steak, cut thick

Flour

1/2 teaspoon salt

1/2 teaspoon pepper

1 tablespoon David Wade Worcestershire Powder

3 tablespoons butter, margarine, beef or bacon fat

1 1/2 pounds red onions, peeled and sliced

1 pint beer

Cut round steak into 2-inch squares and sprinkle generously on one side with flour. Then sprinkle with salt, pepper and Worcestershire Powder. With mallet or edge of heavy plate, pound seasoning into meat, flattening slightly. Turn and repeat flouring, seasoning and pounding on other side. Melt butter, margarine, beef or bacon fat in heavy skillet over medium heat. Add seasoned meat and onions and cook until brown on all sides. Add beer.

Cover tightly. Reduce heat to low and simmer 1 1/2 to 2 hours or until meat is tender and broth is thick. Serve with boiled potatoes with chopped parsley and butter, scalloped tomatoes and cucumber salad.

Makes 4 to 6 servings.

NOTE: After adding beer, covered skillet may be placed in moderate oven (325 degrees) and baked 1 1/2 to 2 hours. Use oven-proof skillet.

German Spaghetti

1 cup olive oil

4 large onions, finely chopped

1 1/2 pounds veal or round steak, ground

2 green peppers, finely chopped

1 1/2 cans (1 lb. 4 ozs. each) tomatoes

1 can (6 ozs.) sliced mushrooms

1 tablespoon David Wade Worcestershire Powder

Salt, pepper, paprika and cayenne to taste

1 pound cooked spaghetti

1 pound grated sharp Cheddar cheese

Heat olive oil in saucepan over medium heat, add finely chopped onion and saute. Add ground veal or steak and cook until tender but not brown. Add chopped green pepper, tomatoes, mushrooms, Worcestershire Powder, salt, pepper, paprika and cayenne to taste. Mix cooked spaghetti and grated Cheddar cheese and add to other mixture; cook slowly 25 minutes.

Mixture is best when prepared the day before and reheated just before serving.

Makes 10 servings.

Gypsy Steak

1/4 cup cooking oil

  4 small individual round steaks, approximately 1/4-inch thick

Flour, salt and pepper

1/4 cup cooking oil

  1 large yellow onion, finely chopped

  1 medium green pepper, finely chopped

  1 can (4 ozs.) sliced mushrooms

  1 can (4 ozs.) tomato paste

  2 cans (8 ozs. each) tomato sauce

1 can (10 ozs.) tomatoes, drained

1 tablespoon David Wade Worcestershire Powder

Dash Tabasco

  1 teaspoon garlic salt

1/4 teaspoon basil

1/2 teaspoon oregano

Salt to taste

Pepper to taste

  2 cups cooked elbow macaroni

  1 cup grated Cheddar cheese

Heat oil in heavy skillet over medium heat. Score the edges of round steaks and dust each side with flour, salt and pepper. Add steaks to hot oil and cook until brown on each side. Remove from skillet. To oil remaining in skillet add 1/4 cup cooking oil, chopped onion, green pepper and sliced mushrooms and cook until vegetables are tender. Add tomato paste, tomato sauce, tomatoes, Worcestershire Powder, Tabasco, garlic salt, basil, oregano, salt and pepper. Reduce heat to low and continue cooking 5 minutes. Stir in cooked elbow macaroni. Spoon 2 tablespoons of mixture onto center of each steak and top with grated Cheddar cheese.

Shape steaks into rolls by folding sides over mixture and securing with toothpicks. Arrange the four steak rolls in deep baking dish and pour over remaining sauce mixture. Cover and bake in moderate oven (350 degrees) 45 minutes or until meat is fork tender.

Makes 4 servings.

Grilled Lamb Chops

12 loin lamb chops
(1-inch thick)

1/4 cup butter or margarine,
melted

1/2 teaspoon garlic powder

1 tablespoon David Wade
Worcestershire Powder

1/4 teaspoon black pepper

1 tablespoon parsley flakes

1 teaspoon salt

Remove excess fat from lamb chops. Combine remaining ingredients and mix well. Dip chops in seasoned butter mixture. Place on cold broiler grid. Broil 15 minutes, turning to brown both sides.

Makes 6 servings, 2 chops each.

Hominy Casserole

2 tablespoons shortening
or olive oil

2 onions, chopped

1/4 pound ground round
steak

1 can (16 ozs.) hominy,
drained

1 can (8 ozs.) tomato sauce

1 1/2 teaspoons salt

1/4 teaspoon pepper

1/2 teaspoon oregano

1/2 teaspoon thyme

1/2 pound salt pork, sliced

1/2 cup crushed potato chips

Heat shortening or olive oil in skillet over medium heat. Add chopped onion and cook until tender. Add ground round steak and cook until brown, then remove from heat. Add drained hominy, tomato sauce, salt, pepper, oregano and thyme. Pour into greased 1 1/2-quart casserole. Add sliced pork, then cover with crushed potato chips. Bake in moderate oven (350 degrees) 45 minutes.

Makes 6 servings.

Honeydew Game Hens

6 Rock Cornish Game Hens

6 Honeydew or Crenshaw melons

Salt and pepper

2 1-lb. cans fruit salad

6 tablespoons David Wade Worcestershire Powder

Permit game hens to reach a few degrees below room temperature. Season the cavities and outside with salt and pepper to taste. Fill each cavity with approximately 4 tablespoons of fruit salad. Rub one table-spoon of Worcestershire Powder all over the surface of each them.

With a sharp knife, cut each melon in half. Using a large spoon, remove all but 1/4 inch of ripe fruit from each melon half. Place one game hen in one half of a melon. Put the top half of the melon back in place covering the game hen. You can tie a cotton string around the melon in both directions to tightly secure the top half. Place the 6 melons with game hens enclosed into a shallow baking pan approximately 3 inches tall. Do not use a lid for the pan. Preheat your oven to 400 degrees. Place the pan into the center of the oven and cook for one hour. Lower the temperature to 300 degrees and continue cooking for 3 hours.

When you remove the melon game hens from the oven, the melons will appear perfectly horrible but once you remove the top half, you will be surprised at the astonishing results found within.

Recipe serves 6.

Hong Kong Bacon Medley

1 cup regular or processed white rice

1/4 pound bacon slices

1 cup sliced onion

1 1/2 cups sliced celery

1 cup sliced mushrooms

2 cups water

1 1/2 tablespoons cornstarch

1 teaspoon salt

1/8 teaspoon pepper

Dash liquid red pepper seasoning

1 1/2 teaspoons soy sauce

2 cups shredded cabbage

1 cup sliced green pepper

1/4 pound bacon slices, halved

Cook rice according to package directions, then keep hot. Fry bacon slices over medium heat until crisp but not brittle. Remove bacon from pan. Add sliced onion, sliced celery, and sliced mushrooms to bacon fat and cook until brown. Reduce heat to low.

Blend water and cornstarch together and stir into onions and simmer 10 minutes. Add salt, pepper, red pepper seasoning, soy sauce, cabbage, green pepper and cooked bacon, broken in pieces. Cover and cook until vegetables are just tender. Meanwhile, fry halved bacon slices over medium heat until crisp. To serve, make ring of rice on serving dish. Pour vegetable mixture in center. Garnish with halved bacon slices.

Makes 4 servings.

Hungry Man's Noodles

1 tablespoon oil

1 pound ground meat (beef, pork, venison or combination of any two)

2 small onions, minced

2 cups chopped celery

1 package (6 ozs.) noodles, cooked and drained

2 cups cooked tomatoes or 1 cup tomato sauce

2 teaspoons David Wade Worcestershire Powder

3/4 cup grated sharp cheese

Salt and pepper to taste

Heat oil in saucepan or kettle over medium heat, add ground meat and cook until browned and partly done. Add minced onion and chopped celery and cook 10 minutes more. Add cooked and drained noodles, tomatoes or tomato sauce, Worcestershire Powder, grated cheese and salt and pepper to taste and mix well. Simmer over low heat 30 minutes or pour into greased baking dish and bake in moderate oven (350 degrees) 45 minutes.

Makes 8 servings.

Jean Baskin's Chicken Cutlets

3 cups flour

1 1/2 teaspoons pepper

3 teaspoons salt

1 1/2 teaspoons David Wade Worcestershire Powder

3 cups milk

1 1/2 cups cooking oil

3 pounds skinless chicken breasts

Mix together in a bowl the flour, pepper, salt and Worcestershire Powder and set aside. Pour milk into a largt bowl. Heat cooking oil in large skillet until frying hot.

Pound each chicken breast to about 1/8 inch thickness. Roll breasts in seasoned flour, then dip in milk and roll again in the flour mixture. Carefully place chicken pieces into hot oil and cook until golden brown on both sides. (About 5 minutes on each side.)

Remaining flour mixture can be used with additional milk and residue from skillet to make sauce to be spooned over cooked chicken.

Recipe serves 6.

John Gary's Chili

2 tablespoons olive oil

2 pounds ground sirloin

1 1/2 green peppers, chopped

2 medium onions, chopped

12 mushrooms, sliced

1 can (1 lb.) tomatoes

1 can (8 ozs.) tomato sauce

1 bottle (20 ozs.) catsup

1 bottle (12 ozs.) chili sauce

1 can (6 ozs.) tomato paste

4 cloves garlic, chopped

1 teaspoon oregano

Pinch of thyme

Liquid red pepper to taste

Heat olive oil in skillet over medium heat. Add ground sirloin, chopped green pepper, chopped onion and sliced mushrooms and saute 20 minutes. Add tomatoes, tomato sauce, catsup, chili sauce, tomato paste, chopped garlic, oregano, thyme and red pepper and reduce heat to low. Cover and simmer 2 hours. Serve on English muffins, omelettes, spaghetti, ravioli, toast or noodles. Meat may be omitted and sauce used on ribs or pork chops.

Makes approximately 3 quarts.

Lakeway Inn Pepper Steak

Cracked black pepper

2 1/2 pounds beef tenderloin cut into 6 steaks

1/3 cup butter or margarine

1/3 cup flour

1 cup tomato juice

2 cups consomme or beef stock

2 tablespoons David Wade Worcestershire Powder

2 teaspoons bottled brown bouquet sauce

1 teaspoon white pepper

1 1/2 teaspoons seasoned salt

Using mallet or edge of heavy plate, pound cracked black pepper into beef steaks. Combine butter or margarine and flour in saucepan and cook over low heat until light brown, stirring frequently. Gradually add tomato juice and consomme or beef stock. Add Worcestershire Powder, brown bouquet sauce, white pepper and seasoned salt and cook until thickened, stirring constantly. Keep warm. Saute peppered steaks in butter or margarine over medium heat until of desired doneness. Serve hot with approximately 1 cup sauce poured over each steak.

Makes 6 servings.

Moscow Chicken

1 cup rice

1 teaspoon salt

1 teaspoon monosodium glutamate

1 onion, finely chopped

1 1/2 can (10 1/2 ozs.) chicken with rice soup

1 1/2 soup cans water

10 pieces chicken

Mayonnaise

Paprika

Combine rice, salt, monosodium glutamate, chopped onion, chicken with rice soup and water in shallow baking pan, stirring until blended. Spread skin side of chicken with mayonnaise then place chicken pieces in pan with rice mixture, skin side up. Sprinkle with paprika.

Bake in low oven (300 degrees) 2 hours. Makes approximately 6 servings.

Maui Pork

(Sweet-Sour Pork)

2 tablespoons shortening

2 pounds lean boneless pork shoulder, cut in 1 1/2 inch cubes

2 medium onions, thinly sliced

1 large green pepper, cut in strips

1 cup diced celery

1 clove garlic, chopped

1/4 cup orange juice

1/4 cup soy sauce

1/4 cup brown sugar, firmly packed

1/2 teaspoon salt

1/4 teaspoon ginger

2 teaspoons David Wade Worcestershire Powder

1/2 cup white wine

3 medium carrots, cut in strips

1/4 pound mushrooms, halved (optional)

2 tablespoons plus 1 1/2 teaspoons cornstarch

2 tablespoons water

Heat shortening in Dutch oven over medium heat. Add pork cubes and cook until brown. Remove meat from pan. If necessary, remove excess fat from pan. Add onions, green pepper, celery, and garlic and cook until tender but not brown. Combine orange juice, soy sauce, brown sugar, salt, ginger and Worcestershire Powder. Then add white wine and slowly pour over vegetables. Return meat to pan. Add carrot strips and bring to boil. Reduce heat to low, cover tightly and simmer until meat is tender, about 1 hour. Add mushrooms and cook 5 minutes.

Blend cornstarch and water and stir into meat mixture. Bring to boil and cook 5 minutes, stirring.

Makes 5 or 6 servings.

Meat-Stuffed Green Peppers

6 large green peppers

1/4 cup olive oil

1/2 cup chopped onion

1 clove garlic, chopped

3/4 pound ground veal, beef, pork or combination of all three

2 cups cooked rice

3/4 cup grated Parmesan cheese

3 tablespoons chopped parsley

3 tablespoons Burgundy or Claret

2 teaspoons David Wade Worcestershire Powder

Salt and pepper to taste

3/4 cup tomato juice

Cut off tops and remove seeds from green peppers. Heat olive oil in large skillet over medium heat, add chopped onion and garlic and cook until onion is transparent. Add ground meat and cook until no longer red. Add rice, Parmesan cheese, chopped parsley, Burgundy or Claret, Worcestershire Powder, salt and pepper to taste. Remove from heat. Cool slightly.

Stuff peppers with meat mixture. Place in greased baking dish. Pour tomato juice around peppers. Bake in moderate oven (350 degrees) 30 to 40 minutes or until peppers are tender. Baste occasionally with juice in pan, adding more liquid if necessary.

Makes 6 servings.

Nevada Baked Steak

2 pounds round steak, cut 1-inch thick

1/2 teaspoon salt

Dash pepper

1 can (6 ozs.) tomato paste

1 teaspoon David Wade Worcestershire Powder

1 1/2 cups water

1 bay leaf

1/4 teaspoon thyme

1/4 cup vinegar

1 clove garlic

Salt and pepper

1/4 cup flour

3 tablespoons oil

1 large onion, sliced and separated into rings

1 green pepper, sliced in rings

Trim fat from round steak and cut into serving pieces. Place in shallow dish or pan. Combine salt, pepper, tomato paste, Worcestershire Powder, water, bay leaf, thyme and vinegar and pour over meat. Refrigerate overnight. After removing from refrigerator drain sauce from meat and reserve. Rub meat with garlic clove then sprinkle meat with salt and pepper. With mallet or edge of heavy plate, pound flour into meat.

Heat oil in skillet over medium heat, add meat and cook until brown. Place meat in baking dish. Drain oil from skillet. Add reserved sauce and heat. Arrange sliced onion rings and green pepper rings on top of meat. Pour hot sauce over all. Cover tightly. Bake in moderate oven (350 degrees) 1 1/2 to 2 hours.

Makes 6 servings.

Pheasants
With Nutted Orange Rice

3 broiler pheasants (1 1/2 lbs. each) split

1/2 lemon

Salt and pepper to taste

1/3 cup butter or margarine

Juice of 3 oranges

1 cup raisins

1 teaspoon grated lemon rind

1/3 cup muscatel wine

1 cup chicken broth

Rub inside of pheasants with lemon. Season with salt and pepper to taste. Place in baking pan, breast side up. Spread with butter or margarine.

Combine juice of oranges, reserving shells, raisins, grated lemon rind, wine and chicken broth and add to baking pan. Bake in moderate oven (350 degrees) 45 minutes, basting with drippings every 10 minutes. Serve with Nutted Orange Rice.

Makes 6 servings.

NUTTED ORANGE RICE

2 cups chicken broth

1 cup regular white rice

2 tablespoons butter or margarine

2/3 cup chopped pecans

2 tablespoons minced parsley

Salt to taste

Combine chicken broth and white rice in saucepan and bring to boil over medium heat. Stir, cover and cook over low heat 14 minutes. Remove from heat. Stir in butter or margarine, chopped pecans, minced parsley and salt. Flute reserved orange shells when preparing pheasant. Spoon rice into shells.

Makes 6 servings.

Pinwheel Ham Loaf

1 pound ground cooked ham	2 cups chopped fresh peaches
1/2 cup finely chopped celery	2 cups sifted flour
1/2 cup finely chopped pecans	3 teaspoons baking powder
1/2 cup fine bread crumbs	1 teaspoon salt
2 tablespoons minced onion	1/4 cup shortening
1 teaspoon ground cloves	1/2 cup milk (approximately)
1 egg, slightly beaten	Melted butter or margarine

Combine ground ham, chopped celery, pecans, bread crumbs, minced onion and ground cloves. Blend in slightly beaten egg and chopped peaches. Sift flour, baking powder and salt together into mixing bowl.

With pastry blender, fork or 2 knives, cut flour mixture into shortening until mixture looks like corn meal. Stir in milk to make dough stiff enough to form ball. Turn out onto lightly floured board and knead lightly. Roll out to 15 x 10-inch rectangle. Spread ham mixture evenly over dough. Starting at long edge, roll up as for jelly roll. Cut into 1 1/2-inch thick slices. Place, cut side down, on greased baking sheet. Brush with melted butter or margarine. Bake in hot oven (425 degrees) 25 minutes. Serve with Fresh Peach Sauce.

Makes 12 to 15 pinwheels.

FRESH PEACH SAUCE

1 1/2 tablespoons cornstarch	1 tablespoon grated lemon rind
1/2 cup sugar	
1 teaspoon dry mustard	2 teaspoons lemon juice
1 cup boiling water	1 1/2 cups thinly sliced fresh peaches

Combine cornstarch, sugar and dry mustard in saucepan, add boiling water and cook over low heat until thickened and clear, stirring constantly. Remove from heat. Add grated lemon rind, lemon juice and sliced peaches.

Makes about 1 1/2 cups.

Pork Casserole Oriental

1 1/2 pounds pork

2 tablespoons fat

1 1/2 cups sliced celery

1 medium onion, chopped

1 can (10 1/2 ozs.) condensed cream of chicken soup

1 can (10 1/2 ozs.) condensed cream of mushroom soup

1 1/3 soup cans water

2 tablespoons soy sauce

1/2 cup uncooked rice

Salt to taste

Minced parsley

Chow mein noodles

Cut pork in julienne strips. Heat fat in skillet over medium heat, add pork and cook until brown. Remove from heat. Add sliced celery, chopped onion, cream of chicken soup, cream of mushroom soup, water, soy sauce, rice and salt to taste. Pour into 2-quart baking dish. Cover and bake in moderate oven (325 degrees) 1 1/2 hours, stirring after the first 1/2 hour. Garnish with minced parsley and serve with warmed chow mein noodles.

Makes 6 servings.

Portuguese Chicken

3 tablespoons butter or margarine

2 pound broiler-fryer, cut in serving pieces

1 tablespoon chopped onion

1 tablespoon flour

1 clove garlic, finely chopped

1/4 cup dry white wine or water

1/2 cup chicken broth

1/2 cup canned tomatoes, drained

1 tablespoon David Wade Worcestershire Powder

Salt and pepper to taste

2 fresh tomatoes, peeled and chopped

Chopped parsley for garnish

Heat butter or margarine in skillet over medium heat. Add chicken pieces and fry until brown on all sides. Remove chicken from skillet and keep hot. Reduce heat to low and add chopped onion to skillet. Cook 3 or 4 minutes, stirring occasionally. Add flour and chopped garlic, stirring with wire whisk. Add wine or water and chicken broth and cook until thickened and smooth. Add tomatoes, Worcestershire Powder, salt and pepper to taste and return chicken to skillet. Cover and simmer 30 minutes or until tender. Remove chicken to warm serving platter and keep hot. Add tomatoes to skillet. Simmer 15 minutes. Pour sauce over chicken. Sprinkle with chopped parsley.

Makes 4 servings.

Ricotta Meatloaf

2 pounds lean ground beef	**Salt and pepper to taste**
2 eggs	**1 lb. Ricotta cheese**

Mix meat thoroughly with eggs then add salt, pepper and Ricotta cheese. Mix thoroughly; stir in 1 1/2 cups Tomato Sauce (recipe below). Place meat mixture into casserole dish and form into loaf. Top with remaining tomato sauce and place uncovered, into a preheated 375 degree oven. Bake for approximately 45 minutes or until done.

TOMATO SAUCE

2 tablespoons cooking oil	**2 tablespoons David Wade Worcestershire Powder**
1 large onion, finely diced	
1 (1 lb. 1 oz.) can tomatoes and liquid	**1/2 teaspoon salt**
	1/2 teaspoon pepper
1 (12 oz.) can tomato sauce	**1 teaspoon garlic powder**
	1/2 teaspoon oregano
1 small can tomato paste	**1 1/2 teaspoons sugar**
Few drops Tabasco sauce	

Heat cooking oil in saucepan then add onion. Saute until onion is soft; add tomatoes with liquid, tomato sauce and tomato paste. Cook slowly until rawness is removed from tomatoes. Add Tabasco sauce, Worcestershire Powder, salt, pepper, garlic powder, oregano and sugar. Simmer slowly for approximately 3 minutes.

Recipe serves 6.

Sauteed Calf's Liver With Avocado

1 1/2 pounds calf's liver

2 tablespoons butter or margarine

2 medium avocados

2 tablespoons butter or margarine

1/4 cup butter or margarine

1/2 cup chicken broth

1/3 cup white wine

1/4 cup lemon juice

1 tablespoon snipped chives

1 teaspoon snipped parsley

2 teaspoons David Wade Worcestershire Powder

Slice calf's liver in 12 thin slices. Heat 2 tablespoons butter or margarine in skillet over medium heat and add liver, cooking until brown on both sides. Remove liver to platter and keep warm. Peel and slice avocados into 9 whole slices each. Add 2 tablespoons butter or margarine to skillet in which liver was cooked and add avocado slices and cook approximately 1 minute on each side. Remove to platter with liver and keep warm. Add 1/4 cup butter or margarine to drippings in skillet and cook until brown. Add chicken broth, white wine, lemon juice, chives, parsley and Worcestershire Powder and bring to boil. Pour mixture over liver and avocado slices and serve.

Makes 6 servings.

Southern Style Beef Hash

2 tablespoons butter or margarine

1/2 cup diced white onion

1/2 cup diced green pepper

1 cup diced raw potatoes

2 cups finely diced roast beef

1 cup beef stock or 1 beef bouillon cube in 1 cup hot water

Salt and pepper to taste

2 tablespoons minced parsley

Heat butter or margarine in skillet over low heat. Add diced onion and green pepper and cook, covered, 10 minutes. Add potatoes, diced roast beef, stock or beef bouillon cube in hot water, salt and pepper, and continue cooking 40 minutes or until potatoes are tender. Add water if necessary to prevent sticking. Fold in 1 tablespoon minced parsley. Place in serving dish. Garnish with 1 tablespoon minced parsley. For back-yard supper, serve hash right from iron skillet, resting it on large wooden plate or iron griddle.

Makes 6 servings.

Sour Cream Enchiladas

2 tablespoons cooking oil

2 pounds lean ground beef

1 onion, diced finely

1 green bell pepper diced finely

Salt and pepper to taste

4 tablespoons canned chili without beans (slightly thinned with water)

2 tablespoons Picante Sauce

1 tablespoon chili powder

1/2 teaspoon cumin powder

1/2 teaspoon coriander

1 tablespoon garlic powder

1 tablespoon David Wade Worcestershire Powder

4 drops Tabasco sauce

1/2 cup ripe sliced, pitted olives

12 corn tortillas

1/4 cup Picante Sauce

2 cups water

1/4 pound butter

4 tablespoons flour

1 1/2 cups milk

1 pint sour cream

1 pound grated mild Cheddar cheese

1/2 cup whole, pitted ripe olives

In large, heavy skillet or Dutch oven, heat oil, then brown ground beef, stirring constantly. Add onion and green bell pepper and continue cooking until soft. Add salt, pepper, chili, Picante Sauce, chili powder, cumin powder, coriander, garlic powder, Worcestershire Powder, Tabasco sauce and sliced ripe olives. Continue stirring while recipe simmers for approximately 5 minutes.

Using mixing bowl, place 1/4 cup Picante Sauce in 2 cups water and blend with fork. Place tortillas in Picante water and permit to soak for a few minutes.

In separate saucepan, melt butter and stir in flour. Add milk and continue to stir until sauce is slightly thickened. Blend in sour cream and continue to heat slowly for 1 minute.

Select a large casserole dish and grease lightly. Drain each tortilla slightly and fill with 2 tablespoons of meat mixture. Sprinkle some grated Cheddar cheese (reserving 1/2 pound) over meat mixture and fold over in enchilada style. Arrange the stuffed tortillas in the dish and top thoroughly with sour cream sauce. Sprinkle remaining 1/2 pound of grated Cheddar over top of enchiladas. Locate whole ripe olives on surface and place enchiladas into a preheated 375 degree oven. Bake for 25 minutes or until sauce is bubbling. Remove from oven and serve immediately on heated plates.

Makes 12 enchiladas.

Spanish Lamb Stew

2 teaspoons salt

2 tablespoons flour

4 pounds shoulder of lamb, cut into 2-inch pieces

1/4 cup olive oil

1/4 cup salad oil

3 onions, chopped

2 or 3 cloves garlic, crushed

2 ripe tomatoes, peeled and chopped

1 teaspoon powdered cumin

1 teaspoon cinnamon

1/4 teaspoon ground cloves

1 cup dry sherry

2 1/2 cups water

1 package (10 ozs.) frozen butter beans

Combine salt and flour and coat lamb pieces with mixture. Heat olive oil and salad oil in heavy saucepan or kettle over medium heat; add lamb and cook until browned on all sides. Add chopped onion, crushed garlic and chopped tomatoes and cook until onion is soft. Add cumin, cinnamon and cloves and cook 1 minute. Add sherry and water, cover, and simmer over low heat 3 or 4 hours, skimming occasionally. Remove from heat. Cool and chill in refrigerator at least 24 hours. Skim fat from surface.

Before serving, add butter beans and cook over low heat 20 to 30 minutes. Serve with plain or saffron rice.

Makes 10 servings.

Note: 1 cup canned tomatoes may be used in place of fresh tomatoes. Add to stew after onion is soft. This dish freezes well and can be made ahead of time.

Stuffed Flank Steak With Sour Cream Gravy

1 1/2 pound flank steak	1/8 teaspoon pepper
1/2 pound pork sausage	2 tablespoons butter or margarine
1 1/2 cups fresh bread crumbs	
2 green onions, chopped	1 can (10 1/2-ozs.) beef consomme
1/2 cup chopped celery	
1 teaspoon salt	1 cup water
1/4 teaspoon pepper	2 tablespoons butter or margarine
2 teaspoons David Wade Worcestershire Powder	1/2 pound fresh mushrooms, sliced
3 tablespoons flour	
1/2 teaspoon salt	1/2 cup sour cream

If desired, have butcher cut pocket for stuffing in flank steak. Cook sausage in skillet over medium heat until done. Add bread crumbs, chopped onion, celery, salt, pepper and Worcestershire Powder. Stuff pocket in steak or spread on surface. Roll and fasten with skewers or tie with string. Combine flour, salt and pepper. Dredge steak in seasoned flour. Heat butter or margarine in skillet over medium heat and add steak, cooking until brown on all sides. Place steak in casserole. Add any remaining seasoned flour to drippings in skillet. Add beef consomme and water and stir to loosen drippings. Pour consomme mixture over steak. Cover and bake in moderate oven (350 degrees) 1 hour and 15 minutes, turning once or twice. Remove from oven. Place steak on heated platter.

Heat butter or margarine in saucepan over low heat; add mushrooms and saute. Blend in drippings from casserole. Gradually add sour cream and heat to serving temperature being careful not to boil. Pour over steak and serve.

Makes 4 to 6 servings.

Texas Meatballs

1 **pound ground chuck**	1 **teaspoon ground cumin**
1 **egg, slightly beaten**	1 **teaspoon ground coriander**
1/2 **cup milk**	
3/4 **cup crushed corn chips**	1 **teaspoon dried oregano leaves**
2 1/2 **teaspoons salt**	
2 1/2 **tablespoons flour**	1 **teaspoon David Wade Worcestershire Powder**
2 **tablespoons shortening**	1 **can (1 lb. 3 oz.) tomatoes, undrained**
2 **cups onion, sliced**	
1 **clove garlic, crushed**	1 **square unsweetened chocolate**
2 **tablespoons sugar**	
1 **tablespoon chili powder**	3 **cups cooked white rice**
	1 **cup water**

In large bowl, mix ground chuck lightly with egg, milk, corn chips, and 1 teaspoon salt. Refrigerate, covered, for 1 hour. Remove from refrigerator and gently shape into 20 meatballs, using 2 tablespoons meat mixture for each. Roll meatballs lightly in 2 tablespoons flour, coating completely.

In large, heavy skillet with tight-fitting lid, heat shortening slowly. When hot, saute meatballs, a few at a time, until nicely browned all over. Remove meatballs from skillet as they are browned. In same skillet, cook sliced onion and crushed garlic, stirring occasionally, about 5 minutes, or until tender. Remove from heat.

Combine sugar, chili powder, cumin, coriander, oregano, Worcestershire Powder and remaining salt and flour. Stir into skillet along with tomatoes, chocolate and water, mixing well. Bring mixture to boiling, stirring constantly. Reduce heat and simmer, covered, stirring occasionally 45 minutes. Add meatballs to skillet and simmer, covered, 15 minutes. Uncover and simmer 15 minutes. Turn meatballs and sauce into chafing dish. Serve over hot rice.

Makes 4 to 6 servings.

Upside-Down Peach Ham Loaf

1 pound ground cooked ham

1 pound ground lean pork

2 eggs, slightly beaten

1 cup corn flake crumbs

1 cup milk

1/4 teaspoon pepper

1/2 cup light brown sugar, firmly packed

1 tablespoon prepared light mustard

2 teaspoons lemon juice

4 medium peaches

2 tablespoons slivered blanched almonds or fresh strawberry halves

Mix ground ham, ground pork, beaten eggs, corn flake crumbs, milk and pepper together. Combine brown sugar, mustard and lemon juice mixing well. Peel peaches, cut in half and pit. Place peaches, cut side down,. in bottom of 9x5x3-inch pan. Spread 2/3 sugar mixture over peaches. Press meat mixture over peaches and spread remaining sugar mixture over meat. Bake in moderate oven (375 degrees) 1 1/2 hours. Turn out onto serving platter. Place 2 tablespoons slivered, blanched almonds or fresh strawberry halves in center of peach halves.

Makes 8 to 10 servings.

Neptune's Treasure

The waterways of the world provide us with some of our most interesting and nutritional foods. This section presents exciting creations for your seafood menu. It is suggested, because of the valuable nutrients found in fish products, that they be served about twice a week. The items of cuisine should never be overcooked or their natural flavor hidden by too many seasonings and batters.

Baked Tuna-and-Cheese Casserole

1 cup elbow macaroni

2 cans (7-oz. size) chunk-style tuna, drained

1 can (8-oz.) diced carrots, drained

1/4 cup slivered ripe olives

5 tablespoons butter or margarine

1/2 cup packaged seasoned dry bread crumbs

1/4 cup sliced onion

1/4 cup unsifted all-purpose flour

1 1/2 teaspoons salt

1/8 teaspoon pepper

2 1/2 cups milk

3/4 cup grated sharp Cheddar cheese

Cook macaroni as package label directs then drain. Preheat oven to 375 degrees.

In a 2-quart casserole, toss macaroni with tuna, carrots and olives then mix well.

Melt butter in medium saucepan. Toss 1 tablespoon melted butter with bread crumbs in a small bowl and set aside. In rest of hot butter, saute onion until golden — about 5 minutes. Remove from heat and add flour, salt and pepper, stirring until smooth. Gradually stir in milk. Bring mixture to boiling and boil 1 minute. Reduce heat and add cheese, stirring until it is melted.

Pour cheese sauce over tuna mixture, toss to mix well. Sprinkle buttered crumbs over the top and bake 20 minutes or until golden-brown and bubbly. Makes 6 servings.

Barbecued Shrimp

Juice of 1 lemon

1 tablespoon onion juice

1 cup catsup

2 tablespoons David Wade Worcestershire Powder

1 teaspoon chili powder

1 teaspoon salt

2 dashes liquid red pepper seasoning

1/4 cup white wine

2 pounds cleaned, deveined jumbo shrimp

Combine lemon juice, onion juice, catsup, Worcestershire Powder, chili powder, salt, red pepper seasoning and white wine in saucepan and heat over very low heat until mixture begins to bubble. Remove from heat and let stand 10 minutes. Place, in single layer, in shallow pan or on foil-covered broiler pan the jumbo shrimp and top with sauce. Broil 3 inches from medium heat until shrimp is golden brown.

Makes 4 servings.

Brunch Shrimp Supreme

2 tablespoons butter or margarine

1 cup sliced fresh mushrooms

2 tablespoons flour

1/2 cup light cream

1 can (10 1/2 ozs.) condensed cream of mushroom soup

1/3 cup cooking sherry

3 tablespoons grated Parmesan cheese

2 packages (7 ozs. each) frozen shelled shrimp, cooked

1 can (15 ozs.) artichoke hearts, drained and halved

1/4 cup toasted, slivered, blanched almonds

Melt butter or margarine in saucepan over medium heat and saute mushrooms until tender. Reduce heat to low and push mushrooms to side of pan. Blend flour into liquid in pan and gradually stir in cream. Bring to boil and boil 1 minute, stirring frequently.

Blend in cream of mushroom soup, sherry and grated Parmesan cheese then stir in cooked shrimp and artichoke hearts. Heat thoroughly, stirring gently. Place in chafing dish to keep warm. Sprinkle slivered blanched almonds on top and garnish with watercress. Serve over tiny biscuits or patty shells.

Makes 6 servings.

Crab Meat Mornay Supreme

4 tablespoons butter or margarine

4 tablespoons flour

2 cups milk

Salt and pepper to taste

1/4 cup Madeira

1 pound crab meat

Grated Parmesan cheese

Buttered bread crumbs

Melt butter or margarine in saucepan over very low heat, then blend in flour. Remove from heat. Add milk gradually, stirring until smooth. Return to heat and cook until thickened, stirring constantly. Add salt and pepper; blend in Madeira and crab meat. Pour into greased casserole or individual ramekins. Top with grated Parmesan cheese and buttered bread crumbs.

Bake in hot oven (425 degrees) 15 minutes or until brown and bubbly. Makes 4 servings.

Crab Sauce With Spaghetti

1 pound fresh, thawed frozen or pasteurized crab meat or 3 cans (6 1/2 or 7 1/2 ozs. each) crab meat

1/4 cup butter or margarine

1/2 cup chopped onion

1/2 cup chopped celery

2 cloves garlic, finely chopped

2 tablespoons chopped parsley

1 cup canned tomatoes

1 can (8 ozs.) tomato sauce

1/4 teaspoon salt

1/2 teaspoon paprika

2 teaspoons David Wade Worcestershire Powder

Dash pepper

3 cups cooked spaghetti

Grated Parmesan cheese

Drain crab meat, remove any shell or cartilage and cut into 1/2 inch pieces. Melt butter or margarine in saucepan over medium heat and add onion, celery, garlic and parsley and cook until tender. Add tomatoes, tomato sauce, salt, paprika, Worcestershire Powder and pepper and simmer over low heat 20 minutes, stirring occasionally. Add crab meat and continue cooking until hot.

Place cooked spaghetti in serving bowl or platter and pour sauce over it, then sprinkle with grated Parmesan cheese.

Makes 6 servings.

Dishwasher Fish

If you enjoy poached fish the way that I do, you will thoroughly enjoy this recipe and have much fun in the process.

Select as many fish fillets (any type) as may be desired for serving. Make certain the fish is just slightly below room temperature. Sprinkle approximately 1 tablespoon of lemon juice over each fillet. Brush approximately 1 tablespoon of melted butter over each fish selection. Sprinkle 1/2 teaspoon of David Wade Worcestershire Powder over each fillet. Securely seal each fillet, with seasoning, in freezer bags (the type used in freezing foods.) Carefully place the individual pouches in the top racks of your automatic dishwasher. Close the dishwasher and set control to full cycle. Activate dishwasher and remove fish 15 minutes following the termination of the dishwasher operation. You will find these poached fish to be delightful.

Various seasoned vegetables can be sealed in freezer bags and placed in the lower racks to cook during the process. These vegetables will be served crisp tender.

Hot Salmon Loaf

1 1/4 cups toasted almonds (about 7 ozs.)	4 drops liquid red pepper seasoning
1 1/2 cups medium white sauce	2 teaspoons salt
3 egg yolks, slightly beaten	1/2 teaspoon pepper
1 can (1 lb.) finely flaked salmon	1/2 teaspoon paprika
1 1/2 cups soft bread crumbs	3 egg whites
	Parsley
1/4 cup finely chopped onion	Lemon slices

Using fine blade of food chopper, grind almonds to make 1 1/4 cups. Prepare white sauce according to favorite recipe and stir 3 tablespoons

73

of hot sauce into slightly beaten egg yolks. Vigorously stir egg mixture into remaining white sauce. Remove from heat. Stir ground almonds, flaked salmon, bread crumbs, chopped onion and red pepper seasoning into sauce. Add salt, pepper and paprika.

Beat egg whites until rounded peaks form then spread over salmon mixture and fold together. Turn mixture into 9 x 5 x 3-inch pan with bottom greased. Set loaf pan in larger pan on oven rack. Fill larger pan with boiling water to depth of salmon mixture in loaf pan. Bake in moderate oven (350 degrees) 1 hour and 10 minutes. Remove from oven. Turn out of pan. Garnish with parsley and lemon slices. Serve immediately. Makes approximately 6 servings.

Macaroni And Bean Salad With Shrimp

2 whole cloves stuck in
1 small yellow onion

1 1/4 pounds medium fresh raw shrimp

1/2 lemon

1 celery stalk top

2 sprigs parsley

Water

2 cups elbow macaroni

1 package (9 ozs.) frozen French green beans with toasted almonds

1 small purple onion, sliced and separated into rings

1 pimiento, chopped

1/3 cup lemon juice or vinegar

1/3 cup salad oil

1 small clove garlic, minced

1 teaspoon salt

1/2 teaspoon thyme

1/4 teaspoon oregano

Combine cloves stuck in onion, shrimp, lemon, celery top and parsley in saucepan. Add water to cover and bring to boil over full heat. Cover and remove from heat; let stand 5 minutes. Drain. Rinse shrimp with cold water, remove shells and devein. Split shrimp and set aside. Cook macaroni according to package directions and drain. Rinse with cold water and drain thoroughly. Cook green beans with almonds according to package directions, reserving almonds.

Combine shrimp, macaroni, green beans, onion rings and pimiento in large bowl. In small bowl, combine lemon juice or vinegar, salad oil, minced garlic, salt, thyme and oregano, mixing well. Then pour dressing over shrimp mixture and toss until thoroughly coated. Cover and let stand in refrigerator at least 1 hour. Serve in lettuce cups, if desired. Garnish with reserved toasted almonds. Makes 8 or 9 servings.

Mushrooms And Clams Supreme

50 fresh steamer clams	1 1/4 teaspoons lemon pepper
50 medium-size fresh mushrooms	2/3 cup finely chopped green onion
2/3 cup butter or margarine, melted	10 slices bacon

Scrub clams and place on broiler pan. Broil in preheated broiler compartment as far from full heat as size of compartment will permit. When shells have opened, remove from broiler and cool. Remove clams from shells.

Rinse mushrooms, pat dry and remove stems. Brush with melted butter or margarine then dust cavities of mushrooms with lemon pepper. Place one clam in each mushroom cavity. Sprinkle with chopped onion.

Cut each bacon slice into 5 pieces and place one piece bacon on top of each clam-stuffed mushroom. Place on broiler grid. Broil 3 inches from full heat until bacon is crisp.

Makes 50.

Note: In place of fresh clams, 5 jars (7 ozs. each) whole little neck clams may be used. Drain and cut large whole clams in half.

Nebraska Scalloped Oysters

1/4 cup butter or margarine

1/4 cup light cream

1/2 teaspoon salt

1/8 teaspoon pepper

1 teaspoon David Wade Worcestershire Powder

2 tablespoons snipped parsley

1/2 teaspoon lemon juice

1 1/4 cups coarsely broken saltines

1/2 cup grated process Cheddar cheese

2 dozen shucked oysters, drained

1 can (12 ozs.) whole kernel corn, drained

Combine butter or margarine, light cream, salt, pepper, Worcestershire Powder, snipped parsley and lemon juice in small saucepan and heat over low heat just until butter is melted.

In greased 10x6x2-inch baking dish, place half of the broken saltines, then sprinkle grated Cheddar cheese over saltines. Place drained oysters on cheese along with drained corn. Pour butter mixture over all. Top with remaining saltines. Bake in hot oven (400 degrees) 20 to 25 minutes. Serve immediately.

Makes 4 to 5 servings.

Note: Pick over oysters to remove any bits of shell.

Salmon-Cheese Casserole

1 1/2 cups milk

2 tablespoons butter or margarine

1 cup soft bread crumbs

3 eggs, well beaten

2 tablespoons minced parsley

2 tablespoons finely chopped onion

1 1/2 cups shredded sharp Cheddar cheese

1 teaspoon David Wade Worcestershire Powder

1/8 teaspoon pepper

Dash paprika

1 can (1 lb.) salmon, drained, skinned and broken into pieces

Heat milk and butter or margarine in saucepan over very low heat until butter is melted. Combine bread crumbs and well beaten eggs and stir milk into this mixture. Add parsley, onion, shredded Cheddar, Worcestershire Powder, pepper and paprika, mixing well. Spread salmon pieces in bottom of greased 1 1/2-quart casserole. Pour custard mixture over salmon. Place in pan with hot water to a depth of at least 1 inch. Bake in moderate oven (350 degrees) 1 hour or until custard mixture is set.

Makes 4 to 6 servings.

Salmon Louis

Dressing

1/2 cup mayonnaise or salad dressing	2 hard-cooked egg whites, chopped
2 tablespoons heavy cream	1 tablespoon chopped olives
2 tablespoons chili sauce	1/2 teaspoon lemon juice
2 tablespoons chopped green pepper	Dash salt
2 tablespoons chopped green onion	Dash pepper

Combine all ingredients and chill thoroughly.

Salad

1 head lettuce	2 tomatoes
1 can (1 lb.) salmon, drained and flaked	2 hard-cooked egg yolks, sieved

Place lettuce in shallow salad bowl. Arrange flaked salmon on lettuce. Cut tomatoes into 6 wedges each and place around edge of bowl. Pour chilled dressing over all. Sprinkle with sieved egg yolks.

Makes 6 servings.

Salmon-Stuffed Peppers

3 large green peppers

1 cup flaked, cooked or canned salmon

1 cup medium white sauce

Salt and pepper to taste

2 tablespoons chili sauce

1 hard-cooked egg, chopped

Buttered fine bread crumbs

Cut green peppers in half, lengthwise and remove seeds and membrane. Cook in boiling water over low heat 5 minutes. Drain. Mix salmon, white sauce, salt and pepper, chili sauce and chopped egg together. Fill pepper halves with salmon mixture. Cover with buttered bread crumbs. Place in greased baking dish. Pour small amount of hot water in bottom of dish. Bake in moderate oven (350 degrees) 25 to 30 minutes.

Makes 3 servings.

Sauteed Scallops With Scallions

1/2 cup packaged dried bread crumbs

1/4 teaspoon paprika

1 pound (1 pint) bay scallops

6 tablespoons butter or margarine

1/3 cup finely sliced scallions or minced onion

1/2 teaspoon salt

1/8 teaspoon pepper

Combine bread crumbs and paprika. Roll bay scallops in crumbs. Heat butter or margarine, finely sliced scallions or minced onion, salt and pepper in skillet over medium heat. Add scallops and saute until golden on all sides.

Makes 3 or 4 servings.

Savory Baked Fish

1 1/2 pounds haddock fillet

Salt to taste

   1 teaspoon instant
     minced onion

   1/4 teaspoon tarragon
     leaves

   1 teaspoon David Wade
   Worcestershire Powder

1/16 teaspoon pepper

1/2 teaspoon dry mustard

   2 teaspoons water

   1 teaspoon lemon juice

1/2 cup mayonnaise

Paprika

Wipe haddock fillets with damp cloth and place in shallow baking dish. Sprinkle with salt. Combine minced onion, tarragon leaves, Worcestershire Powder, pepper, mustard and water and let stand 10 minutes. Add lemon juice and mayonnaise to spice mixture and spread on fish.

Bake in hot oven (425 degrees) 25 to 30 minutes or until browned. Sprinkle with paprika.

Makes 6 servings.

Shrimply Delicious

1/2 cup finely chopped garlic

1/2 cup finely chopped celery
   hearts

Water

   1 cup lemon juice

   1 cup parsley, finely chopped

Salt and pepper to taste

1 teaspoon David Wade
   Worcestershire Powder

2 pounds peeled, deveined
   shrimp

2 cups flour

1 cup grated Parmesan cheese

2 eggs, slightly beaten

Saute chopped garlic and celery hearts in butter or margarine over medium heat and place in large saucepan or kettle; cover with water. Add lemon juice, parsley, salt, pepper and Worcestershire Powder. Add the shrimp and boil over low heat. Remove from heat. Remove shrimp and drain. Combine flour, grated Parmesan. Dip shrimp in the slightly beaten eggs, then dip in flour-cheese mixture. Fry in deep hot fat over medium heat until brown.

Makes 4 servings.

Shrimp With Green Peppers

1 pound raw shrimp, shelled and deveined

6 tablespoons unsifted all-purpose flour

2 tablespoons grated Parmesan cheese

1 3/4 teaspoons salt

1/2 cup olive or salad oil

1 clove garlic, crushed

6 medium green peppers, cut into strips

1/4 cup dry white wine

Dash pepper

Toss shrimp with flour, cheese and 1 teaspoon salt, coating well. Slowly heat oil in large, heavy skillet and add shrimp and garlic. Cook about 5 minutes, or until shrimp are golden. Remove shrimp from the skillet and set aside.

Add pepper strips to skillet. Cook, covered, over medium heat for 10 to 15 minutes or until crisp-tender. Add the shrimp, rest of the salt, wine and pepper to the skillet and cook, covered, until heated through. Serve with rice. Makes 6 servings.

Tuna Supper Pilaf

2 cans (6 1/2 or 7 ozs. each) tuna

1 cup sliced celery

1/3 cup minced onion

1 large green pepper, slivered

3 cups cooked rice

1/3 cup diced canned pimiento

1 can (3 or 4 ozs.) sliced mushrooms and liquid

1/2 cup sliced Brazil nuts

1 teaspoon salt

1/2 teaspoon monosodium glutamate

1/4 teaspoon pepper

1 teaspoon rosemary leaves

1 teaspoon marjoram leaves

Drain oil from tuna and place in large skillet. Heat oil over medium heat, add sliced celery, minced onion and slivered green pepper and cook 3 minutes or until crisp tender. Add drained tuna, cooked rice, diced pimiento, sliced mushrooms and liquid, sliced Brazil nuts, salt, monosodium glutamate, pepper, rosemary leaves and marjoram leaves. Heat to serving temperature. Serve immediately.

Makes 4 to 6 servings.

Wheel Of Fortune Crabmeat

2 tablespoons butter or margarine

2 tablespoons flour

1/2 teaspoon liquid red pepper seasoning

1 cup milk

1/2 cup grated or crumbled American cheese

2 cans (6 ozs. each) crabmeat

1 can (16 ozs.) asparagus spears

Melt butter or margarine in saucepan over very low heat and stir in flour and red pepper seasoning. Gradually add milk and continue cooking until thickened, stirring constantly. Add grated or crumbled American cheese and cook until melted. Add crabmeat.

Heat asparagus spears over low heat then drain and place on serving plate. Spoon hot crabmeat mixture over asparagus. Makes 6 servings.

Red Snapper Ponchartrain

2 eggs

4 10 oz. portions filet of red snapper

4 tablespoons white flour

Salt and pepper to taste

8 uncooked jumbo shrimp

1 stick sweet butter

1 clove garlic, crushed

3 green onions, finely chopped

1/2 cup chopped green parsley

1 1/2 cups fresh or canned mushrooms

Juice of 1 and 1/2 lemons

1 cup dry vermouth

Beat whole eggs and set aside. Dip red snapper fillets into beaten eggs. Place flour, salt and pepper into a small paper sack and insert fish fillets and jumbo shrimp. Shake sack until fish is well coated.

Melt butter in a heavy skillet and add crushed garlic. Place red snapper fillets and shrimp into the butter and cook slowly for 3 to 5 minutes. Turn fish to other side and cook until red snapper starts to flake slightly. Add finely chopped green onion and chopped parsley, then add mushrooms and lemon juice. Cook slowly until mushrooms and green onions are lightly browned, then add dry vermouth. Permit this sauce to reduce by cooking for approximately one additional minute. Serve on a heated plate garnished with parsley and a slice of lemon. Makes 4 servings.

Desserts

The menu finale' is most often the course which leaves the lasting impression on your guests. Shouldn't it be special? Here is a collection of especially tasty treats which are sure to join your current list of favorites.

Almond Macaroons

1/2 pound (1 cup) almond paste, chopped

1 cup unsifted confectioners' sugar

3 egg whites or less

Dash salt

1/2 teaspoon vanilla

Granulated sugar

Work chopped almond paste and confectioners' sugar together with fingers until blended. Add, one at a time, the egg whites, blending well after each addition. Use only enough egg white to make soft mixture that will hold its shape when dropped from a spoon. Add salt and vanilla. Press through plain pastry tube into rounds on baking sheet covered with unglazed paper. Leave 2 inches between rounds. Sprinkle with granulated sugar. Bake in low oven (300 degrees) 20 minutes. Remove sheet of macaroons, paper side down, to a damp cloth to loosen cookies for easy removal. Remove from paper and cool on wire rack.

Makes approximately 3 dozen.

Apple Trifle

1 package (3 1/4 ozs.) coconut pudding mix

2 1/2 cups milk

1/2 teaspoon brandy extract

1 can (1 lb. 4 ozs.) pie-sliced apples, drained

1/2 cup apricot preserves

1/2 cup heavy cream, whipped

12 ladyfingers

Combine coconut pudding mix and milk in saucepan and cook according to package directions. Add brandy extract and cool. Combine sliced apples and apricot preserves in skillet and simmer over low heat 3 to 4 minutes or until apples are glazed. Remove from heat and cool. Fold whipped cream into pudding mixture.

Split ladyfingers and place in 6 dessert bowls or glasses. Spoon layer of pudding then layer of apples over ladyfingers. Chill.

Makes 6 servings.

Apple And Pretzel Pie

FILLING

1 can (1 lb. 4 ozs.) apple
slices

3/4 cup sugar

4 tablespoons cornstarch

1/8 teaspoon salt

Apple juice or cider

1/2 cup raisins

1-inch piece stick cinnamon

2 tablespoons lemon juice

Whipped cream (optional)

Drain liquid from can of apple slices, reserving. Combine sugar, cornstarch and salt in saucepan and gradually add apple liquid plus cider or apple juice to make 1 cup. Stir in drained apples, raisins and stick of cinnamon. Bring to boil over low heat then cook 5 minutes longer, stirring constantly. Add lemon juice and cool 5 minutes, stirring once or twice. Pour into pretzel pie shell. Serve with sweetened whipped cream, if desired.

SHELL

5 egg yolks

1/2 cup sugar

1 teaspoon vanilla

5 egg whites

1/2 cup sugar

1 teaspoon baking powder

1 cup pretzel crumbs

1 cup chopped walnuts

Beat egg yolks until thick and lemon colored. Gradually add sugar, beating until thick and fluffy, then add vanilla. Beat egg whites and sugar until stiff. Stir baking powder, pretzel crumbs and chopped walnuts into yolk mixture then fold into egg whites. Pour into 2 greased and floured 8-inch cake pans. With back of spoon spread on bottom and sides of pan to form shell. Bake in moderate oven (350 degrees) 20 minutes or until firm. Remove from oven. Loosen edges with spatula and remove from pans. Cool on cake racks.

Apple Strudel

2 1/2 cups flour

1 teaspoon salt

2 tablespoons shortening

2 eggs, slightly beaten

1/2 cup warm water

2 cans (1 lb. 4 ozs. each) sliced apples, drained

1/2 cup seedless raisins

1/2 cup chopped nuts

1 cup brown sugar, firmly packed

1/2 teaspoon cinnamon

Grated rind of 1 lemon

3 tablespoons melted butter or margarine

Sift flour and salt together. With pastry blender, fork or 2 knives cut in shortening until mixture looks like coarse corn meal. Add slightly beaten eggs and warm water, mixing well. Turn out on lightly floured board and knead well. Beat dough by pounding with edge of heavy plate or slamming against board until dough is blistered. Cover with cloth and let stand in warm place 20 minutes. On table covered with floured cloth, lightly roll dough to thin rectangle with floured rolling pin. Carefully ease hands under dough. With dough resting on sides of hands, gently pull to paper thinness working from center to each edge. Combine apples, raisins, nuts, brown sugar, cinnamon, lemon rind and butter or margarine and spread over dough. Fold in edges of dough to keep filling from spreading. Shape into roll about 4 inches wide. Place on baking sheet. Bake in hot oven (450 degrees) 10 minutes then reduce to moderately hot (400 degrees) and continue baking 20 minutes. Cool. Slice to serve.

NOTE: To re-heat, wrap in foil and heat in low oven (300 degrees) 10 minutes removing foil last 2 to 3 minutes.

Apricot Nut Bread

2 3/4 cups sifted flour	1 1/2 cups sugar
2 teaspoons soda	1 tablespoon melted fat
1/2 teaspoon salt	1 egg
2 cups dried apricots, chopped	1 1/2 cups Dr Pepper
1 cup pecans, chopped	1 tablespoon vanilla

Sift flour, soda and salt together. Add chopped apricots and pecans. Blend sugar and melted fat in mixing bowl and add egg, beating until light and fluffy.

Beginning with flour mixture, add flour mixture to sugar mixture alternately with Dr Pepper. Add vanilla and pour into greased and floured 9 x 5 x 3-inch loaf pan or two 8 x 4 x 2 1/4-inch loaf pans. Bake in moderate oven (350 degrees) 1 hour.

Makes 1 large or 2 small loaves.

Bananas Foster

3 tablespoons butter	2 tablespoons brandy
1 tablespoon brown sugar	1 banana, quartered
1 teaspoon cinnamon	1 tablespoon brandy
2 tablespoons banana liqueur	2 dishes vanilla ice cream
1 tablespoon rum	

Blend butter, brown sugar, cinnamon. banana liqueur, rum, brandy and quartered banana in skillet and bring to simmer over low heat. Simmer about 1 minute. Add brandy. Ignite sauce with match. Spoon over ice cream and serve immediately.

Makes 2 servings.

Baklava

6 cups sugar

3 cups water

1 cup honey

Juice of 1 lemon

1 stick cinnamon

Peel of 1 lemon
(not grated)

2 pounds pecans, finely
chopped (Do not grind.)

1 cup sugar

3 tablespoons cinnamon

2 1/2 pounds butter or
margarine (5 cups)

2 pounds filo leaves

Combine sugar, water, honey, lemon juice, cinnamon and lemon peel in saucepan. Cook over medium heat until small amount forms a soft ball in cold water (234 degrees on candy thermometer.) Remove from heat. Remove cinnamon and lemon peel. Cool.

Combine chopped pecans, sugar and cinnamon and mix well. Melt butter or margarine in saucepan over very low heat. If frozen, thaw filo leaves.

Place 8 sheets filo, one at a time, in bottom of 17 1/2 x 11 1/2 x 2-inch pan, brushing each sheet with melted butter. Sprinkle top sheet generously with nut mixture. Top with buttered filo sheet and continue until all nut mixture is used. Top with 8 more sheets filo, brushing each sheet with melted butter. Before baking, cut through top 3 or 4 sheets filo, only, with sharp knife. Cut into 8 long strips and cut strips diagonally into 8 or 9 pieces. Bake in moderate oven (350 degrees) 30 minutes. Reduce temperature to low (300 degrees) and continue baking 45 minutes longer. Remove from oven and pour cold syrup over hot baklava immediately. Cool before cutting along lines cut before baking.

Makes 5 1/2 to 6 dozen pieces.

Banana Split Pie

Chocolate cookies or macaroons

1 quart softened vanilla ice cream

Sliced bananas

Chocolate fudge syrup

Pineapple preserves

Whipped cream

Maraschino cherries

Line bottom and sides of 9-inch pie pan with cookies or macaroons. Spoon softened ice cream over cookies. Cover with foil to prevent ice crystals from forming. Freeze 10 minutes or until firm. Cover ice cream with sliced bananas. Add syrup and preserves and top with whipped cream and maraschino cherries.

Blueberry Break Cakes

2 1/3 cups unsifted flour

2 1/2 teaspoons baking powder

1/2 teaspoon salt

1/2 teaspoon nutmeg

1/2 cup vegetable shortening

3/4 cup sugar

2 eggs

3/4 cup milk

1 1/2 cups fresh blueberries

1/2 cup melted butter or margarine

3/4 cup sugar

1/4 teaspoon cinnamon

Sift flour, baking powder, salt and nutmeg together. Cream shortening until light and fluffy and gradually add sugar. Beat in eggs. Beginning and ending with dry ingredients, add dry ingredients to creamed mixture alternately with milk. Fold in blueberries.

Fill greased muffin cups 3/4 full. Bake in moderate oven (350 degrees) 20 to 25 minutes. Remove from oven and cool slightly. Mix sugar and cinnamon together. Roll muffins in melted butter or margarine, then roll in sugar-cinnamon mixture. Serve warm.

Makes 18.

Blueberry Orange Chiffon Pie

1 package (3 ozs.) orange-
flavored chiffon pie filling

1 1/2 cups fresh blueberries

Baked 9-inch pastry shell

1 cup heavy cream

2 tablespoons confectioners'
sugar

1 teaspoon vanilla

Prepare pie filling according to package directions then fold in 1 cup blueberries. Pour into pastry shell and chill until firm, about 2 hours.

Whip heavy cream, confectioner's sugar and vanilla. With toothpick, lightly mark top of pie into 6 wedges. Fill 3 alternate wedges with whipped cream. Fill remaining wedges with 1/2 cup fresh blueberries. Cut so each slice is covered with half cream and half blueberries.

Christmas Nutmeg-Pecan Cake

2 cups sifted flour

1 teaspoon baking powder

1/4 teaspoon salt

1 cup seeded raisins

1 1/2 cups finely chopped
pecans

3/4 cup butter or margarine

1 teaspoon nutmeg

1 teaspoon vanilla

1 cup sugar

1/3 cup light brown sugar,
firmly packed

3 eggs

2 tablespoons milk

Sift flour, baking powder and salt together. Mix sifted dry ingredients with raisins and pecans.

Blend butter or margarine, nutmeg and vanilla together. Gradually add sugar and brown sugar, beating well after each addition. Add eggs, one at a time, beating well after each addition. Gradually stir in dry ingredients and milk.

Pour into greased and floured 9 x 5 x 3-inch pan. Bake in low oven (300 degrees) 1 hour and 50 minutes. Remove from oven and let cool 20 minutes before removing from pan. Remove from pan and finish cooling on wire rack. If desired, wrap in clean cloth soaked in brandy or wine. Let stand at least 7 to 10 days before serving. Slice thin to serve.

Chocolate Cinnamon Torte

Pastry

2 3/4 cups sifted flour	2 cups sugar
2 tablespoons cinnamon	2 eggs
1 1/2 cups butter (do not substitute)	

Grease 2, 3 or 4 round 9-inch cake pans. Line bottom with waxed paper and grease again. Sift flour and cinnamon together. Cream butter and sugar together then add eggs and beat until light and fluffy. Gradually add sifted dry ingredients to creamed mixture, mixing until smooth. With spatula or back of spoon, spread 1/3 cup dough in thin layer in each prepared pan. Bake in moderate oven (375 degrees) 8 to 12 minutes or until golden. Remove from oven and carefully remove from pan at once. Cool on wire rack. Continue baking layers until all dough is used. (Make at least 12 layers.) These may be made several days before use. Store, carefully stacked, in airtight container.

Filling

1 one-ounce square unsweetened chocolate	Sugar
	2 tablespoons cocoa
2 one-ounce squares semi-sweet chocolate	12 candied or maraschino cherries
4 cups heavy cream	12 walnut halves

Grate unsweetened chocolate medium fine. With vegetable parer, peel semi-sweet chocolate into curls. Whip cream until stiff and sweeten to taste with sugar.

On serving plate, stack pastry layers, spreading each one with 1/4 to 1/3 cup whipped cream. Fold cocoa and grated unsweetened chocolate into remaining whipped cream. Heap chocolate cream on top of torte. Decorate with candied or maraschino cherries and walnut halves. Heap semi-sweet chocolate curls in center. Chill at least 30 minutes.

Makes 12 servings.

Coconut Pound Cake

3 cups sifted flour

1/2 teaspoon salt

1 teaspoon baking powder

1 cup less 2 tablespoons butter or margarine

2/3 cup vegetable shortening

3 cups sugar

5 eggs

1 cup milk

1 teaspoon coconut extract

1/2 teaspoon vanilla

1 can (3 ozs.) flaked coconut

Sift flour, salt and baking powder together. Cream butter or margarine, vegetable shortening and sugar. Add eggs, one at a time, beating well after each addition. Beginning and ending with dry ingredients, add dry ingredients to creamed mixture alternately with milk. Blend in coconut extract, vanilla and flaked coconut. Pour into greased and floured 10-inch tube pan. Bake in moderate oven (325 degrees) 1 1/2 hours. Remove from oven and let cool in pan 5 minutes. Remove from pan and finish cooling on wire rack.

Crazy Crust Apple Pie

1 cup flour

1 teaspoon baking powder

1/2 teaspoon salt

1 tablespoon sugar

1 egg

2/3 cup shortening

3/4 cup water

1 can (1 lb. 5 ozs.) apple pie filling

1 tablespoon lemon juice

1/2 teaspoon apple pie spice

Combine flour, baking powder, salt, sugar, egg, shortening and water in small mixing bowl. Blend well. Beat 2 minutes at medium speed. Pour into 9-inch pie pan.

Combine apple pie filling, lemon juice and apple pie spice and pour into center of batter. Do not stir. Bake in hot oven (425 degrees) 45 to 50 minutes.

Note: Mincemeat pie filling may be substituted for apple.

French Coconut Pie

1 cup milk

3 tablespoons butter

3 eggs

1/2 cup sugar

1/2 cup light corn syrup

1/2 teaspoon vanilla

1/2 teaspoon coconut extract

1 cup grated coconut

Unbaked 9-inch pastry shell

Heat milk and butter together in saucepan over very low heat until butter is melted. Beat eggs until foamy then add sugar, light corn syrup, vanilla and coconut extract. Combine milk and egg mixtures, mixing well. Spread grated coconut in pastry shell then pour milk and egg mixture over coconut.

Bake in moderate oven (350 degrees) 40 minutes or until set.

Fresh Grape Lemon Chiffon Pudding

5 egg yolks

1 cup sugar

1/3 cup fresh lemon juice

1 teaspoon grated lemon rind

1 tablespoon unflavored gelatin

1/4 cup water

5 egg whites

1/8 teaspoon salt

1 teaspoon vanilla

1 cup Emperor (red Tokay) grapes, seeded

Beat egg yolks until lemon colored then add sugar and beat until thick. Add lemon juice and grated lemon rind. Soften unflavored gelatin in water then place in pan of hot (not boiling) water until gelatin is melted. Cool. Beat egg whites and salt until stiff. Stir in gelatin. Fold gelatin-egg white mixture into lemon-egg yolk mixture and add vanilla. Stir in grapes.

Pour into individual serving dishes. Chill in refrigerator. Garnish with additional grapes, if desired.

Makes 8 servings.

Fresh Peach Meringue Pie

2 pounds fresh peaches
(about 2 1/2 cups prepared
peaches)

1 teaspoon lemon juice

1/2 cup sugar

2 tablespoons cornstarch

1/2 teaspoon cinnamon

1/4 teaspoon nutmeg

Dash salt

2 egg yolks, slightly beaten

9-inch graham cracker crust

2 egg whites

Dash salt

1/4 cup sugar

Peel, pit and crush peaches and mix in lemon juice.

Combine sugar, cornstarch, cinnamon, nutmeg and salt in saucepan, then stir in peach mixture. Cook over medium heat until mixture reaches boiling point, stirring constantly. Reduce heat to low and cook 3 minutes, stirring constantly. Stir small amount of hot mixture into slightly beaten egg yolks then add egg yolks to remaining hot mixture and cook until thickened, stirring constantly. Remove from heat. Cool 10 minutes. Pour into graham cracker crust and cool to room temperature.

Beat egg whites with salt until soft peaks form. Gradually add sugar and continue beating until stiff peaks form. Spread meringue over filling so it touches crust all around edge. Bake in moderate oven (350 degrees) 10 minutes.

Grasshopper Dessert

1 package (4 3/8 ozs.) lime-
flavored self-layering dessert
mix

2/3 cup boiling water

1 cup cold water

3 tablespoons brandy

2 tablespoons green creme de
menthe

6 baked 3 1/2-inch graham
cracker tart shells

Place dessert mix in deep narrow bowl. Add boiling water and blend at low speed of mixer or with rotary beater 30 seconds. Whip at high speed 4 minutes. (Do not underwhip.) Add cold water, brandy and creme de menthe, beating at low speed just enough to blend. Immediately pour into graham cracker tart shells filling each only half full, then pour remaining mixture into tart shells. Let stand at room temperature 10 minutes. Chill until set, about 3 hours.

Makes 6 tarts.

Note: Mixture may be poured into tall parfait glasses instead of tart shells. Makes 4 servings.

Greek Spice Cake

1 cup sugar	1 teaspoon baking powder
1 cup brown sugar, firmly packed	1 cup salad oil
2 1/2 cups sifted cake flour	3 eggs, slightly beaten
1 teaspoon cloves	1 1/3 cups buttermilk
1 teaspoon nutmeg	2 teaspoons almond extract
1 teaspoon cinnamon	1 cup chopped nuts
1 teaspoon salt	3/4 cup water
1 teaspoon soda	2 cups sugar

Mix sugar, brown sugar, cake flour, cloves, nutmeg, cinnamon, salt, soda and baking powder in mixing bowl. Add salad oil and beaten eggs, blending well. Slowly add buttermilk. Mix in almond extract and chopped nuts. Pour into greased 13 x 9 x 2-inch pan. Bake in moderate oven (350 degrees) 35 minutes.

Boil water and sugar together over medium heat until sugar is thoroughly dissolved. While cake is hot, cut in squares and pour hot sugar syrup over cake.

Note: Cake may be cooled 10 minutes, then turned out of pan and cut into squares or it may be cut into squares while in pan.

Ice Cream Muffins

2 cups self-rising flour	1 pint softened vanilla ice cream

Combine flour and vanilla ice cream in mixing bowl, beating until smooth. Pour greased muffin cups 3/4 full. Bake in hot oven (425 degrees) 20 minutes or until golden brown. Makes 12.

Layered Nut Bars

1 cup sifted flour

1 cup brown sugar, firmly
packed

1/2 cup shortening (may be half
butter)

2 tablespoons flour

1/2 teaspoon baking powder

1/4 teaspoon salt

2 eggs

1 cup brown sugar, firmly
packed

1 teaspoon vanilla

3/4 cup chopped pecans or
walnuts

1 cup flaked coconut

Confectioners' sugar (optional)

Grease and line with paper, and grease again, a 9x9x2-inch pan.
Mix flour and brown sugar together. With pastry blender, fork or 2
knives, cut in shortening and mix until crumbly. Press mixture into
prepared pan. Bake in moderate oven (350 degrees) 15 minutes.

Combine flour, baking powder and salt. Beat eggs until very light.
Gradually add brown sugar and beat until fluffy. Add vanilla. Blend
in dry ingredients. Stir in chopped pecans or walnuts and flaked coconut. Pour over baked base. Return to oven and continue baking 30
minutes. Cool in pan. Turn out of pan and cut into bars or squares.
If desired, sprinkle with confectioners' sugar.

Makes 18 bars or 36 squares.

Love Cakes

1/2 cup butter or
margarine

1 cup graham cracker
crumbs

1 can (3 1/2 ozs.)
flaked coconut

1 cup semi-sweet
chocolate pieces

1 cup chopped pecans

1 can (15 ozs.) sweetened
condensed milk

Melt butter or margarine in saucepan over very low heat and blend
with graham cracker crumbs. Place in 9 x 9 x 2-inch pan. Top with
half of flaked coconut, then sprinkle with chocolate pieces. Top with
remaining coconut. Spread chopped pecans over top, then pour condensed milk over all. Bake in moderate oven (350 degrees) 30 minutes.
Remove from oven and cool. While still slightly warm, cut in squares.

Makes approximately 4 dozen.

Mace Cherry Pie

1 can (1 lb. 13 ozs.) tart, pitted pie cherries

1 cup sugar

3 tablespoons cornstarch

3/4 teaspoon mace

1/4 teaspoon salt

1 tablespoon lemon juice

Unbaked 9-inch pastry shell

2 tablespoons butter or margarine

Drain liquid from can of cherries reserving 1/2 cup. Combine sugar, cornstarch, mace and salt in saucepan then blend in cherry liquid and cook over medium heat until mixture is clear, stirring. Remove from heat and cool. Stir in drained cherries and lemon juice and turn into unbaked pastry shell. Dot with butter or margarine. Adjust top crust. Cut slits in top crust to allow steam to escape. Bake in hot oven (425 degrees) 10 minutes. Reduce temperature to moderate (375 degrees) and continue baking 30 minutes. Remove from oven and cool before serving.

Molasses Bread Pudding

2 1/4 cups day-old bread cubes

1/2 cup raisins

2 eggs

2 1/2 cups milk

1/8 teaspoon salt

1/4 cup dark molasses

1 tablespoon butter or margarine

2 tablespoons sugar

1/4 teaspoon cinnamon

Combine bread cubes and raisins in 1 1/2-quart casserole. Beat eggs, milk and salt together, then blend in molasses. Pour milk mixture over bread cubes. Dot with butter or margarine.

Combine sugar and cinnamon and sprinkle evenly over top. Bake in moderate oven (350 degrees) 30 to 35 minutes or until knife inserted near center comes out clean.

Makes 6 servings.

Note: For Molasses Rice Pudding, 1 1/2 cups cooked rice may be substituted for bread cubes. Bake in 1 1/2-quart casserole or six 5-ounce custard cups.

Pinto Bean Fruit Cake

1 cup sifted flour

1 teaspoon soda

1/2 teaspoon salt

1 teaspoon cinnamon

1/2 teaspoon cloves

1/2 teaspoon allspice

1 cup sugar

1/4 cup butter or margarine

1 egg, beaten

2 cups cooked pinto beans, mashed

2 cups diced raw apples

1/2 cup chopped nuts

1 cup raisins

2 teaspoons vanilla

Sift flour, soda, salt, cinnamon, cloves and allspice together. Cream sugar and butter or margarine together; add beaten egg and pinto beans and mix well. Add sifted dry ingredients to bean mixture, mixing well. Add diced apples, chopped nuts, raisins and vanilla and mix well. Pour into greased 10-inch tube pan. Bake in hot oven (475 degrees) 45 minutes. Remove from oven and let stand 5 minutes before removing from pan. Remove from pan and finish cooling on wire rack. If desired, glaze and decorate with candied cherry halves and walnuts.

Prairie Cake

2 cups brown sugar, firmly packed

1 cup shortening

2 eggs

1 cup chopped nuts

2 cups chopped dates

1 teaspoon cinnamon

1/2 teaspoon allspice

1/2 teaspoon cloves

3 cups sifted flour

2 teaspoons baking powder

1/2 teaspoon salt

2 cups beer or ale

Confectioners' sugar (optional)

Cream brown sugar and shortening together; stir in eggs, chopped nuts, chopped dates, cinnamon, allspice and cloves. Sift flour, baking powder and salt together into mixing bowl and stir in beer or ale. Add beer mixture, to creamed mixture, blending well. Pour into greased and floured 10-inch tube pan. Bake in moderate oven (350 degrees) 1 hour and 15 minutes or until wooden pick inserted in center comes out clean. Remove from oven and let stand 5 minutes before removing from pan. Remove from pan and finish cooling on cake rack. Top may be sprinkled with confectioners' sugar, if desired.

Quick Banana Kolatchen

1/4 cup finely chopped pecans

1/4 cup brown sugar, firmly packed

1/4 teaspoon cinnamon

1 can (8 ozs.) refrigerated crescent dinner rolls

1 tablespoon softened butter or margarine

2 bananas

1 teaspoon lemon juice

2 tablespoons honey

1/2 cup sifted confectioners' sugar

1 to 2 teaspoons hot water

Mix pecans, brown sugar and cinnamon together. Unroll dinner rolls and separate into 4 rectangles then place on ungreased baking sheet. Spread with softened butter or margarine and sprinkle with nut mixture. Peel bananas and cut in quarters, crosswise. Place 2 pieces banana on each rectangle, crosswise.

Combine lemon juice and honey and pour over bananas. Bring dough up around bananas and seal by pinching edges together. Bake in hot oven (400 degrees) 12 to 15 minutes. Mix confectioners' sugar and hot water together until smooth. Spread frosting on top of hot rolls. If desired, sprinkle with extra chopped nuts.

Makes 4.

Sun Blushed Peach Cheese Cake

1 cup graham cracker crumbs	2 egg yolks
1/4 cup sugar	3/4 cup sugar
1/4 cup softened butter or margarine	1 pound cream cheese, softened
3 envelopes (3 tablespoons) unflavored gelatin	2 egg whites
3/4 cup water	1/2 teaspoon salt
2 pounds peaches	1/4 cup sugar
1 tablespoon lemon juice	1 cup heavy cream

Blend graham cracker crumbs, sugar and softened butter or margarine together and press on bottom of 9-inch spring-form pan. Soften gelatin in water. Peel, pit and thoroughly crush peaches to make 3 cups puree. Stir in lemon juice.

Beat egg yolks in saucepan; add 1/2 cup of crushed peaches and sugar and cook over very low heat until thickened, stirring. Add softened gelatin, stirring until dissolved. Remove from heat. Combine softened cream cheese with remaining peaches and add the gelatin mixture to cheese mixture. Chill until mixture mounds when dropped from spoon.

Beat egg whites and salt until foamy; gradually add sugar and continue beating until stiff peaks form. Whip cream until stiff. Fold egg whites and whipped cream into peach mixture. Pour into crumb-lined pan. Chill at least 4 hours or until firm. Serve with Crushed Peach Sauce.

Makes 12 servings.

Crushed Peach Sauce

2 pounds peaches   1/3 cup sugar

Peel, pit and slightly crush peaches, then stir in sugar. Makes approximately 2 1/4 cups.

Toll House Marble Squares

1 cup plus 2 tablespoons sifted flour

1/2 teaspoon soda

1/2 teaspoon salt

1/2 cup softened butter or shortening

6 tablespoons sugar

6 tablespoons brown sugar, firmly packed

1/2 teaspoon vanilla

1/4 teaspoon water

1 egg

1/2 cup coarsely chopped nuts

1 package (6 ozs.) semi-sweet chocolate pieces

Sift flour, soda and salt together. Blend butter or shortening, sugar, brown sugar, vanilla and water together in mixing bowl, beat in egg. Add sifted dry ingredients, mixing well. Stir in chopped nuts. Spread in greased 13 x 9 x 2-inch pan. Sprinkle with semi-sweet chocolate pieces.

Bake in moderate oven (375 degrees) 1 minute. Remove from oven and run knife through batter to marbleize. Return to oven and continue baking 12 to 14 minutes. Remove from oven. Cool and cut in 2-inch squares.

Makes 2 dozen.

Note: To make Toll House Oatmeal Marble Squares, reduce flour to 3/4 cup and add 1 cup rolled oats.

Top Of The Sixes
Cherries Jubilee

1 lemon	**2 tablespoons Triple-Sec**
1/2 cup confectioners' sugar	**1/4 cup Triple-Sec**
1 can (1 lb.) tart red cherries and liquid	**Vanilla ice cream**

Heat chafing dish blazer pan or skillet over very low heat. Cut lemon in half and squeeze into warmed pan, reserving shells. Lift pan and revolve so lemon juice covers surface. Add confectioners' sugar, stirring constantly until dissolved. Add cherries and liquid and continue cooking and stirring until liquid is reduced by half. Rub bottom of pan with cut sides of lemon shells, tilting as necessary to avoid liquid. Add 2 tablespoons Triple-Sec and cook until alcohol is evaporated, stirring constantly. Turn heat to high and add 1/4 cup Triple-Sec. When slightly warmed, ignite with match. Flame until alcohol is greatly evaporated. Place vanilla ice cream in 4 dessert dishes and make a well in top of each scoop ice cream. Pour cherries over ice cream. Serve immediately.

Makes 4 servings.

Yorkshire Apple Squares

1/3 cup butter or margarine

1/2 cup light brown sugar, firmly packed

1 can (1 lb. 4 ozs.) pie-sliced apples, well drained

1 1/2 cups sifted flour

3/4 teaspoon salt

3 eggs

1 1/2 cups milk

Melt butter or margarine in 13 x 9 x 2-inch pan in hot oven (450 degrees). Remove from oven. Sprinkle brown sugar evenly over bottom of pan. Arrange apple slices over sugar. Sift flour and salt together and set aside. Beat eggs with rotary beater or mixer until thick and light, then add sifted dry ingredients and 1/2 cup of milk and beat until well blended. Gradually add remaining milk (1 cup) and continue beating 1 to 2 minutes or until smooth. Pour over apples in pan. Bake in hot oven (450 degrees) 25 to 30 minutes. Serve immediately.

Makes 6 servings.

Miscellaneous

Avocado-Garlic Salad Dressing

1 cup salad oil

2 tablespoons sugar

3/4 teaspoon salt

1 teaspoon paprika

1/4 teaspoon dry mustard

1/8 teaspoon black pepper

1/4 teaspoon garlic powder

1/4 medium avocado

1/4 cup lemon juice

Combine salad oil, sugar, salt, paprika, mustard, black pepper and garlic powder and let stand 1 hour. Press avocado through sieve and add this, along with lemon juice to oil mixture. Beat with rotary beater until thickened. Serve over mixed salad greens or fruit salad.

Makes 1 1/2 cups.

Brown Derby Split Pea Soup

1/4 cup butter or margarine

1 medium onion, sliced

2 small stalks celery, sliced

1 pound green split peas, quick-cooking variety

1 ham hock or whole ham bone

3 pints chicken or beef stock

1/2 bay leaf

1 1/2 teaspoons black peppercorns

Salt to taste

1 cup heavy cream, heated

1/2 cup croutons

Melt butter or margarine in heavy saucepan or kettle over low heat, add onion and celery and simmer 4 minutes. Add peas, ham hock or bone, chicken or beef stock, bay leaf, peppercorns and salt and cook 1 1/2 hours. Strain through fine sieve. Add heated cream and pour into heated tureen. Sprinkle with croutons.

Makes 8 servings.

Note: If using regular split peas, soak overnight in water.

Brennan's Eggs Benedict

Canadian-style bacon

Crisp rusk or English muffin

Soft poached egg

Hollandaise Sauce

Paprika

Truffle slices

Parsley

Place slice of grilled Canadian-style bacon on crisp rusk or English muffin. Place soft poached egg on bacon slice. Top with generous amount of Hollandaise Sauce. Sprinkle with paprika. Garnish with truffle slices and sprigs of parsley. Serve immediately.

Soft Poached Eggs

Fill saucepan with water to depth of 3 to 4 inches. Bring just to boiling over low heat. Add small amount of vinegar and salt. Break each egg into small sauce dish. Stir simmering water to make a swirl, following direction of swirling water. Reduce heat to very low and cook 3 to 5 minutes or until desired doneness. Do not let water boil. Remove egg from water with slotted spoon or pancake turner. To keep hot until serving time, place egg in lukewarm water, 3 inches deep.

Hollandaise Sauce

4 egg yolks

1 to 2 tablespoons lemon juice

1 cup butter, melted

Salt and pepper to taste

In saucepan or top of double boiler, beat egg yolks slightly and stir in lemon juice. Place over very low heat or over hot water in lower part of double boiler (do not let water touch bottom of upper pan). Add butter, a small amount at a time, stirring constantly with wooden spoon. Add salt and pepper to taste. Continue cooking until mixture thickens, stirring constantly.

Makes 1 cup.

Banana Chips

Salad oil or melted shortening

Firm bananas

Salt

Pour salad oil or melted shortening 1/2-inch deep in skillet and heat over medium heat. Peel and slice bananas into thin rounds. Fry in hot oil until golden brown, turning once. Drain well on absorbent paper. Sprinkle with salt.

Number of chips depends on amount of bananas used.

Calico Cheese Soup

1/2 clove garlic

1/4 cup salad oil

1/2 cup finely chopped carrots

1/2 cup finely chopped celery

1/4 cup butter or margarine

2 tablespoons minced onion

3 tablespoons flour

2 cups scalded milk

2 cups canned chicken broth

1/2 pound process Cheddar cheese, shredded

2 cups small fresh bread cubes

1/4 cup grated Parmesan cheese

Combine garlic and salad oil and let stand overnight at room temperature. Remove garlic from oil and set aside. In covered saucepan, cook chopped carrots and chopped celery in boiling, salted water to cover, over low heat until just crisp-tender. Drain. Melt butter or margarine in saucepan over low heat; add minced onion and saute until tender. Reduce heat to very low and blend in flour, milk and chicken broth. Cook and stir until slightly thickened. Add shredded Cheddar cheese, stirring until melted. Add carrot mixture and cook 10 minutes. Heat garlic-flavored oil in skillet over medium heat; add bread cubes and saute until lightly browned and crisp, then remove from oil. Sprinkle with grated Parmesan cheese. Serve cheese croutons on soup.

Makes approximately 6 servings.

California Rice

1/2 cup butter or margarine

1 cup peeled, diced eggplant

1 small zucchini or summer squash, diced

2 large mushrooms, sliced

1 clove garlic, minced

1 ripe tomato, peeled, seeded and chopped

3 pimientos, minced

1 teaspoon salt

1/4 teaspoon pepper

1 cup uncooked rice

1 can (13 1/4 ozs.) chicken broth

Melt butter or margarine in saucepan over medium heat, add diced eggplant, zucchini or squash, mushrooms, garlic, tomato, pimientos, salt and pepper and cook 10 minutes, stirring occasionally. Stir in uncooked rice. Add chicken broth and bring to boil. Reduce heat to low, cover tightly and cook 30 minutes.

Makes 4 servings.

Caribbean Fiesta Mold

1 cup water

1 package (3 ozs.) orange-flavored gelatin

1 can (11 ozs.) mandarin oranges

Dry sherry or water

1/4 cup chopped nuts

2 bananas, peeled and sliced

Bring water to boil over medium heat, add orange-flavored gelatin, stirring until dissolved. Drain can of oranges placing liquid in measuring cup. Add sherry or water to liquid to make 1 cup. Add to gelatin. Chill until mixture begins to thicken.

Fold in orange sections, chopped nuts and sliced bananas and pour into 4 or 5-cup mold. Chill until firm.

Makes 4 to 6 servings.

Cheese Nut Croquettes

3 tablespoons peanut oil	1/8 teaspoon pepper
1/4 cup unsifted flour	2 cups cooked rice
1 cup milk	1 cup chopped pecans
1 cup grated sharp cheese	2 eggs
2 tablespoons grated onion	2 tablespoons water
3/4 teaspoon salt	Fine bread crumbs
1/2 teaspoon dry mustard	

Combine peanut oil and flour in saucepan and bring to boil over low heat, stirring constantly. Remove from heat. Add milk gradually and cook over low heat until mixture comes to boil, stirring constantly. Simmer 1 minute, then remove from heat. Add grated cheese stirring until melted. Add grated onion, salt, mustard and pepper. Fold in cooked rice and chopped pecans. Chill thoroughly. Shape into 12 balls. Beat eggs and water together. Coat balls with bread crumbs, dip in egg mixture then coat with more bread crumbs.

Chill until ready to fry. Fry in deep hot peanut oil over medium heat until golden brown. Serve hot.

Makes 12.

Chilaquiles De Huevo

(TORTILLA HASH)

2 tablespoons butter or margarine	2 tablespoons minced onion
6 tortillas, cut in eighths	3 eggs, beaten
2 medium tomatoes, peeled and cubed	Salt and pepper to taste
	1 tablespoon grated Parmesan cheese

Heat butter or margarine in skillet over medium heat; add tortilla pieces and fry lightly. Add cubed tomatoes and minced onion and fry until onion is limp. Add beaten eggs, salt and pepper and cook over very low heat until of desired consistency, stirring as for scrambled eggs. Sprinkle with grated Parmesan cheese. Serve immediately.

Note: For spicier flavor, Mexican chili sauce may be added with salt and pepper.

Makes 4 servings.

Coconut-Carrot Salad

1 cup flaked coconut	1/4 cup mayonnaise
1 1/2 cups shredded carrots	Lettuce
1/4 cup seedless grapes	Orange sections and mayonnaise for garnish
2 tablespoons lemon juice	
1/2 teaspoon ground ginger	

Combine coconut, carrots, grapes, lemon juice, ginger and mayonnaise. Chill. Serve on lettuce leaves. Garnish with orange sections and mayonnaise.

Makes 4 servings.

Cold Cucumber Soup

1 can (10 1/2 ozs.) condensed cream of mushroom soup	1 soup can milk
	1 teaspoon onion juice
1 can (10 1/2 ozs.) condensed cream of chicken soup	1 cup finely shredded, unpeeled cucumber

Combine all ingredients in mixing bowl. Mix well and chill until serving time.

Makes 4 servings.

Corn Bread Supper Dish

1 cup sifted flour

3/4 cup corn meal

1 tablespoon baking powder

1 tablespoon sugar

1 egg

3/4 cup milk

1/4 cup shortening, melted

2 packages (8 ozs. each) frozen mixed vegetables with onion sauce

Sift flour, corn meal, baking powder and sugar together in mixing bowl. Add egg, milk and melted shortening and stir until just blended and pour into greased and floured 3 or 4-cup ring mold. Bake in hot oven (425 degrees) 20 minutes. Remove from oven and cool in pan 5 minutes. Remove from pan and place on serving plate.

Prepare mixed vegetables with onion sauce according to package directions. Thin with small amount of milk, if desired, and pour over and around corn bread ring.

Makes 6 servings.

Cream of Curry Soup

2 tablespoons butter or margarine

2 tablespoons finely chopped onion

2 teaspoons curry powder

1 tablespoon flour

2 cans (14 ozs. each) clear chicken broth

4 egg yolks, slightly beaten

1 cup heavy cream

1 cup crushed pineapple, drained

Heat butter or margarine in large skillet over medium heat. Add chopped onion and saute 5 minutes or until golden. Remove from heat. Stir curry powder and flour into fat to make smooth paste, then gradually add chicken broth. Bring to boil over low heat, stirring. Blend small amount of hot mixture into slightly beaten egg yolks, then stir yolk mixture into soup. Continue cooking 1 minute or until slightly thickened, stirring. Strain into large bowl. Cool. Chill in refrigerator several hours. Just before serving, stir in the heavy cream and crushed pineapple.

Makes 7 to 8 servings.

Deviled Tomatoes

4 tomatoes

Salt

Pepper

Cayenne

2 tablespoons buttered bread crumbs

2 tablespoons butter or margarine

1/2 teaspoon prepared mustard

Dash liquid red pepper seasoning

1 tablespoon David Wade Worcestershire Powder

1 teaspoon sugar

4 1/2 teaspoons vinegar

1 egg yolk, beaten

Cut tomatoes in half crosswise and place on baking sheet, cut side up. Sprinkle lightly with salt, pepper and cayenne and top with buttered bread crumbs. Melt butter or margarine in very small saucepan over low heat; add mustard, red pepper seasoning, Worcestershire Powder, sugar and vinegar and bring to boil. Stir small amount of vinegar mixture into beaten egg yolk, then add yolk mixture to remaining vinegar mixture and cook over very low heat until thickened, stirring constantly. Broil tomato halves 3 inches from low heat until crumbs are brown. Serve with spoonful of sauce on each half.

Makes 4 servings.

Dutch Chicken Dressing

1 cup Ricotta cheese

1/2 cup bread crumbs

1 egg

1/2 cup chopped ham

1 clove garlic, chopped

2 teaspoons chopped parsley

3 tablespoons grated Romano cheese

2 tablespoons olive oil

Salt and pepper to taste

Combine all ingredients, and mix well. Use to stuff 4 to 5 pound roasting chicken. Roast as usual.

Eggs Rebecca

6 eggs, hard cooked

2 tablespoons dry sherry

1 tablespoon finely chopped onion

1 bay leaf

6 peppercorns

2 tablespoons butter

1 tablespoon flour

1 cup beef bouillon

1/2 cup finely chopped mushrooms

1 teaspoon minced parsley

1 teaspoon lemon juice

1/4 cup cream, whipped

Ground nutmeg

1 teaspoon salt

Freshly ground black pepper

Combine sherry, onion, bay leaf, peppercorns and 1 tablespoon butter in saucepan and simmer for 5 minutes. Stir in flour and mix thoroughly. Add bouillon and cook until thickened, stirring constantly. Strain and return to saucepan. Add mushrooms and simmer for 5 minutes. Add parsley and lemon juice. Meanwhile cut eggs in half lengthwise. Remove yolks and mash them. Add the remaining 1 tablespoon butter, whipped cream, a dash of nutmeg, the salt and freshly ground black pepper and blend thoroughly. Fill egg whites with yolk mixture and arrange them in a shallow baking dish. Pour the hot sherry sauce over the eggs.

Bake in a hot oven (400 degrees) for 15 minutes. Serves 6

Farmer's Market Salad

1 head romaine lettuce, shredded

1 head iceberg lettuce, shredded

3 tomatoes, cut in wedges

4 hard-cooked eggs, cut in wedges

1 can (1 lb.) green peas, drained

Place all ingredients in salad bowl. Toss with Farmer's Market Salad Dressing.
Makes 8 to 12 servings.

Farmer's Market Salad Dressing

2 tablespoons chopped green onion

1 clove garlic, crushed

1/4 cup chopped parsley

1 cup mayonnaise

1 tablespoon lemon juice

1/4 cup vinegar

1/4 cup (2 ozs.) bleu cheese, crumbled

1/4 cup sour cream

Salt and freshly ground pepper to taste

Combine all ingredients, mixing well. Chill. Makes 2 1/4 cups.

Goldenrod Eggs

6 hard-cooked eggs

2 cups medium white sauce

Salt and pepper to taste

1/2 cup grated Cheddar cheese

Toast points

Separate whites and yolks of hard-cooked eggs and chop whites. Combine white sauce and salt and pepper to taste. Stir in chopped egg whites. Add grated Cheddar cheese and heat over very low heat. Arrange toast points on plates and pour sauce over toast. Crumble yolks or press through sieve and sprinkle on sauce.

Makes 4 servings.

Gazpacho Salad

2 cucumbers, peeled and finely diced

4 tomatoes, seeded and finely diced

2 green peppers, seeded and finely slivered

1 onion, finely chopped

salt and pepper to taste

5 or 6 rolled anchovies

5 or 6 black olives

2 garlic cloves

pinch of ground cuminseed

1/4 cup vinegar

1/2 cup olive oil

1 tablespoon finely chopped parsley

2 teaspoons finely chopped shallots

Juice of one lemon

In a deep bowl or glass jar, arrange alternate layers of cucumbers, tomatoes, green peppers and onion. Sprinkle the layers lightly with salt and pepper and intersperse the vegetables with the anchovies and olives. In a wooden mixing bowl, mash to a paste the garlic cloves with a little salt and cuminseed, beat in vinegar and olive oil and stir in parsley and shallots. Pour the dressing over the salad and chill it for 2 or 3 hours. Sprinkle the vegetables with the lemon juice and serve in chilled bowls as an hors d'oeuvre.

German Cabbage Soup

2 cans (10 1/2 oz. each) condensed beef broth

2 1/2 cups water

1 can (8 oz.) tomato sauce

2 teaspoons lemon juice

3 cups shredded cabbage

2 cups diced apples

1/3 cup onion flakes

1 tablespoon caraway seed

1 teaspoon sugar

1/4 teaspoon garlic powder

1 tablespoon David Wade Worcestershire Powder

1/8 teaspoon ground black pepper

In a large saucepan combine broth, water, tomato sauce and lemon juice; bring to boiling point. Add remaining ingredients. Cover and simmer 20 minutes. Serve with sliced rye bread, if desired.

Makes 6 to 8 servings.

Grapefruit Cole Slaw

1 small head cabbage
(1 pound)

1/2 teaspoon salt

1 small grapefruit, peeled
and cut in sections

1/4 cup mayonnaise

1 teaspoon lemon juice

1 teaspoon horseradish
sauce

Slice cabbage in paper-thin shreds and sprinkle with salt. Add grape-fruit sections. Combine mayonnaise, lemon juice and horseradish sauce and lightly toss this mixture with cabbage and grapefruit. Garnish with sliced toasted almonds or peanuts, if desired.

Makes 8 servings.

Green Goddess Dressing

1/4 cup parsley flakes

3 tablespoons white wine
vinegar

1 tablespoon lemon juice

1 cup mayonnaise

1/2 cup dairy sour cream

1 can (2 oz.) flat anchovies,
drained and minced.

2 tablespoons freeze-dried
chives

3/4 teaspoon garlic powder

1/2 teaspoon tarragon leaves,
crumbled

1/4 teaspoon coarse ground
black pepper

1/8 teaspoon salt

In a small bowl combine parsley flakes with vinegar and lemon juice. Blend well until mixture turns green. Stir in remaining ingredients. Serve over salad greens.

YIELD: About 2 cups

Green Mansion Salad

1 head cabbage

1 cup drained pineapple tidbits

1 cup green seedless grapes

1/2 cup diced celery

1/2 cup shredded cucumbers

2 tablespoons pineapple juice

Salad dressing

Remove center from head of cabbage, leaving outer leaves to form shell, and shred cabbage removed from center. Add pineapple tidbits, grapes, celery, cucumbers and pineapple juice mixed with salad dressing, mixing lightly. Chill. Fill cabbage shells.

Makes 6 servings.

Menehune Salad

1 head iceberg lettuce

1/2 cup sliced radishes

1/2 cup chopped green onion

1/3 cup oil (part olive, part corn)

2 tablespoons lemon juice

2 teaspoons sugar

1/2 teaspoon salt

Pepper to taste

4 ounces feta or Romano cheese

1 can (2 ozs.) flat anchovy fillets

Whole pitted ripe olives (about 2/3 cup)

Crumbled dry oregano

Core, rinse and drain lettuce. Place in plastic bag and chill. Cut in half lengthwise. Shred crosswise then chop. (Should make 5 cups.) Combine lettuce, radishes and chopped green onion in salad bowl.

Combine oil, lemon juice, sugar, salt and pepper and toss with lettuce mixture. Crumble cheese coarsely and sprinkle on salad near rim of bowl. Drain anchovy fillets and wrap around olives. Place in center of cheese ring on top of salad. Sprinkle with crumbled oregano. Toss before serving.

Makes 6 servings.

Molded Salad
With French Green Beans And Almonds

1 package (9 ozs.) frozen
French green beans
with almonds

1 package (3 ozs.) lemon-
flavored gelatin

1 cup boiling water

2 teaspoons vinegar

1/2 tray (7 to 10) ice cubes

1/2 cup diced celery

Cook frozen green beans with almonds according to package directions omitting butter or margarine and increasing water to 3 tablespoons. Do not drain. Combine lemon-flavored gelatin and boiling water, stirring until gelatin is dissolved. Add vinegar and ice cubes and stir until thickened. Remove unmelted ice. Fold in green beans and diced celery and pour into 3-cup mold or individual molds. Chill until firm. Serve on crisp greens with mayonnaise, if desired.

Makes 6 servings.

Nachos

Crisp tortilla chips

Sliced or grated sharp
Cheddar cheese

David Wade Worcestershire
Powder

Jalapeno pepper slices

Place tortilla chips on baking sheet and place sliced or grated Cheddar cheese on each. Sprinkle lightly with Worcestershire Powder and top with slice of jalapeno pepper. Bake in hot oven (400 degrees) until cheese melts. Serve hot. If desired, stuffed olive slices may be used instead of jalapeno peppers.

Old-Country Borsch

6 cups water

1 pound beef brisket, cut into 6 pieces

2 onions, sliced

2 stalks celery, cut into 1-inch pieces

4 medium beets, peeled and sliced (about 2 cups)

4 carrots, peeled and thinly sliced (about 1 1/2 cups)

1 small head cabbage, cut into wedges

1 bay leaf

2 teaspoons salt

2 beets, coarsely grated (about 1 cup)

1 can (6 ozs.) tomato paste

2 tablespoons vinegar

1 tablespoon sugar

2 teaspoons salt

1 cup sour cream

The day before or early in the day on which soup is to be served, place water, beef brisket pieces, sliced onions, celery pieces, sliced beets, sliced carrots, cabbage wedges, bay leaf and salt in large kettle. Cover and simmer over low heat about 2 hours. Add another cup of beets, tomato paste, vinegar, sugar and salt, cover and simmer 15 to 20 minutes. Cool. Refrigerate.

To serve, skim fat from soup. Bring to boil over medium heat. Reduce heat to low and simmer 10 minutes. Serve topped with sour cream.

Makes 4 to 6 servings.

Note: Leftover soup may be frozen. Cool, then pack in straight-sided jars or containers. Freeze immediately.

Pear Waldorf Salad

3 cups diced fresh pears

1 tablespoon lemon juice

1 cup diced celery

1/2 cup chopped nuts

2 tablespoons mayonnaise

Lettuce

Toss diced pears, lemon juice, celery, nuts and mayonnaise together lightly. Serve on lettuce leaves.

Makes 6 servings.

Polish Stuffed Eggs

6 hard-cooked eggs

1 can (4 3/4 ozs.) liverwurst spread

2 tablespoons mayonnaise

1 tablespoon chopped chives

Cut hard-cooked eggs in half and remove yolks. Mash yolks with liverwurst spread and mayonnaise. Add chopped chives (pickle relish, chopped celery, chopped green pepper or chopped walnuts may be used, if desired, and mix well. Stuff egg whites with mixture. Chill thoroughly.

Makes 6 servings.

Ricotta Cheese Pie

2 cups sifted flour

1/2 teaspoon salt

2/3 cup butter or margarine

2 tablespoons dry sherry

1/4 cup cold water

1/4 pound toasted almonds, finely chopped

2 tablespoons chopped pistachio nuts

1 1/2 pounds Ricotta cheese

4 eggs

1/3 cup sugar

1 teaspoon vanilla

1 tablespoon chopped citron

3 maraschino cherries, chopped

Milk

Sugar

Confectioners' sugar

Sift flour and salt together into mixing bowl. With pastry blender, fork or 2 knives, cut in butter or margarine until mixture looks like coarse corn meal. Add sherry, a few drops at a time, then add cold water a few drops at a time. Blend with fork just until mixture holds together. Roll out dough 1/8-inch thick. Fit circle of dough into greased 9-inch pie pan. Cut remaining dough into lattice strips.

Combine chopped almonds and pistachio nuts. Add Ricotta cheese and mix well. Beat eggs and sugar together thoroughly. Add vanilla, chopped citron and chopped cherries. Add egg mixture to Ricotta mixture, blending until smooth. Pour into pastry shell. Place lattice strips crisscross fashion over filling and seal to edges of pastry. Flute edge of pastry. Brush with milk and sprinkle with sugar. Bake in moderate oven (375 degrees) 40 minutes or until pastry is golden brown. Remove from oven and cool. Sprinkle with confectioners' sugar.

Rinctum-Diddy

1 tablespoon butter or margarine

1 tablespoon flour

1 cup milk

1 egg, beaten

1/2 pound American cheese, grated

1 can (16 1/2 ozs.) condensed tomato soup

1 teaspoon soda

1 teaspoon salt

Dash red pepper

Melt butter or margarine in 1 1/2 quart saucepan over very low heat; stir in flour. Combine milk and beaten egg and gradually stir into flour mixture. Continue cooking 1 minute. Add grated American cheese and continue cooking until melted, stirring. Combine tomato soup and soda and stir into cheese mixture; bring to boil over low heat. Add salt and red pepper and continue cooking until thickened. Serve hot on toast or crackers.

Makes approximately 3 cups.

Rosy Fruit Cocktail Slices

2 packages (3 ozs. each) cream cheese, softened

1 cup mayonnaise

1 cup heavy cream, whipped

1 can (1 lb. 13 ozs.) fruit cocktail, drained

1/2 cup drained maraschino cherries

2 1/2 cups marshmallows

Red food coloring or cherry juice

Lettuce & maraschino cherries for garnish

Blend cream cheese and mayonnaise together and fold in whipped cream, fruit cocktail, maraschino cherries, marshmallows and food coloring or cherry juice. Pour into two 1-quart round ice cream or freezer containers. Freeze at least 6 hours or overnight. To serve, remove from freezer and let stand few minutes. Remove from container and slice. Serve on lettuce leaves, garnished with maraschino cherries and small lettuce leaves.

Makes 10 to 12 servings.

Shirred Eggs Gruyere

1 teaspoon butter or
margarine

2 eggs

Grated Gruyere cheese

1/4 cup hot heavy cream

Melt butter or margarine in individual flameproof ramekin. Add eggs and cook over low heat 1 minute. Remove from heat. Cover eggs with grated Gruyere cheese and pour hot cream over top. Place ramekin in pan of hot water. Bake in moderate oven (350 degrees) until eggs are set and cheese is melted.

Makes 1 serving.

Swiss Cream-of-Potato Soup

4 medium potatoes, peeled

2 slices bacon, diced

1/4 cup minced onion

2 tablespoons butter or
margarine

1 tablespoon snipped parsley

2 teaspoons salt

1/2 teaspoon nutmeg

Dash cayenne

1/4 teaspoon dry mustard

1 teaspoon David Wade
Worcestershire Powder

3 cups milk

1/2 cup grated natural Swiss or
process Cheddar cheese

Cook potatoes in covered saucepan in 1-inch boiling water over low heat until tender, then drain. Saute diced bacon and minced onion in skillet over low heat until brown and tender. Mash potatoes. Add bacon and onions, butter or margarine, snipped parsley, salt, nutmeg, cayenne, mustard and Worcestershire Powder. Stir in milk and heat over very low heat, stirring. Sprinkle with grated Swiss or Cheddar cheese. Serve immediately.

Makes 4 servings.

Tropical Turkey Salad

2 cans (5 ozs. each) boned
turkey

3/4 cup mayonnaise

1/4 teaspoon liquid red pepper
seasoning

1 teaspoon David Wade
Worcestershire Powder

1 teaspoon lemon juice

1 can (15 ozs.) pineapple
slices

1/4 cup peanuts, chopped

1/4 cup diced celery

Shred turkey and set aside. Mix mayonnaise, red pepper seasoning, Worcestershire Powder and lemon juice together. Drain can of pineapple slices, reserving 6 whole rings. Cut remaining slices into pieces then toss together with shredded turkey, chopped peanuts, diced celery and seasoned mayonnaise. Mound salad on whole pineapple slices. Chill.

Makes 6 servings.

Tuna Summer Salad

1 can (7 ozs.) tuna, drained
and flaked

1/2 cup crushed corn chips

4 tablespoons chopped green
pepper

4 tablespoons chopped celery

1 teaspoon chopped onion

1/8 teaspoon pepper

Mayonnaise

Combine tuna, corn chips, green pepper, celery, onion and pepper. Add mayonnaise to moisten and mix well. If desired, garnish with corn chips and sliced stuffed olives.

Makes 3 to 4 servings.

Watermelon With Rum

Cut a 3-inch plug from a watermelon and reserve. Pour rum into melon through hole, a small amount at a time, until melon will absorb no more. Fit plug back into melon. Seal cut with tape or butter or margarine. Let stand in cool place overnight or longer. Cut into wedges to serve.

Syndicated
Newspaper Column

While many people enjoy recipes in cookbooks, there are those who enjoy searching out colorful and historical backgrounds of the recipes and their ingredients. In this section are many of Mr. Wade's outstanding food reports published previously in his syndicated newspaper column. With these creative editorials, David Wade stirs interest, excitement and romance into even the most ordinary food preparations.

Avocado and Cheese
Stuffed Celery

Celery was known for centuries only as a medicine. Its taste was bitter. In the 17th Century, some unknown gardener in Italy or southern France, who set a great store by celery as a cure-all, transplanted wild celery (or "smallage") to a choice garden spot where the soil was deep, rich and moist. To his amazement the ribs and leaves from these plants had a pleasing taste. The flavor was so pleasing, in fact, that this gardener's family began munching ribs of the fragrant plants.

Celery is one of the most recently developed of all the world's popular vegetables. In the early 17th Century still a medicine; in the 20th, one of America's most popular vegetables, so highly esteemed that it takes an annual total of 1,500,000,000 pounds to satisfy our appetite.

Celery growing is tricky. The soil must be of medium texture, constantly moist, neither acid or alkaline. Temperature during its growing season must average somewhere in the 60's. It takes its good old time about growing, even at that, requiring some 125 days from seed to harvest.

A celery grower needs a great deal of equipment, most of all he needs a "mule train", a huge tractor-drawn packing shed which moves along the length of the rows at harvest time. The crew of about 75 people who work this "mule train" cut, trim, wash and grade stalks 24 rows at a time. Such a machine costs more than $30,000. Conveyor belts, like outspread arms, carry the cut stalks from each row to the machine, then to a truck being pulled by the machine.

As each truck is filled with boxed, graded celery, it is sped to the nearby hydrocooler. Here it is traveled slowly through an ice-cold shower to remove field heat. Before it is packed for transportation to our food markets a blizzard of snow-ice is blown over the layers of celery crates. This is how our celery reaches us so fresh, crisp and sweet.

Celery growers point out that there is still a certain amount of confusion in some cookbooks which call for "stalk" of celery when they mean "ribs". A "stalk" or "bunch" is the whole plant. The "rib" is only a part of the stalk—the part we eat with such gusto and a sprinkling of salt.

There are hundreds of good dishes which require celery—appetizers, salads, soups, stews, sandwich fillings, stuffings, and many cooked vegetable dishes. Get into the habit of using the leaves, too, for they are good, healthful food.

RECIPE

1/3 cup cream cheese

1/3 cup mashed avocado

1/4 teaspoon salt

1/2 teaspoon lime juice

1/16 teaspoon ground white pepper

16 three-inch celery lengths

Thin radish slices for garnish

Combine cream cheese, mashed avocado, salt, fresh lime juice and ground white pepper. Mix until smooth. Stuff 3-inch celery lengths with mixture and garnish with radish slices.

YIELD: 16 pieces celery

Bacon Flavored Corn Casserole

It was peppery 18th Century Jonathan Swift who said "Whoever could make two ears of corn . . . grow upon a spot of ground where only one grew before, would deserve better of mankind, and do more essential service to his country, than the whole race of politicians put together."

He might have been talking about present-day Florida where some 10,769 refrigerator cars of sweet corn were shipped north last year compared with 744 cars twenty years ago. Florida grows more sweet corn than any other state. From the rich black soil of the Sunshine State comes corn-on-the-cob almost the entire year.

Actually, it has taken many men to double and re-double this supply of sweet corn. First credit goes to the plant breeders who succeeded in developing strains of corn which would thrive in southern fields; strains which can develop and mature despite the shorter days of winter, which even come to sub-tropical areas.

It takes all the resources of big business, too, to rush sweet corn to market in best condition. Huge motorized packing sheds or "mule trains" as they are called, move down the long fields with crews of about 75 workers picking the tender corn, crating it then and there and speeding it to hydro coolers where the temperature is immediately dropped from field heat to 40F. This prompt cooling slows down enzyme action which would otherwise change sugar to starch.

Time and temperature are of the essence, too, on road and rail. The crates of corn, showered with snow ice, can be sped from a Florida field to a table full of hungry corn-eaters a thousand miles away in 48 hours. Florida sells its corn mostly to the eastern half of the country, while Texas and California corn is enjoyed in the west.

Corn has been a cultivated crop in the Western Hemisphere for at least 4,000 years. The first mention of corn in what is now the United States described it as growing in Florida. This was 1528. Ten years later, De Soto landed in Florida and found "maes" not only in that peninsula, but all along the route to the Mississippi River.

We will never know how much, if any, of this corn was what we would now call sweet corn, for the earliest written record of this delicacy was dated 1801. (It began to be listed in seed catalogues in 1828, but was still unnamed.) It is possible, however, that sweet corn originated among the high civilizations of the Andes and that they ate it as a green vegetable and used its sweet juices in a beverage called "chicha". Today Andean gardeners are likely to hide their planting of sweet corn right in the center of fields of non-sweet maize. This is to keep unwelcome visitors from helping themselves to the delicious corn.

As is obvious from all the new sweet corn varieties developed for Florida, corn is very easily hybridized. Corn historians single out Golden Bantam as the one most important ancestor of most of today's corn varieties. A sweet corn resembling Golden Bantam was grown a century ago, but wasn't called that until 1902.

I suggest this great corn recipe.

RECIPE

6 **ears fresh Florida corn**

1/4 **cup chopped onion**

1/3 **cup diced green pepper**

2 **tablespoons bacon fat**

6 **strips crisp bacon**

1 **cup soft bread crumbs**

1 **cup milk**

1 **egg, beaten lightly**

1 **teaspoon salt**

1/8 **teaspoon ground black pepper**

2 **tablespoons butter or margarine**

Remove corn kernels from cob (makes about 2 cups); set aside. Saute onions and green pepper in bacon fat. Add corn and cook 3 to 4 minutes. Break bacon into small pieces and add along with 1/2 cup of the bread crumbs, beaten egg, milk, salt and black pepper; mix well. Turn into a buttered 1-quart casserole. Sprinkle with remaining bread crumbs. Dot with butter. Bake in a preheated moderate oven (375 F.) 20 minutes or until crumbs are deep brown. YIELD: 6 portions

Baked Lake Bass

Cooks gifted with a flair for seasoning have always agreed that basil is one of the most delightful of culinary herbs.

Not so, however, the doctors and herbalists of ancient times. As medicine and magic, basil was a bone of contention. That may be mixing metaphors a bit, but these old time medicine men disagreed violently on the curative values of basil. Nicholas Culpeper, in his 17th Century herbal says, "This is the herb which all authors are together by the ears about, and rail at one another like lawyers." He agreed that it might be good for the "bite of venomous beasts," but beyond that, he didn't think much of it as a medicine.

On the other hand, John Gerard, who'd lived at the time of Shakespeare, loved the fragrant herb and wrote in his herbal. "A smell of Basil is good for the hart and head—cureth the infirmities of the hart, taketh away sorrowfulness which cometh of melancholie, and maketh a man merrie and glad."

When it came to Basil as a symbol, people really dug in their heels. In Italy, it was—and still is—a symbol of love. (They call it Kiss-Me-Nicholas in some parts of Italy.) Any girl carrying a basil sprig is encouraging her beau to propose. In Romania, the same thing is true! If a young man reaches out his hand and takes the sprig of basil offered by a girl, he may as well consider himself engaged to her.

In Greece, on the other hand, Basil has always been the symbol of hate. The word "Basil" has two possible origins. One, from the Greek for "royal" or "kinglike". The other from a tongue-twister, also Greek, meaning "lizard." In Greek mythology, this was a very special lizard. The basilisk (Bass-uh-lisk) had but to look at or breathe on his victims to kill them! These two different word origins started all the argument among the men of the medical profession.

Basil is an herb of the mint family. There are some 60 varieties, but here in the United States, we like the Sweet Basil best. The shiny leaves are a sort of golden green and the entire surface of the leaf is spotted with tiny wells filled with this exquisitely fragrant oil. The fields in which basil grows have a heavenly scent, especially if someone brushes up against a basil bush. Or, for that matter, if the wind stirs the leaves. Once you've become familiar with the smell—and flavor—of basil, you'll find more and more exciting ways of using it.

Basil rivals oregano as a pizza herb. Use it too, in all other dishes which include tomatoes or cheese. Broiled tomato halves, for instance, are excellent and easy to prepare. Dab tomato halves with butter. Sprinkle with salt, pepper and grated Italian cheese. Then, as a finishing touch, scatter a little pinch of basil over each half and broil.

Next time you're preparing sauteed zucchini, add a little basil, about one teaspoonful for six servings, just minutes before the zucchini is done. Cucumbers are very good prepared the same way. Slice them about 1/4 inch thick and saute 3 or 4 minutes. They're done so quickly you'd better put the basil on as they begin to cook.

I suggest that fishermen try this recipe.

RECIPE

1 pound bass

2 teaspoons salt

1/2 teaspoon ground black pepper

1 teaspoon basil leaves

1 teaspoon instant minced onion

1/4 cup olive or salad oil

1/2 cup fine dry bread crumbs

Place the cleaned bass in dish. Combine salt, black pepper, basil, instant minced onion and oil. Mix well and pour over bass. Marinate 2 hours. Place in a 8 X 8 X 2-inch baking dish. Pour the marinade over the fish. Sprinkle with the bread crumbs and bake in a preheated oven (400 degrees) for about 20 minutes. Serve at once. YIELD: 6 servings

Bẽchamel Sauce

The French have a way with sauces. Ever since the days of the famous Caréme, sauce-making has been the key to French haute cuisine, ranking foremost among the many skills that any aspiring cook must learn, practice, and finally master.

"A sauce-maker", according to the celebrated chef, Escoffier, "must be adroit and sensitive to the most delicate nuance as sauce-making includes chemistry, harmony, flavor, voluptuousness, vigilance, and other virtues, all crossed by the lightning stroke of genius." No wonder so many cooks hesitate to look into this awesome subject and discover for themselves that, given a few practice rules and a little experience, the whole magic realm of sauce-making is theirs for the asking. Don't misunderstand me, however, I do not contend that after a few lessons in sauce-making that your Quenelles de Brochet will equal the ethereal Pain de Poisson served with an unctuous Sauce Cardinale that is featured at the famous French Restaurant Alexandre Dumaine's.

Yet, sauces, like soups and stocks, have their place in everyday good cooking as well as in the kitchens of international hotels and restaurants. A homemade sauce can lend certain magic to the simplest ingredients and make a memorable meal out of humble beginnings.

Béchamel, named after the maítre d' hótel of Louis XIV, is the mother sauce of all white sauces and is exceedingly simple to negotiate. A simple Béchamel can be constructed with just flour, butter, milk, and a little minced onion, but I think you will find that the following classic recipe which includes chopped veal, adds greatly to the flavor of this delicious sauce. The secret of making a good white sauce, and most other sauces, is to romance it slowly. Try this sauce to dress up almost any cooked vegetable.

RECIPE

6 tablespoons butter	1 stalk celery, finely chopped
1/2 onion, finely chopped	2 tablespoons butter
6 tablespoons flour	1 small sprig thyme
4 cups hot milk	1/2 bay leaf
2 ounces lean veal, or ham, chopped	White pepper corns
	Freshly grated nutmeg

In a thick-bottomed saucepan, or in the top of a double boiler, melt butter and cook onion over a low heat until it is transparent. Stir in flour and, stirring constantly, cook for a few minutes or until mixture cooks through but does not take on a color. Add hot milk and cook, stirring constantly until the mixture is thick and smooth. In another saucepan, simmer finely chopped lean veal (or ham) and celery in butter over a very low heat. Season with thyme, bay leaf, white peppercorns, and grated nutmeg. Cook for 5 minutes, stirring to keep veal from browning. Add veal to the sauce and cook over hot water for 45 minutes to one hour, stirring occasionally. When reduced to the proper consistency (two-thirds of original quantity), strain sauce through a fine sieve into a bowl, pressing meat and onion well to extract all the liquid. Cover surface of sauce with tiny pieces of butter to keep film from forming. Makes about 2 1/2 cups.

Bouillabaisse

It takes only the sketchiest knowledge of French to realize that most of the culinary terms of the Western World are of that language. The words **cuisine, chef, saute, souffle, fricassee** and **parfait** just start this list.

Unless we have eaten our way across France, we are familiar only with the **haute cuisine** as served in big hotels and restaurants all over the world. But there's great fun in discovering that most Frenchmen eat the **cuisine de famille,** home cooking—"like **maman** cooks." And then there is **cuisine du paysan** or peasant cooking to be found in rural areas.

French cooking differs according to regions. Seasonings can give us a clue in the most flavorful sort of way. Samples of provincial cooking can be found in the many big and little restaurants of Paris, so let's note the spicing and seasoning techniques of some typical provinces.

Alsace-Lorraine is famous for marvelous sausages, spiced as they are across the Rhine in Germany. Sauerkraut is cooked with onion, clove and an herb bunch. Cheese is studded with anise, fennel or caraway seeds.

Burgundy demands lusty, well-spiced sauces and in this province we find Dijon, world-famous for mustards and fancy gingerbreads. Provence, on the Mediterranean, means Marseille and **bouillabaisse,** that omnium-gatherum of seafood and spices. Provence cooks with a wide variety of highly aromatic herbs; thyme, sage, bay leaf, tarragon. Garlic has been called "the truffle of Provence." In Nice, at the eastern border of Provence, cooks swap recipes with neighboring Italians.

Westward from Provence lies the province of Languedoc. One of its most interesting cities is Montpellier, a seaport which was very active in the spice trading in the Middle Ages. The name of the city is significant, a simplified name which once meant "Mount of the Spice Merchants." As might be expected, foods are bravely seasoned in this region.

Southwestern France borders on Spain, so in Roussillon we find a generous use of garlic, saffron and red pepper, seasoning resembling that of Spanish dishes.

Bordeaux, which lies along the Atlantic is one more proof of the saying that, in France, the best cooking is to be found in the best wine country. Thyme, bay leaf, parsley, rosemary, nutmeg and cloves are among their pet aromatics, along with ever-present wine.

Normandy, on the English Channel, is cream and apple country, with a wide use of cider and apple brandy. In **Tripe a la Mode de caen** the famous **bouquet garni** is used, in this case combining thyme, tarragon, celery, parsley and bay leaf.

RECIPE

1/4 cup olive oil

1 stalk celery, chopped

1 medium onion, chopped

1 clove garlic, finely chopped

1 leek, diced

1/2 teaspoon thyme

1/2 bay leaf

2 cups crushed tomatoes

1 cup bottled clam juice

1 cup dry white wine

1/4 fennel, chopped, or 1/2 teaspoon crushed fennel seeds

Pinch of saffron

2 tablespoons chopped parsley

1 small lobster, cut into pieces

12 mussels, well scrubbed and debearded

12 raw shrimp, shelled and deveined

12 scallops

1 pound red snapper or cod, cut into serving pieces

In a large kettle heat the oil, add the celery, onion, garlic, leek, thyme and bay leaf and cook five minutes. Add the tomatoes, clam juice, wine, fennel, saffron and parsley and simmer fifteen minutes. Add the seafood and cook fifteen minutes longer. Yield: 6 servings

Braised Carrots and Onions

Every poet must surely have written many poems on love, for there are more than 900 separate references under the heading of love in "Bartlett's Quotations."

One practical bit of information which wasn't included comes from the 16th century herbalist, Gerarde. He declared that the carrot "serveth for love matters," but declared that the wild carrot was even better than the nice sweet carrots we eat. Scotch girls in the Hebrides, off the coast of Scotland, must have known this a long time ago, for girls used to take carrot chunks to dances and give them to their favorite young men. English girls, several centuries ago, used to wear the lacy-looking carrot leaves in their hair.

EVEN IF OUR MODERN WILD AND WONDERFUL HAIR STYLES SHOULD SUDDENLY DECREE CARROT LEAVES OR TOPS, THESE WOULD BE HARD TO FIND IN OUR MARKETS. A decade or two ago all tender young carrots came to markets wearing their leafy tops. Only the mature "soup carrots" in the fall were topped before they reached our produce counters.

SINCE THAT TIME RESEARCH HAS SHOWN THAT IT MAKES LESS THAN NO SENSE TO MARKET CARROTS WITH THEIR TOPS ON. The leafy tops draw moisture and nutrients from the root, so that carrots wilt much more quickly. Much of the weight of a carrot plant consists of top. To ship these for several thousand miles, along with the roots, would increase greatly the cost of packing, icing and transportation. We ought all to be very happy that we now can buy nicely scrubbed and topped carrots in film bags. If you leave them in their film bags you needn't put them in an already overcrowded vegetable hydrator — they'll make out fine right on the open shelf.

BUT TO GET BACK TO THIS LOVE BIT: AN APPEARANCE OF GOOD HEALTH IS A BASIC INGREDIENT IN PHYSICAL ATTRACTIVENESS. Girls may think that boys are taken with all the buttons and bows and gorgeous hairdos, but a nice, slim figure; clear skin; shiny eyes and peppy personality give a girl much more sex appeal.

CARROTS ARE ENORMOUSLY RICH IN VITAMIN A. This vitamin is one we need to keep skin nice and soft, for instance. A deficiency of vitamin A can result in rough, dry, scaly skin. It's tremendously important in eye health. Vitamin A is necessary for vision, especially being able to see in twilight or in a darkened room. A very bad lack of vitamin A—such as is common in part of the Orient—is said to be the cause of much of the blindness found there.

CARROTS AND VITAMIN A INFLUENCE THE DEVELOPMENT OF TEETH IN CHILDHOOD. That's why it's a good idea to let youngsters munch raw carrots between meals. Carrots have a certain sweetness which makes them popular with people of all ages, but children in particular.

IF YOU ARE A COMPULSIVE NIBBLER, WHY NOT KEEP SOME WELL-CHILLED CARROT STICKS IN FRONT OF THE REFRIGERATOR? A scant cup of grated carrots has only 42 calories; one small carrot 5 1/2 inches long and 1-inch in diameter on top has only about 20 calories.

RECIPE

8 medium-size fresh carrots	2 tablespoons butter or margarine
1/2 inch boiling water in saucepan	1/16 teaspoon ground black pepper
1 1/2 teaspoons salt	Chopped fresh parsley
1/2 cup small white onion rings	

1. Peel carrots and cut into chunks.

2. Place in saucepan with 1/2 inch boiling water and 1 teaspoon of the salt.

3. Cover and cook only until crisp-tender, 20 minutes. Drain.

4. Saute carrots and onion rings in butter or margarine until vegetables begin to brown.

5. Remove from heat and toss lightly with ground black pepper.

6. Serve hot sprinkled with chopped fresh parsley.

YIELD: 4 servings.

Carpetbag Steaks

There are only eight basic recipes in the entire world. In view of this, it is a thought of astronomical and gastronomical proportions when you consider what the people of the world have invented, created, and produced with only eight recipes. To be exact, the eight recipes are actually eight different methods of cooking: broiling, roasting, stewing, baking, braising, sauteing, steaming and frying.

With this as a point of departure, the various nations have struck out on their own and given us a wonderful international world of food. From Asia to South America, from North America to Europe, from the tropical islands to the frozen North, there exists an array of gourmeting designed to overwhelm any appetite.

Food is a topic of interest to everyone. I cannot recall meeting a person who was not, at least to some extent, interested in food. I shall never forget an experience I had several years ago when I was working on a project at the United Nations. I was interviewing representatives of several governments on the African Trusteeship Council. The outcome of these meetings, which were then in progress, was of international importance. One of the key figures I wanted to interview was Sir Andrew Cowan of the United Kingdom.

I called for an appointment, went to his hotel suite, and told Sir Andrew the information I wanted to record. He replied, "Mr. Wade, Her Majesty's Government has published a full report on this and it is on display in the lobby of the United Nations Building. There is nothing I can add to Her Majesty's stated views."

Abruptly, apparently, the interview was over before it had begun. So it would not be a total loss, I asked if he was possibly familiar with the recipe for Carpetbag Steaks which I had enjoyed at his club in London. His eyes lit up like a neon sign. He was obviously pleased. "So you've had Carpetbag Steaks . . . . and at my club?" I told him of my interest in food, and about my television show, "The Gourmet", and that I would like to have the recipe.

"Quite", he assured me. "I know that recipe well. Glad to give it to you." Whereupon he not only dictated the recipe but offered many interesting facts about its creation, and the difference in various chefs' versions of it in England. We talked at some length about food.

Then he said, "Now, David, what was that interview you wanted?"

136

I hooked up the recorder and off he went with a brilliant thirty minute discussion about the African Trusteeship.

So the language of food is a language we all speak, a subject in which we are all interested. Of all the subjects which have tempted scholars, writers, actors, businessmen, artists, as well as gourmets, none have been more prolific from their pens than the subject of food. Some take the view of philosophy, some of taste, others of economy, still others of cooking, but every man is an expert on food, because he knows what he likes, and he is bound to like something.

I want to give you that recipe for Carpetbag Steaks. See how you like Sir Andrew's club favorite.

RECIPE

4 cyc-of-round steaks about 1 1/2 inches thick

Salt and pepper to taste

Paprika

1/2 pint oysters

2 cups sherry

1/4 pound butter

Cut pockets into each of the steaks. Marinate oysters in one cup of sherry for one hour. Place two or three oysters into each steak with a little sherry. Place butter into a large skillet and melt. Add one cup of sherry to butter. Place the steaks into wine-butter sauce and steam on each side for one minute. Remove steaks from skillet and salt and pepper to taste. Sprinkle paprika on steaks and place in pre-heated broiler. Broil desired amount of time, then baste with wine and butter sauce.

Cherry Parfait

These days, when we're all likely to be studying maps of Asia Minor and the Mid-East we may note Northeast Turkey and the Caucasus Mountains, bounded by the Black Sea on the west and the Caspian on the east. This was a country called Pontus more than 2,000 years ago.

Pontus had a King named Mithridates, who had a touch of the mad chemist about him. He supposedly loved puttering around with poisons and antidotes for poisons. Horticulture was another hobby and even though he was King, he is said to have transplanted and grafted cherry trees with his own hands. Stories about King Mithridates say he was a cherry fancier.

The King's thoughts may have been home in the royal orchards because at one point he was soundly defeated by the Roman Army under Lucullus. General Lucullus was the great epicure, whose banquets are famous in history. It's only natural that General Lucullus would "liberate" some of the sweet cherry trees belonging to Mithridates, or such is the story.

Cherries arrived in Italy about 100 B.C. Within the century, cherry trees were found growing throughout the Roman empire. The Romans took the cherry tree as far as Britain. About five centuries later came the Dark Ages and the cherry tree seems to have disappeared from Britain, along with a lot of other good things the Romans had brought. A thousand years later it is said to have been re-introduced by Henry VIII and its cultivation encouraged. If it hadn't been for Henry VIII, Robert Louis Stephenson couldn't have written, "Up Into The Cherry Tree, Who Should Climb But Little Me?"

English settlers brought the cherry tree to America as early as 1629. Today cherry trees grow in every state. Oregon, California, and Washington, however, lead in the production of the sweet cherry, with New York State growing five times as many sour cherries or "pie cherries." We might sum this up by saying that while Michigan is far and away the leader in the production of sour cherries, the Western states are primarily growers of sweet cherries.

Sweet cherries are in the market mostly June and July. There are numerous varieties but the leader is the Bing cherry. It gets its name, Bing, from a Chinese gardener, who helped in developing this beautiful cherry. This is the sweet cherry we are likely to see often on the produce counter; it is extra large, heart-shaped, and deep maroon to black in color. The skin should be smooth and glossy. Another important variety is the Lambert, red and quite large, meaty and sweet.

138

Sour cherries are on the market from mid-June to mid-August. July is the peak month for sour cherries. Pie cherries are not nearly as available as sweet cherries, although we may find them near cherry-growing areas at harvest time. They are very fragile, very perishable, and that's the reason we see them altogether too seldom. Pie cherries are delectable in pies, tarts, and cooked desserts. And, of course, cherry jellies and jams—their flavor will remind you of summer all winter long.

Since cherries are so perishable, they should be kept cold all the way from shipping point, in the store, and at home. Rinse them before serving.

Experimenting with fresh cherries I have found that a fresh cherry sauce is extremely pleasing with poultry of any kind. Fresh cherries blend beautifully with other fruits such as blueberry in the construction of compotes. The recipe I would like to chronicle for you, however, is one that utilizes fresh cherries but canned cherries could be substituted.

RECIPE

2 cups fresh sweet cherries, halved and pitted	1/4 cup cold water
1/4 cup sugar	3 eggs, separated
1/4 cup fresh lemon juice	1/3 cup sugar
2 tablespoons water	1/4 teaspoon salt
1 envelope unflavored gelatin	1/4 cup sugar

Combine 1 cup of the cherries, the 1/4 cup sugar, lemon juice, and 2 tablespoons water; simmer covered, over low heat for 5 minutes. Drain, reserving 3/4 cup juice and cherries; chill.

Soften gelatin in 1/4 cup cold water. Combine egg yolks and the 1/3 cup sugar in the top part of a double boiler. Stir in salt and chilled cherry juice. Cook over hot water (not boiling) or very low heat until mixture coats metal spoon, stirring constantly. Remove from heat. Add softened gelatin. Chill until mixture is about as thick as fresh egg whites. Fold in chilled cherries. Beat egg whites until they stand in soft peaks; gradually beat in the remaining 1/4 cup sugar. Fold into gelatin mixture. Chill. Just before serving fill parfait glasses with layer of gelatin mixture and remaining one cup of cherries, starting and ending with gelatin mixture. Garnish, if desired, with whipped cream.

Recipe yields 6 servings.

Chicken Divan

One of the questions asked me most often is "what is the single most important talent for a cook to have?" The first time I answered impetuously but I've given a lot of thought to the question since and have not changed my mind. The art of Saucery will do more for a cook's reputation than any other one thing.

Learn to make a good basic brown sauce and a good basic white sauce. Get acquainted with their versatility and their almost infinite variations and you'll never serve a monotonous meal again; even when the end of the money comes before the end of the month or you are snowed in with a shelf full of nothing but tuna fish.

I think the greatest thing about sauces is that they are actually fun. The basic sauces are so simple and easy to make and then it is only a short step to something absolutely exotic—to a finishing touch that makes the difference between eating and dining.

Every country has its own sauces, but it is to France that we owe a large debt of gratitude. At the wonderful restaurants of Paris, the most famous in all the world, the Saucier is second in rank only to the head chef. The success of many of the most elaborate dishes in French cuisine depend on his skill, to say nothing of the success of the restaurant.

The Saucier's day begins with the making of the "basic" or "mother" sauces. From these he goes on a veritable whirl of creativity. He adds onion to Bechamel (a basic white sauce) for Sauce Soubise, one of the most versatile of sauces which is good with lamb, veal, vegetables and poultry. Mornay is white sauce with grated cheese, usually Gruyere or Parmesan, or a combination. Bordeau wine added to Sauce Espagnole (basic brown sauce) and the Saucier has Bordelaise. Chasseur, great with veal, is Espagnole with tomatoes, garlic and herbs. Madeira wine and Truffles added to Espagnole produce Perigueux, which adds the gourmet flair to eggs, veal and ham as well as the elegant fillet of beef. The flavorsome Sauce Robert, so popular with both pork and beef, is simply Sauce Espagnole with a touch of mustard.

One of the first things you should learn to make is Sauce Espagnole. You will probably find a number of recipes in your basic cookbooks. The very best, I believe, starts with a good strong beef stock. It takes a little planning, but very little time and is certainly worthwhile. Not the least of its virtues are the wonderful memories it will recall of the redolent soup pot bubbling on the back of Grandma's stove. She

140

added cracked bones and bits of meat (about 1/3 bones to 2/3 meat), vegetables and seasonings and simmered for hours (maybe even days!). After straining and removing the fat, she had a base par excellence for soups and gravies as well as sauces.

Often a recipe will call for a roux; which, despite the elegant-sounding name, is simply a mixture of butter and flour for thickening. There are white rouxs and blond and brown. Each has a distinctive flavor and color achieved by the degree of browning of the flour.

Hollandaise Sauce is one of the most popular in our country and one that many people find a little scary. There is no reason to avoid it. It is really quite simple to make. It does require you to keep a hawk's eye on the measuring and the cooking temperature, but just follow the instructions as I have outlined them in the recipe and you should have no trouble at all.

RECIPE

1 Five-pound stewing chicken	2 cups White Sauce
5 cups water	1/2 cup Hollandaise Sauce
2 teaspoons salt	1/2 cup heavy cream, whipped
1 large bunch broccoli	3 tablespoons sherry
1 cup grated Parmesan cheese	1 teaspoon David Wade Worcestershire Powder

Place the chicken on a rack in a large kettle. Add about 5 cups boiling water and the salt. Bring to a boil, lower heat, cover and simmer until tender, about 3 hours. Cool the chicken in the broth.

When the chicken has cooled, remove the skin and slice the breast and leg meat. Reserve the remainder of the chicken and the broth for another purpose.

Cook the broccoli in salted water until tender, drain and arrange on a deep heatproof serving platter. Sprinkle lightly with some of the cheese. Arrange the sliced chicken meat on the broccoli.

Combine the White Sauce with the Hollandaise Sauce. Add the whipped cream, sherry and Worcestershire Powder. Pour the sauce over the chicken and broccoli and sprinkle with the remaining cheese.

Place about 5 inches below high heat in a preheated broiler and broil until browned and bubbly.

White Sauce

1/2 cup butter

3 tablespoons flour

3 cups milk

1/2 teaspoon nutmeg

Melt the butter in a saucepan. Add the flour and stir with a wire whisk until blended. Bring the milk to a boil and add all at once to the butter-flour mixture, stirring vigorously with the whisk until the sauce is thickened and smooth. Stir in the nutmeg. Keep hot.

Hollandaise Sauce

3 egg yolks

1 tablespoon cold water

1/2 cup soft butter

1/4 teaspoon salt

1/2 teaspoon lemon juice, or to taste

Combine the egg yolks and water in the top of a double boiler and beat with a wire whisk over hot (not boiling) water until fluffy.

Add a few pats of butter to the mixture and beat continually until the butter has melted and the sauce starts to thicken. Care should be taken that the water in the bottom of the boiler never boils. Continue adding the butter bit by bit, stirring constantly.

Add the salt and the lemon juice. If a lighter texture is desired, beat in a tablespoon of hot water.

Chicken Enchiladas

Climb aboard our flight into the land below the Rio Grande. We'll go adventuring and seeking the pleasures of the table of Old Mexico.

We are bid welcome with a hearty "bienvenido!" as we board. One brief stop at San Antonio, the Air-Port-of-Entry for Mexico, and we are winging southward toward Mexico City.

Night time now. As we approach, the spectacular lights of the National Palace and the Cathedral of Mexico flicker a welcome too. The Palace of Montezuma once occupied that spot, later Cortez built himself a palace there, still later Maximilian re-designed it. Ah, here is history, down there in Mexico City, and you are hungry for some good authentic Mexican food.

Occupying Mexico on your own two feet now, you go through customs, get comfortably settled in your hotel, and inquire about the dining room. You scan the menu. Nothing there that you recognize as a favorite Mexican food. The waiter politely refers the senor to Chicken Mole listed on the menu—the national dish of Mexico. You nod affirmatively, and the mole is served. It is good, very good, but not exactly what you were expecting. Oh, well, manana, manana.

Manana comes and with it sightseeing. Popocatepetl, the National Palace, the Cathedral, shopping on the famous Paseo de la Reforma (Reforma Boulevard—the Champs Elysees of Mexico City), where you dine on Paella Valenciana, a popular dish in Mexico, but it comes from Spain (Spanish rice with pork and shrimp), then in the evening you will be entertained by Mexican guitars which set a fiesta mood, and flamenco singers and dancers. Here, along with your Tequila Cocteles you'll be served, oh, perhaps, Carnitas (little meat pieces, baked), or Empanaditas (tiny Mexican pastry turnovers), or with your cafe you may be served Quemada (burnt sugar candy), or Bizcochitos con Nueces (little nut cookies).

You ask senor guide where you can get some really authentic Mexican food. He knows the very place. Their specialty is Pescado Relleno (large fish stuffed with small shellfishes and seasoned with butter, lemon, and capers). Good? Couldn't be better! Delicious! But about that really authentic Mexican food—? As you drift dreamily off to sleep you wonder if perhaps—manana?

"Ai, Chihuahua, amigo", you are forever doomed to disappointment. You have been enjoying the typical cuisine of Old Mexico. The kind of Mexican food you are thinking of you left in your own backyard—in the United States. You will find nothing like that in Mexico.

The recipe I am chronicling for you now is a genuine blend of native tortillas and chili sauce, with the refinements of a sauce, which a Spanish-speaking French chef gave to me on one of my food adventures to Mexico.

RECIPE

1 chicken (approximately 3 1/2 lbs) disjointed

2 cups water

Salt to taste

1 cup chicken stock

1 tablespoon flour

2 cups sour cream

2 cups sweet cream

2 teaspoons grated onion

2 teaspoons salt

Pepper to taste

Jar of canned pimiento strips

12 tortillas

Grated, dry Monterrey Jack cheese

Place chicken which has been disjointed in about two cups of water. Salt to taste. Cook over medium heat until tender. Cool and remove chicken meat from bones. Measure your chicken stock. If much more than 1 cup remains, cook until more concentrated. Combine in saucepan and cook over low heat until thickened the chicken stock and flour. Stir in sour cream, sweet cream, and grated onion. Add salt, pepper to taste, and bring to boil.

Dip the tortillas one at a time into the cream mixture and place in large, shallow baking pan. Arrange chicken down center of each tortilla. Cover chicken with 2 or 3 strips canned pimiento. Roll each tortilla and push to end of baking dish. Continue dipping and rolling until all tortillas are filled. Pour remaining cream mixture over enchiladas. Bake in moderate oven (350 degrees) for 30 minutes. Sprinkle with grated, dry Monterrey Jack cheese. Serve with Salsa Verde. Makes 6 servings.

Salsa Verde

2 cans (8 oz ea) tomato sauce or 2 cups tomato puree

2 hot green chiles, finely chopped

1 small clove garlic, minced

1 medium onion, chopped

Salt to taste

1 1/2 teaspoons David Wade Worcestershire Powder

Combine all of the above ingredients in a saucepan and cook over low heat for several minutes. Serve in a bowl and let each person take as much as desired. For those who prefer really "hot" enchiladas, Salsa Verde may be substituted for cream mixture and poured over the enchiladas after they are rolled and filled. If you wish to do this, double the Salsa Verde recipe. Salsa Verde is very hot. Treat it with respect. It is this sauce which controls the "hotness" of Chicken Enchiladas.

Chicken Souffle

The awe-inspiring souffle is one of the creations of French haute cuisine. It is, in reality, nothing more than a simple airy mixture of eggs, butter, flour, and a puree of vegetables, meat, fish, or fowl. These purees are unexciting and unpretentious and very often, are left-overs.

Try the souffle as a perfect beginning to a meal, whether it be a simple cheese affair (try a combination of gruyére and Parmesan), a concoction of fish or shellfish, or one made with a well-seasoned base of pureed vegetables (endive, onion, or mushroom and cheese).

Savory souffles also make light-as-air entrees of distinction for luncheon or supper parties and there you can always let your imagination run riot. You will find that souffles are quite easy to make if a few basic rules are followed. First and foremost; a souffle must be eaten when ready. A souffle will not wait for your guests. Your guests must wait for this delicate and sometimes temperamental dish. A rich, smooth sauce is the base of all souffles. Many French souffle recipes simply require a thick well-flavored Béchamel sauce. The egg yolks and egg whites must be beaten separately; the yolks until thick and lemon-colored, the whites until stiff but not dry. In separating the eggs, be sure there is no speck of yolk left in the whites. Otherwise, you will not be able to beat your whites stiff. Use an unbuttered souffle dish for your first attempts so that the souffle can cling to the sides of the dish and rise to its full height. For added flavor, when you butter the dish, sprinkle the buttered surface with fresh bread crumbs or a little finely grated Parmesan cheese. A slow to medium oven, 325 degrees to 350 degrees, is essential. If your oven is too hot, the souffle will be well-cooked on top and undercooked inside. As long as it remains in a warm oven a souffle is pretty sturdy. The best way to determine when a souffle is done is to open the door of the oven after 20 or 25 minutes and give the dish a slight shove. If the top crust moves only very slightly, the souffle is done. However, if it really trembles, leave it in for a few more minutes.

RECIPE

1/4 cup butter

1/4 cup flour

1 1/4 cups hot milk

2 tablespoons Cognac

Salt and freshly ground white pepper

Dry mustard

5 egg yolks

1/2 pound ground cooked chicken

6 egg whites, beaten stiff

Melt butter in a double boiler, blend in flour. Add hot milk and stir over fire until mixture comes to a boil. Remove from fire and add Cognac. Season with salt, white pepper, and a pinch of dry mustard. Beat in egg yolks, one at a time. Add puree of cooked chicken. Fold the beaten egg whites into chicken mixture. Butter an 8-inch souffle dish and tie a band of buttered wax paper completely around the outside. Fill about three quarters full with souffle mixture and bake for 40 minutes in a preheated oven 350 degrees or until top is slightly browned and souffle feels firm to the touch. Remove from oven, take off paper, and serve immediately. Recipe serves 4.

Chili Cocktail Cheese Pot

October's a busy, busy month. Not only Halloween with its horri-pilated cats and air-borne witches, but numerous special holidays. There is for instance, State Fair Day in Texas. Also Missouri Day; Oklahoma Day; Alaska Day or Pulaski Day (in Nebraska). In the Virgin Islands they celebrate Thanksgiving Day in October because it's the end of the hurricane season.

October is also Chili Con Carne Month and brings us Child Health Day; Poetry Day and Columbus Day. So, in honor of Chili Con Carne month, Child Health and Poetry Day, here's a home-made jingle:

> "I'm hungry, Maw!" cried little Willie,
> "Please let me have a bowl of Chili!"

It's good "little Willie" rhymes with "bowl of Chili" because youngsters love chili con carne. (So do their elders, for that matter.)

IT'S ALSO VERY APPROPRIATE THAT COLUMBUS DAY SHOULD COME DURING CHILI CON CARNE MONTH! Because, of course, chili peppers and all the many other kinds of capsicum (cap-si-cum) peppers, were some of the most valuable treasures dis-covered in the New World. While other American plants, such as pota-toes and tomatoes, were ignored at first, Spanish explorers loved the nippy, red podded capsicum peppers immediately. As early as 1493, historian Peter Martyr wrote that Columbus had found "pepper more pungent than that from Caucasus".

SO POPULAR WERE THESE CAPSICUMS THAT THEY WERE SOON BEING GROWN IN MANY PARTS OF THE KNOWN WORLD. In India, for instance, where they quickly got into the habit of adding a few red peppers to their traditional curry dishes. Since the early 16th century, all Indian curries have contained capsicums.

IT WAS AN ENGLISHMAN FROM INDIA WHO CREATED THE FIRST CHILI POWDER, SO THE STORY GOES. This man had loved curry dishes in India. Once he'd reached Texas, in far-off America he kept longing for curry. Chili peppers and oregano were easy to come by. So were cumin seeds, garlic and salt. One day—if we may believe the legend—he ground these ingredients together. It wasn't curry powder, for certain spices were missing, but it was just as richly flavorful. It was a completely right spice blend for beef and beans, for dishes starting with corn and cornmeal. Just as curry powder was made to simulate the typical flavor of Indian curries, chili powder produced the flavor of Mexican dishes.

CHILI POWDER IS VERY AROMATIC, BUT NOT NECESSARILY "HOT". It's a convenient and pleasing spice blend for all kinds of every-day dishes. Add it to stews of all kinds: beef, chicken, seafood. Add it to taste during the last few minutes of cooking. It's a delightful addition to canned soups: Pea soup and tomato soup, mixed. Or in bean-and-bacon soup. Or pepper-pot. Not too much—just enough to give it a tingle of flavor. Then try chili in salad dressings—especially if it's to be mixed with fish or meat salads. One of the best and easiest sauces for broiled fish or vegetables such as asparagus, green beans or corn is chili butter. Simply add 1/2 teaspoon chili powder to 1/4 cup butter or margarine and melt.

This is a great party recipe.

RECIPE

1/4 cup crumbled Roquefort cheese

1/2 cup grated mild Chedder or Monterey Jack cheese

2 pkgs. (6 ounces) cream cheese

1/4 teaspoon onion powder

1/16 teaspoon garlic powder

1 3/4 teaspoons chili powder

1 teaspoon David Wade Worcestershire Powder

1. Mix all cheeses together until well blended.

2. Blend in remaining ingredients.

3. Serve in a crockery cheese jar or in a small bowl as a spread for crackers, cucumber slices or black bread.

YIELD: 1 cup.

Chili Rellenos, El Fenix

Go where you will in Texas and there is not a town worth stopping in that doesn't have a Mexican restaurant. Cities like San Antonio, Houston, and Dallas, provide the diner with an overwhelming choice of fine Mexican restaurants. It is, therefore, no small accomplishment to achieve what the Martinez family has achieved in Dallas—to wit, the best Mexican food you will find anywhere.

How did it all begin?

First, let us go back, back, back to those thrilling days of yester-year when Texans-to-be were swarming into the state. They came from the South, mostly, and from South of the Border. Here in Texas, the impact of their cultures met head-on. Who would have thought that those Southern-fried-chicken-eaters and tamales would ever be so happy together? No one. But miracles are always happening and a food taste happened then. This taste of Mexico was enough to make them **forget the Alamo!**

Now to this background of history enters on the Dallas scene, Mike Martinez. The time is 1918, the place is McKinney and Griffin near downtown Dallas, the facility is one room turned into a restaurant. Ah, but the real success formula Mike Martinez possessed was a philosophy which has been proved by the test of time—his knowledge of the right way to cook Mexican food, his belief in very hard work, and his family.

You know, there are almost as many types of Mexican food as there are Mexican cooks, but to combine the best of all and reach that happy medium that pleases the taste of everyone is genius indeed. El Fenix does this superbly.

The pace of hard work is an example set by Mike Martinez that the sons and daughters still apply to their grown-up and still growing operation. "Work! Work! and Stay With It!" is their theme and their strength.

The sons, Alfred, Gilbert, Henry and Rueben, and two sisters, Irene Garcia and Tina McDonald carry on the El Fenix tradition as a family enterprise. They have been joined by in-laws, aunts and uncles, and cousins to bring the best in Mexican food to all who go in at the door under the sign of El Fenix.

From the little one room where the Martinez family began, they have come a long way, growing with Dallas, and even out of Dallas. This growing success is evident in their spacious new headquarters building in the industrial area, and their new restaurants in Fort Worth, Houston, Richardson and Longview.

Here is a little bit of El Fenix you can take to your own kitchen and serve in the best tradition of Texas-Mexican cuisine—El Fenix Chili Rellenos.

RECIPE

1/2 cup oil
1 onion, finely diced
3/4 cup flour
4 cups tomato juice
1 1/2 teaspoons salt
1/8 teaspoon cumin
1/2 teaspoon white pepper
1 small clove garlic, crushed
1 pound ground round
1 large potato, finely diced
2 tomatoes, peeled and diced
1 onion, finely diced

1 1/2 teaspoon salt
1/4 teaspoon cumin
1/2 teaspoon white pepper
1 small clove garlic, crushed
2 tablespoons chopped pimiento
6 tablespoons finely chopped almonds, if desired
1/2 cup chopped raisins, if desired
2 cups oil
6 large chilis poblano
4 egg whites
4 egg yolks

Heat oil in skillet over medium heat, add onion and saute until tender. Add flour and cook until lightly browned, then add tomato juice gradually and cook until thickened. Add salt, cumin, white pepper and garlic and simmer over low heat 15 minutes.

Keep sauce warm over low heat. Fry ground round in skillet over medium heat until medium done, then add potato and cook until done.

Reduce heat to low temperature, add tomatoes, onion, salt, cumin, white pepper, garlic, pimiento, almonds and raisins and simmer 15 minutes. Remove from heat.

Heat oil in skillet over medium heat and cook chilis poblano until skins look white. Remove from oil and drain. Wrap in moistened cloth. Peel, dipping in water to help loosen skin. Slit and remove veins. Fill with beef mixture. Sprinkle a little flour over filling. Beat egg whites until soft peaks form. Fold in egg yolks and beat until fluffy.

Dip stuffed chilis in egg mixture. Fry in hot oil over medium heat until golden brown. Remove from oil and place in warm tomato sauce. Heat over very low temperature 5 minutes.

Garnish with parsley. Makes 6 servings.

Note: Chilis may be stuffed with pasteurized process cheese instead of meat filling if you prefer. Use 1/4 pound cheese to stuff each chili.

Cinnamon Deep-Dish Apple Pie

Today we can trundle our shopping carts past the spice shelves at the supermarket and think nothing of dropping in a container of cinnamon: Lined up neatly behind the one we reach for are dozens more just like it. But there was a time when cinnamon was as difficult to reach as the Golden Fleece of mythology.

CINNAMON IS THE WORLD'S GREATEST SWEET SPICE AND HAS BEEN A PRECIOUS COMMODITY THROUGHOUT THE AGES. It has been used not only as a flavoring for foods, but as medicine, as perfume and quite often in love charms.

The Chinese, forty centuries ago, believed that cinnamon was the sacred Tree of Life which grew high up in Paradise, up in the Tibetan Mountains. Anyone who ate even a small bit of this tree or its fruit, they believed, would live forever.

At the time of the Crusades—a thousand years ago—many people in Europe thought spices, such as cinnamon, came from the Garden of Eden. Eden, they'd been told, was a "place of delight, full of beautiful trees and fragrant perfumes." These spices were carried out of Eden by the Ganges River and the Tigris. This would have seemed likely to them, for the Garden of Eden was somewhere in the East and cinnamon came from that direction, brought by spice traders from Arabia.

THE ROMANS USED CINNAMON IN THEIR RELIGIOUS CEREMONIES—even by the reprobate Nero. After he'd kicked his wife Poppaea to death, he ordered the annual cinnamon supply of the entire city of Rome burned at her funeral!

NATURALLY, THE ARAB SPICE TRADERS KNEW WHERE CINNAMON CAME FROM, BUT THEY WERE TOO SMART TO SAY. To keep competition out of cinnamon country they told frightening tales of weird dangers: That cinnamon came from deep glens filled with deadly snakes. That cinnamon thickets were guarded by ferocious birds. That only priests were allowed to collect cinnamon and that the sun god claimed the first bundle for his own, igniting it with a spark of divine fire.

CINNAMON IS THE BARK OF AN EVERGREEN TREE. It is native to the Far East and today we get it from Indonesia and South

Vietnam. The bark is first split, then peeled off the tree. As it dries it is rolled into tight quills or sticks. These are cut into lengths of from two to three feet and then shipped that way to the United States. Here we either grind the sticks into a fine powder or cut them into pieces three or four inches long for sale as cinnamon sticks.

CINNAMON GIVES DELIGHTFUL AROMA TO HUNDREDS OF DISHES. FOR INSTANCE: Add a teaspoon of ground cinnamon to a graham cracker crust for pies.

When making rolled out cookies, sift together confectioners' sugar and cinnamon and sprinkle over the pastry board in place of flour.

Add a teaspoon of ground cinnamon to the dry ingredients of a chocolate pudding mix.

Tuck one-inch piece of stick cinnamon in the water when cooking carrots which are to be candied. Or dust ground cinnamon over candied sweet potatoes.

RECIPE

5 cups (5 medium) sliced cooking apples	1 1/2 tablespoons quick-setting tapioca
2 sticks cinnamon, 2 inches long	2 tablespoons butter or margarine
3/4 cup sugar	Pastry, using 1 cup flour
1/2 teaspoon salt	

1. Place apples in an 8 x 8 x 2-inch pan.
2. Add cinnamon.
3. Mix sugar, salt and tapioca. Sprinkle over apples.
4. Dot with butter or margarine.
5. Cover with pastry rolled 1/8-inch thick.
6. Trim, turn under and flute edge.
7. Cut a gash in pastry to allow for escape of steam.
8. Bake in a preheated very hot oven (450°F.) 10 minutes.
9. Reduce heat to moderate (350°F.) and bake 40 minutes or until apples are tender.

YIELD: 8 servings.

Coconut Rice Pudding

Look at a map of the Caribbean Sea and you'll realize there are dozens of islands, some big, most of them mere dots on the map. They pop up here and there through three-quarter million square miles of beautiful blue water.

The ancestors of the people who live on these islands came from Spain, France, Great Britain, Denmark, India, Africa, China, and many other places around the globe. Like people in other regions, they eat what is most easily available. The waters of tropical America are rich with thirteen-hundred varieties of fish. Fruits and vegetables of many kinds grow profusely in tropical gardens and orchards.

All spice, nutmeg, mace, ginger, turmeric and chili peppers are produced in commercial amounts—one of our good sources of these spices. As may be expected, Caribbean cooks use these spices daily in preparing regional dishes.

Remember Ponce de Leon who came to the Caribbean seeking the Fountain of Youth? We almost never hear of his wife, Dona Inez. She brought European herbs and vegetables to their garden in Puerto Rico. She not only showed the Indian women how to use these new flavoring ingredients but, in turn, became acquainted with the use of native foods and seasonings. She serves as a for-instance of early homemakers and mixed-and-matched cooking skills and recipes with the native peoples.

There are variations in cooking and seasoning, but popular in most of the Caribbean are rice, beans, sweet potatoes, corn, cassava, black-eyed peas, cooking bananas, breadfruit, okra, eggplant and many, many peppers. With these rather starchy foods they like lemon and sour orange juice, garlic, onions, pepper, cinnamon, cloves, ginger. Green coriander leaves, called **cilantro,** and oregano are important herbs. This is mortar and pestle country for they like to grind together mixtures of seasonings.

Sofrito is a spiced sauce made of salt pork, ground ham and such spices as onions, garlic, peppers, and oregano for flavor. The islanders also add coriander leaves and achiote (ah-she-oaty) seeds for red color. But coriander seeds and paprika may be used instead. This sauce is made up in quantity and a few tablespoons are used to flavor soups, meats, vegetables.

As we get down to islands nearer the South American coast, meals become lighter, less rich because of the heat. More spiced cold dishes and iced beverages are served to excite the appetite. Hospitality is charming, without ceremony, but guests are genuinely welcomed by their generous hosts.

As a little taste of what one might eat at a Caribbean dinner table, do try this recipe.

RECIPE

In a small saucepan combine:

1 1/2 cups milk

1 can (4 oz) shredded coconut

Bring to boiling point. Remove from heat and cool.

In a medium saucepan bring to boiling point:

2 1/2 cups milk

Stir in:

1 cup raw regular cooking rice

Reduce heat; cover and simmer 25 minutes or until rice is tender. Meanwhile, squeeze milk from coconut through a fine sieve or cheese-cloth; set milk aside. Sprinkle coconut on a baking sheet. Toast under hot broiler until lightly browned; set aside.

Stir into cooked rice:

Reserved coconut milk	**2 egg yolks, beaten lightly**
1/2 cup sugar	**1 teaspoon ground cinnamon**

Cook 5 minutes, stirring constantly. Turn into serving dish. Chill thoroughly. Garnish with reserved toasted coconut. Yield: 6 portions

Cold Ham Mousse

It's strange, the round-about way in which modern words have acquired their meanings. Take the word "garnish", for instance. First this meant "to warn", then it was extended to include battle equipment and armor. Armor was often very beautifully adorned. So, eventually garniture or garnishing meant anything handsomely decked out and that included things to eat. To the present-day American cook, a garnish has come to mean, first of all, a dash of gay red paprika!

Great-grandmother—if she lived in America—probably never used paprika in the course of her lifetime. Today, however, we use about 12 million pounds of this brilliant spice. Paprika is right up there among the first five of America's favorite spices.

Paprika does for dozens and dozens of dishes what rosy cheeks do for a tree-top apple—makes food look good enough to eat. We should be able to enjoy our food with all of our senses: its color, shape and arrangements should delight the eye. Crispness, smoothness please the sense of touch. Fragrance excites the appetite almost as much as does the taste.

Keep paprika close at hand; you can use it to garnish foods for every meal. Dash some on the breakfast scrambled eggs. At lunch time send a cheese rarebit to the table with a rosy-red cast of paprika. Shake up a tomato juice cocktail with a little paprika to intensify the tomato color and increase the tang of the tomato. Pork and beans, salad dressings, meat, fish, chicken, potatoes, noodles, macaroni and a long list of creamed dishes all look more attractive, more appetizing if you'll remember to reach for your container of paprika.

RECIPE

1/2 teaspoon powdered mustard	Dash ground black pepper
1/2 teaspoon warm water	1 cup milk
2 packages unflavored gelatin	1 chicken bouillon cube
2 egg yolks, beaten lightly	2 cups chopped cooked ham
1/2 teaspoon salt	1 teaspoon paprika
1/2 teaspoon instant minced onion	1 teaspoon parsley flakes
	1/2 cup heavy cream, whipped

Blend mustard and water; let stand 10 minutes for flavor to develop.

Soften gelatin in 1/2 cup cold water and set aside. Combine mustard egg yolks, salt, minced onion and black pepper in top of double boiler. Gradually stir in milk, 1 cup water and bouillon cube. Cook over hot water 15 minutes or until thickened, stirring constantly. Stir in softened gelatin, ham, paprika, parsley flakes and vinegar. Chill until mixture begins to thicken. Fold in whipped cream. Turn into a 6-cup ring mold which has been rinsed in cold water. Chill until firm. Just before serving, unmold on serving plate. Serve with watercress and mayonnaise, if desired.

YIELD: 8 servings

Columbian Cuchuco

(Barley Soup)

All the South American countries naturally have their own characteristic dishes, according to their produce and to their climate conditions. But if you tried to discover where their overall ideas in gastronomy were derived, you would find a definite Spanish trait.

From Argentina, the land of the beef, comes some very interesting and highly flavored meat dishes, like the Puchero. The other fascinating dish from the same country is the Argentine carbonado, an exotic mixture of sweet and savory flavors. It seems to me that in the land of plenty of Argentine beef, they are inordinately fond of mixing fruit and meat in their cookery; probably because "just steak" is such an everyday occurrence that good cooks hardly give their thoughts to it. I am told that until quite recently the Argentines served steak with every meal, in much the same way we get bread on the table without ordering it separately.

The Bolivians, too, are very partial to highly seasoned food, but the Bolivian recipes can be served without risk of offending the most sensitive palates. Their stuffed avocados will lend style and elegance to any dinner table and will start off a dinner party on a high note of gastronomic finesse.

From Venezuela, the land of contrast and exotic, unexplored jungles, comes a real work of art in the shape of meat pies: Venezuela Hallacas. In spite of the fact that these meat pies contained no outlandish ingredients, they are a real gourmet's joy. What I like about them is their mundane and ordinary outer appearance coupled with their most luscious filling. It is always fun to watch your guests lift up an ordinary-looking meat pie and go into raptures of praise after the first bite.

From Columbia, comes a very filling and satisfying soup called Columbian Cuchuco, a very palatable soup without any sharp or spicy ingredients.

RECIPE

1 pound soup bones

4 pints water

1 bay leaf

3 peppercorns

1 large onion, chopped

1 pound barley

Water to cover

8 ounces fresh green peas

8 ounces cabbage, finely chopped

2 teaspoons salt

1/2 teaspoon pepper

1 teaspoon David Wade Worcestershire Powder

Place the bones in the 4 pints water, then add onion, bay leaf and peppercorns. Simmer in a covered container for 2 hours. Wash the barley and place in another container, cover with water, and bring to boil. Strain the barley and recover with water and cook for 3 additional minutes. Strain this mixture and add to the strained bone stock when cooked. Bring this mixture to a boil and add vegetables and seasonings. Gently simmer until the soup thickens and the barley is cooked.

Coquilles St. Jacques

The gourmet's richest rewards are found in the haute cuisine of France. Haute cuisine means, literally, "high-class cooking". Even the smallest bistro in Paris is justifiably jealous of its culinary reputation, but the haute restaurants are famous for the elegance of their creations.

Americans have always made Europe their first overseas vacation choice. France is an integral part of the grande tour. Naturally, Americans look forward to tasting the world famous **cuisine francaise.** They have heard of it all their lives. Now, they are in Paris—the world center of gastronomy. So what happens? We are often frightened away from really magnificent foods by the odd names on the menu.

Unless you speak, write, or understand French (gourmet French, too, please), it can be disturbing to see "Le Pigeonneau Roti le Riz Sauvage Americain", staring back at you from a cafe programme. The best we are apt to come up with, lacking a knowledge of the language, is something like "American Pigeon." This is not very appetizing. Indeed, it makes us downright uncomfortable. But, "Le Pigeonneau Roti le Riz Sauvage Americain", is only roasted squab, with wild rice, American style.

If we are going to enjoy French cooking abroad, or at home, we'll just have to "take a chance" and experiment a little. Keep in mind that this style of cooking has been popular for centuries. Only the best survives that long on a world-wide basis. Usually, your reward is a happy new taste thrill. Another clue for ordering in French: When in doubt, order Specialities de la Maison. This is always a safe choice, because the specialty of the house is the dish, or dishes, they are proudest of, think they prepare best, and so recommend to one and all.

I have never known anyone to return from Europe without "discovering" a new recipe about which they went into exclamations of praise. They could, of course, have enjoyed those same foods right here in America. But in Europe they discover that they were really gourmets at heart all the time.

Transplanted among foreign people who are savoring these strange morsels with gusto; seeing different sights; listening to another language; surrounded by an atmosphere that is exciting and stimulating, the scene is set for a new food experience. Add to this the important fact that they can't get what they are "always accustomed to eating" at home. Voila! A gourmet is born.

It is unnecessary to go abroad to enjoy haute cuisine. America abounds with superb restaurants serving haute style. We can create cuisine francaise in our own kitchen anytime we please. The longest trip you'll have to make is to your supermarket.

I captured this recipe for Coquilles St. Jacques (they are only scallops!) from a very haute restaurant near the Montmartre section of Paris several years ago. It has been a favorite of mine ever since I first tasted its enchanting flavor.

RECIPE

8 scallops	Salt and pepper to taste
1 large tomato, peeled and sliced	1/4 cup butter or margarine
1 small onion, finely chopped	1/4 cup Bechamel Sauce (white or cream sauce)
1 can (4 oz.) finely sliced mushrooms	Parsley, garnish

Wash the scallops, and cover with cold, salted water, and cook over medium heat. Bring them to a boil. (This takes about 8 minutes to cook until soft). Drain and chop the white and red parts together, Mix with tomato, onion, mushrooms, and salt and pepper.

Now we intensify these flavors by melting the butter in a skillet and adding the scallop mixture. Cook 3 to 5 minutes. Add the Bechamel (white or cream) sauce. Stir well. Spoon the entire mixture into four scallop shells. Brown them in your broiling compartment about 3 inches away from the heat. Garnish with parsley before serving. Recipe will serve four people.

Coquilles St. Jacques is the epitome of haute cuisine, yet it is not difficult to prepare.

Crazy Bean Casserole

Obviously the tastemakers have been busy sniffing and sampling their way along the American spice shelf looking for new flavor effects, for 1969 spice import figures show a sharp increase in black and white pepper and cinnamon, and a jump in the quantity of celery and anise seeds and sage leaves which entered the country.

While thousands of tons of stalk on salad celery is grown in this country, the celery seed for the spice shelf must all be imported from India, France and Indonesia, a total of some 3,116,000 pounds.

The botanical name is the same—Apium graveolens—but there is a distinct difference in flavor. Celery seed is the fruit of wild celery or smallage, harvested for many centuries for its medicinal properties: "The disease then to celery yields, conquered by the remedy." Then, as now, only the seeds had appetizing aroma, for the rest of the plant was unpleasantly bitter. "Ungrateful" they would have called it several centuries ago. It took centuries of taming to develop the much sweeter plant which puts celery flakes and diced celery on our spice shelves.

The flavor fillip of the tiny brown celery seed is available whole or as celery salt, which is a mixture of ground celery seed and table salt. Celery seed is one of the important pickling spices. It is excellent, too, in chowders and fish soups; in egg dishes; with sea food and salads of different kinds.

RECIPE

1 pkg. (10 oz) frozen lima beans

1/2 lb. frankfurters

2 tablespoons butter or margarine

1 medium onion, chopped

1 clove garlic, minced

1 can (1 lb.) kidney beans, drained

1 jar (1 lb. 6 oz) baked beans

1/4 teaspoon celery seed

1 teaspoon mustard (prepared)

1 tablespoon brown sugar

1/2 cup catsup

1/2 cup dry red wine

1/2 teaspoon salt

Dash pepper

1/2 cup crushed corn or potato chips

1. Cook lima beans according to package directions; drain.

2. Preheat oven to 350 degrees.

3. Slice frankfurters.

4. Heat butter in large skillet, and saute frankfurter slices, onion, and garlic, stirring occasionally.

5. When onion is tender, stir in lima beans and all remaining ingredients except chips.

6. Spoon mixture into a 2-quart casserole and top with chips.

7. Bake 30 minutes.

Makes 8 servings.

Creamed Mushrooms and Onions A La Romano

Walk into a well-stocked housewares department and there seem to be pots, pans and cookers for all kinds of foods—special egg poachers, fish poachers, potato bakers, asparagus cookers, souffle dishes and many more. This may seem like over-specialization, yet two thousand years ago the Romans had a special pan for cooking mushrooms. They called mushrooms **boleti** and the mushroom cooking vessels were **boletaria.** They were to be used only for mushrooms, never lesser foods.

There must have been instances when other foods were cooked in the **boletaria.** At least the Roman writer, Martial, depicts an unhappy mushroom vessel bewailing its comedown in a carelessly run Roman kitchen. Said this mushroom pot, "Although **boleti** have given me so noble a name, I am now used, I am ashamed to say, for Brussels sprouts."

RECIPE

1/2 **pound fresh mushrooms or 1 can (6 to 8 oz) sliced mushrooms**

1 **package (2 oz) white sauce mix**

1/2 **teaspoon Italian seasoning**

1/8 **teaspoon ground black pepper**

1 **can (15 1/2 oz) small white onions**

1/3 **cup grated Romano or Parmesan cheese**

Slice fresh mushrooms (makes 2 1/2 cups) or drain canned mushrooms. Prepare white sauce according to package directions. Season with Italian seasoning and black pepper. Place mushrooms and onions in buttered one quart casserole. Pour over all. Sprinkle with cheese. Bake in preheated moderate oven 30 minutes.

Yield: 4 portions

Creole Stuffed Green Peppers

When the spice-seeking Spaniards sailed west to accidentally discover the New World, they didn't find the spices of India, but they did find many new taste thrills. They must have been particularly fascinated with the Capsicum family. Not only were the fruits of the pod pepper plant pleasing to the taste, but the plants themselves were a joy to behold, with their glassy green leaves and colorful fruit.

There are hundreds of varieties of the Capsicum family; its fruits vary in size and shape as well as flavor, and they come in a myriad of colors. Some peppers are green at maturity, others are red. Some are yellow, violet, white or brown.

The pod pepper plant is, in fact, so pretty that many gardeners plant it in the flower garden right along with other ornamental plants and it is a particular favorite with kitchen-window gardeners. See for yourself —plant a few seeds in coffee cans in the fall and by Christmas, with very little investment of time or money, you will have wonderful remembrances for your gourmet friends.

In general, the Capsicum family can be divided into two categories— the hot, especially beloved south of the border, and the mild, sweet-flavored bell or bull-nosed pepper, most popular in the United States where a whopping 485,000,000 pounds reach the markets annually.

Most popular of these sweet-flavored peppers are the California Wonder, which has a large, smooth fruit, dark green at maturity, but turning red as it continues to ripen; the Chinese Giant, which is short, chunky and a brilliant scarlet in color; the long, thin, bright-red Ruby King; and the Sunnybrook, which looks a bit like a flattened tomato. The pimento, which is so widely used in its canned version, is also a member of the group.

Let your eye be your guide when selecting peppers. A good pepper looks like a good one! You will avoid blemished and wrinkled fruit, of course, and remember that a pale color denotes immaturity. A good quality pepper is bright-colored, whether red or green, fresh and crisp-looking and well shaped.

There may well be as many recipes for stuffed peppers as there are varieties of pepper but remember this—just as the same 88 notes can be arranged to produce a delightful melody, so can a basic recipe become a work of art!

The following recipe is in that category—simple enough to serve again and again to your family and grand enough to serve on any occasion.

RECIPE

4 large green peppers

1 cup boiling water

Salt

1 pound ground chuck

1/2 cup minced onion

1/2 cup minced celery

1/4 cup minced green pepper (optional)

1 egg, unbeaten

1/2 cup light cream or evaporated milk

1 one lb. 4 oz. can tomatoes (2 1/2 cups)

1 tablespoon sugar

1/4 teaspoon cinnamon

6 whole cloves

1 tablespoon flour

1/4 cup cold water

Wash 4 green peppers; cut thin slice from stem end of each; remove seeds. Boil peppers in boiling water with 1 1/4 teaspoons salt; tightly covered, 5 minutes.

Meanwhile, combine meat, 1/4 cup onion, celery, 1 teaspoon salt, 1/4 cup minced green pepper, egg, cream. Drain boiled peppers; stuff with meat mixture. Place in 8" x 8" x 2" baking dish.

Start heating oven to 350 degrees. In saucepan, combine tomatoes, 1/4 cup onion, 1/2 teaspoon salt, sugar, cinnamon, cloves; simmer, uncovered, 10 minutes; then strain, reserving liquid. Stir flour and cold water until smooth; add to strained liquid; cook, stirring until slightly thickened; pour over peppers. Bake 45 to 50 minutes. Makes 4 servings.

Dolly Madison Pound Cake

In 1779, General George Washington, writing from West Point to a friend, commented about food, as he so often did. "The cook has had the sagacity to discover that apples will make pies." Adding that he wondered how his guests would accept an Apple Pie alongside a Beef-Steak Pie the following evening when he was entertaining at a somewhat (as much as the war allowed) formal dinner. Then he mentioned other items on the menu. But my mind goes back to the picture of those guests tasting the surprising apple pie for the first time. Of course, Washington needn't have wondered about his guests' approval of the pie. Anything the man who was becoming first in war, first in peace, and first in the hearts of his countrymen, and who, even before that shot was fired at Lexington, was known to be a very proper gentleman, served at the table was correct.

Actually, I imagine the guests went home to tell their cooks to cook up a pie "with apples in it." A new pie was presented to a new nation that night. "As American as apple pie" the saying goes, and that pie is as American as George Washington.

The father of our country was not the only Early American Gourmet. He was, indeed, far surpassed by the eminent author of liberty, Thomas Jefferson. The same hand that penned those immortal words, "... we hold these truths to be self-evident ...", also spent much time penning good "receipts" as they were called. Jefferson was such a great epicure and had such a profound fondness of the intricately-prepared dishes of France that Patrick Henry critically remarked that Jefferson was a man "who abjured his native victuals". Henry's preference was for that Virginia menu he had learned to love, to wit: Virginia Ham, batter bread, Brunswick stew, and pound cake.

Jefferson urged his daughter (he was widowed early in life) to collect good receipts and perfect the finer culinary arts. She did and later ran his Monticello home. At Monticello it was not unusual to sit down to dinner with fifty guests, and never fewer than fifteen guests, any evening. The grocery lists which appear in Jefferson's account books attest to his epicurean fancies:

"two pipes Marsalla; two casks of Bucellas; five casks porter; 40 beef tongues; 100 ham of Colonel Mason; 4 kegs tomp and sounds; 40 lbs. crackers; 5 bottles anchovies; 3 dozen pickles; 10 lbs. almonds; 2 ounces cinnamon; 2 ounces nutmeg; 1 lb. allspice; 1 lb. pepper; 6 bottles mustard; 6 lbs. chocolate; 6 lbs. sugar; 20 1/2 lbs. good cheese; 11 3/4 lbs. cheese, ordinary; 40 lbs. coffee; 10 lbs. rice; 25 lbs. raisins."

Like Washington at Mount Vernon, Jefferson found he was running an Inn at Monticello. Eventually, all of this Southern hospitality veered him toward bankruptcy, but he never scrimped on setting a fine table. He introduced macaroni into this country, and vanilla, new wines and the first receipt for ice cream.

Dolly Madison was also famous for her desserts. This cake is an example.

RECIPE

1 **pound butter**	12 **eggs, separated and beaten**
1 **pound granulated sugar**	1 **pound flour, sifted twice**
1/2 **pound pitted dates**	12 **almonds, skinned**
6 **tablespoons honey**	

Cream your butter and sugar together and add well-beaten egg yolks, and stiffly beaten egg whites. Add flour alternately with the eggs to the creamed sugar-butter mixture. Beat. When very light, pour into a well-greased and floured round pan. The pan should be large enough to hold the entire mixture plus an inch or more at the top of the pan. Bake in a moderate oven (350 degrees) until golden brown. Baking should be slow and watched carefully. Allow to cool while in the pan. When cooled, remove from pan and decorate with dates and almonds. Pour honey over the top for glaze.

Dutch Carrot Bread

In the beautiful gardens of King Merodad-Baladan, in ancient Baby-lon, a lacy-leaf ornamental plant grew among the scented herbs. In Elizabethan England, ladies wore the same wispy leaves to adorn their hair.

We don't know whether King Merodad-Baladan ever realized that his pretty plant had such a delicious root, but we do know that the carrot has been cultivated as a much-loved food for centuries.

Carrots, in addition to their many other virtues, are among our most accommodating foods. They are easily grown and they store well, they can become a salad, a vegetable, or a dessert, and they combine well with other foods to become a main dish.

Little girls eat carrots to make their hair curly, pilots eat them to make their eyes sharper, and the diet conscious find them low in calories and high in taste appeal. I can't offer any documented evid-ence to show that carrots do make little girl's hair curly (they haven't done much for mine!) but they are very high in vitamin A, which is necessary for good eyesight.

By the way, while preparing the delectable delight I'll give you later, take just a moment for this little adventure—you'll see what it was that King Merodad-Baladan and the Elizabethan ladies found so appealing. Select a particularly likely-looking carrot top, slice off about 1/2 inch and place it in a saucer of water on your window sill. Before long, you will be rewarded with an exquisite miniature fern!

I often feel that carrots are a very much misunderstood vegetable. Countless adults are certain they "don't like carrots" when in fact, they may never have tasted them properly cooked. Old time cooking meth-ods that left the carrots devoid of flavor (the flavor having been dumped down the drain with the over-abundant cooking water) were the cul-prit. Properly cooked carrots are full of flavor, and vitamins as well.

If you have never tried carrots in baking, I urge you to do so now. They add such a delightful flavor and wonderfully moist texture!

The following recipe is one I know you'll want to create over and over. This Dutch Carrot Loaf stores well—great to have on hand to serve with coffee when unexpected guests appear, and if you have any lunch box carriers in your household, it will be doubly appreciated. Perhaps I shouldn't even mention nutrition—but then surely none of my readers would be so devious as to allow a child to eat his vegetables when he thinks he is eating cake!

RECIPE

2 cups sifted flour	1 1/2 cups oil
2 teaspoons soda	1 1/2 cups sugar
1/2 teaspoon salt	2 tablespoons vanilla
2 teaspoons cinnamon	3 eggs
2 cups grated carrots	

Sift dry ingredients into large mixing bowl. Push to sides of bowl and add all other ingredients except carrots. Beat on medium speed until well blended. Fold in carrots. Turn into greased and floured loaf pans. Cook at 300 degrees for 1 hour. Dust with confectioners sugar if desired. Makes 2 loaves.

Eggplant Parmesan

Cheese is certainly one of the most versatile foods in the world as it can turn up at any point during a meal. It is served more than any other product as an appetizer, provides a perfect topping on soup, excites our appetites in salads, and is the most popular ingredient for casseroles. There must be thousands of variations of the cheese sauce and more and more this hallmark dairy product is being used as a dessert. "A meal without it," according to Brillat-Savarin, "is like a beautiful woman with one eye missing."

Like its classic champions, bread and wine, cheese is made by the process of fermentation, which can transform one substance, at the point it is about to spoil, into something far superior to what it was in the first place. Legend provides the story that cheese was discovered by an Arab merchant who put milk into a pouch made of the stomach of a suckling calf. When he went to drink the milk he found curds of cheese. This metamorphosis had been accomplished by an enzyme called rennet in the calf's stomach. Cheese-making was the earliest manner of preserving milk, and soon became popular as a special product. Cheese soon gained such status that Viking sailors were sometimes paid in cheese rather than money at the end of a voyage. There is even a story which gives cheese a place in history; supposedly the Montevidean Navy once defeated the Buenos Aires Navy by using cheeses as cannon balls.

From its accidental beginnings cheese-making developed into a fine skill. In the Southern part of France is a small town called Roquefort. Surrounding Roquefort is a range of hills that are interlaced with limestone caverns. Around 1000 A.D. monks near the town of Roquefort discovered that milk left in these local cool, humid limestone caverns would, in a matter of months, transform into a delicious cheese veined with blue mold. Soon other monasteries throughout Europe began developing varieties of cheese as a source of income. Today, there are over 500 kinds of cheese, most of them of European origin, although cream and cottage cheeses and Liederkranz are native to America.

While cheese can be a feature attraction at any table, it has become a cardinal trapping in many recipes for great cuisine. The following recipe demonstrates the compatibility of cheese with a garden product.

RECIPE

1 large eggplant

1/4 cup grated Parmesan cheese

1/4 pound Mozarella cheese, sliced

1 egg, lightly beaten

1/4 cup dry white wine

1 cup cracker crumbs

1 garlic clove, minced

1/4 cup olive oil

2 cups canned tomato sauce

2 tablespoons minced parsley

1/4 teaspoon basil

1/4 teaspoon oregano

1 bay leaf, crumbled

1 teaspoon salt

Pare eggplant and cut it crosswise into 1/4-inch slices. Beat egg with wine. Dip eggplant slices in egg and wine, then dip them in cracker crumbs. Saute garlic in oil for 5 minutes. Add eggplant and saute for 10 minutes or until golden brown. Remove eggplant and keep it hot. Add tomato sauce, parsley, basil, oregano, bay leaf, and salt to oil remaining in skillet and simmer for 15 minutes, stirring frequently. Arrange alternate layers of eggplant, Parmesan and Mozarella cheese, and sauce in a casserole. Top with Mozarella. Bake in a moderate oven, 350 degrees, for 30 minutes. Recipe serves 6.

Fresh Pineapple, Luau Style

Some of our most popular fruits such as grapes, apples and oranges have been known for many, many centuries and it is natural that there should have been paeans in recognition of their obvious delights. The pineapple, however, was one of the New World's gifts. But in less than 500 years it has collected the most extravagant compliments from the world's epicures.

The sailors of Columbus found pineapples growing on the island of Guadulupe in 1493. This was in the course of the second of Columbus' journeys to the New World. He and his men might have missed this fragrant fruit if they hadn't wandered off into the dense tropical forests and been lost for several days. While they were trying to find their way back to the ship, they found and gathered as many pineapples as they could carry. Peter Martyr, historian of the expedition, records the excitement of tasting these first pineapples.

Pineapples were found in many other parts of tropical America. On different islands in the Caribbean; in Mexico; Central America; Brazil. Its discoverers were always astonished and delighted with the new fruit. Just how delighted we can judge from some of these records from the 16th and 17th century:

We might start with Sir Walter Raleigh. He wasn't the first, but his name is most familiar. He wrote "Pines, the princess of fruits, that grow under the sun, especially those of Guiana".

Then there was explorer Acosta who noted, "Pineapples have an excellent smell, and it is very pleasant and delightful to taste, it is full of juice, and of a sweet and sharp taste." Early missionaries loved it, too. One, Father Oviedo, wrote, "It—the pineapple—restores a healthy appetite and stimulates people to eat."

One of the most glowing accounts was given by another missionary, Father White, who discovered pineapples in the Barbados. He said: "The rarest of all others that I think is in the world, is the pineapple, of the color of gold, mixed with an orient green. It is not hard to peel, but of soft and thin skin, of delicious taste, not having one membrane or kernel, but all clean through, equally dainty to taste. It is the queen of all meat fruits without exception. The taste, as near as I can express it, is an aromatical compound of wine and strawberries."

When selecting your pineapple, remember these signs of a fine fruit: It will have a pleasing fragrance, also, if you tug at one of the stiff spiky leaves in its top-knot, it will loosen readily. The Spanish Red Pineapple is the best known variety. Its color will be red-gold when ripe. The other common variety called "Sugar Loaf", remains a dark green, even when completely and sweetly ripe.

I have received many requests from my readers to blueprint the directions for serving a luau style fresh pineapple. While it might appear difficult, it is really very simple if you follow these simple directions.

RECIPE

Cut a thick slice from the top and bottom of a fresh, ripe pineapple, saving the bottom slice. Run a sharp, thin, long knife blade around the pineapple between the rind and meat, leaving a shell, 3/8-inch thick, intact. To do this, cut the pineapple from either end to the halfway point, keeping the knife blade pointed toward the rind. Push the pineapple cylinder out the big end by pressing from the small end. Cut the cylinder in half, lengthwise, then cut each half into quarters. Cut away and discard core from each quarter. Cut quarters into lengthwise strips. Place the bottom that was cut from the pineapple on a plate, over which rests the pineapple shell. Fill the shell with pineapple strips.

Green Beans
With Hot Mustard Sauce

It was Alexander Dumas, the Elder, who may be considered the Granddaddy of cloak-and-dagger fiction. D'Artagnan leaps to mind, sword in hand, as do Porthos, Athos, and Aramis. The Count of Monte Cristo, the Chevalier of Maison Rouge (or red house), and a whole parade of fearless men and beautiful women, were Dumas products. Yet, how many know that in addition to more than four hundred volumes of fiction, he made time for a dictionary of cuisine. Father Dumas was a great trencherman.

In the original edition of this dictionary, there appeared an advertisement for mustard. The copy for this ad runs to about 3,000 words and is signed by Dumas. No modern Madison Avenue copywriter would have the slightest little hope of getting such an ad in print, even if he had the energy to write. But, Dumas' mustard copy is very interesting indeed.

Dumas begins his mustard ad with the ancient history of the spice. Both the Greeks and Romans called it, "sinapis" (si-NAH-pis), which is still its botannical name. The Romans in the days of the Caesars did not, however, use it in "its primitive simplicity". They made a sort of suspicious mess called garum (GAH-rum), which started with a little mustard. To this were added the spare parts of anchovies, mackerel, dolphin, mushrooms, and a number of other seasonings.

Dumas did not write his mustard ad for the man who reads as he runs. He mentions the names of forgotten Greeks and Romans who had anything to say about mustard and tells how they used it. He tells us that Charlemagne and his Court, in the ninth century, sat down to dine at 9:00 AM, but apparently never used mustard. Some 500 years later, when the Duke of Burgundy entertained King Phillip of France, 100 gallons of mustard were used at a single meal. Another big mustard eater was King Louis XI in the 15th century. He used to drop in on his noble friends, just to see what they were up to. On all of these surprise visits he carried his own pot of mustard, says Dumas.

There have been twenty-three Catholic Popes named John. Pope John XXII lived almost 600 years ago. Dumas tells us he loved mustard and good food. When this Pope had to find a post for an untalented nephew he named him, "Chief Mustard Maker". It isn't likely that the nephew actually had much to do with the mixing of the papal mustard for, Dumas reminds us the expression "Chief Mustard Maker to the Pope" applied to a stupid and vain person.

Louis XIV was so fond of the nippy flavor of mustard that he granted a coat of arms to the spice. In the 18th century, mustard making had become one of the esteemed arts. One mustard maker, Maille, won for himself the title of Purveyor of Mustard to Madame Pompadour and Vinegar Distiller and Mustard Maker to the King of France and the Emperors of Germany and Russia. He made twenty-four kinds of mustard. One of his rivals invented forty different mustard mixtures.

To bring Dumas up to date, mustard comes to us in three forms. The whole seeds are used for pickles, with boiled beets and as a garnish on salads. Then there is powdered mustard, which is also sometimes called, "dry mustard", or "ground mustard" or "mustard flour". This is one of our important spices. The familiar prepared mustard, which is a mixture of ground mustard with salt, vinegar, and other spices, is a condiment. There are hundreds of variations of this spread, although all team famously with the mighty frankfurter.

RECIPE

1/2 teaspoon powdered mustard	2 large egg yolks, beaten
1/2 teaspoon water	3/4 cup milk
1 tablespoon butter or margarine	2 teaspoons fresh lemon juice
1 teaspoon flour	1 pound (3 cups) hot cooked green beans
1/8 teaspoon salt	Chopped pimiento
1/8 teaspoon ground black pepper	

Combine powdered mustard and water; let stand 10 minutes for flavor to develop. Melt butter or margarine, Stir in flour, mustard, salt and ground black pepper; blend well. Mix egg yolks with milk and stir into the mixture. Cook until slightly thickened, stirring constantly. Do not boil. Add lemon juice and pour over beans. Garnish with chopped pimiento. Recipe serves 6.

Guacamole Salad Dressing

Have you ever wondered how some of our slang expressions came into being? For instance, "He knows his onions!" Who said it first? And when? And why? It's possible we started "knowing our onions" the year the thirteen volumes of the Oxford English Dictionary was published. There are 15,487 pages altogether. Work was started in 1879 and it was completed 54 years later, in 1933. There were four editors in those 54 years. The latest was a Mr. Onions. (Some pronounce his name "oh-NIGH-uns" instead of "onions"). At any rate those who used this thumping big dictionary must be absorbing the wisdom of Mr. Charles T. Onions. They knew their onions. They were smart.

IF YOU KNOW YOUR ONIONS, YOU KNOW THAT THE VERY LATEST THING IN ONIONS IS DEHYDRATION. While drying is probably the oldest means of food preservation known to man, it wasn't until 1931 that the first of the dehydrated onion products became commercially successful. Since then, other forms have been added. Now instant minced onion, instant onion powder, onion salt and onion flakes are sold nationally.

THERE ARE SEVERAL REASONS WHY THE USE OF DE-HYDRATED ONIONS HAS INCREASED TEN-FOLD IN TEN YEARS. They have no-fuss, no-muss convenience; they're ever-ready right on the spice shelf. In finely minced or powdered state, the onion flavor is distributed evenly through mixtures. In this time of high prices, dehydrated onion products cost less than they did ten years ago. One other quality we mustn't overlook: Dehydrated onions have dependable, uniform flavor. They are never too strong or too mild.

There are some 500 known varieties of onions. They differ in color, shape and moisture content. They can also differ enormously in pungency. Chemists have a chemical test for onion juice which turns the juice, pink, pinker, pinkest, depending on the strength of the aroma of the particular onion. California grows the onions best suited to drying. As might be expected they are comparatively low in moisture and high in flavor particles.

ONIONS HAVE BEEN A FAVORITE SEASONING FOR MANY CENTURIES AND IN MANY LANDS. Builders of the Egyptian pyramids consumed enormous amounts of onions, according to the Greek historian, Herodotus. We know from the Holy Bible that the children of Israel developed a great yen for onions when they were crossing the wilderness. Alexander the Great urged his soldiers to eat plenty of onions. This was supposed to make them brave. Several thousand years later, General Grant must have believed the same thing. At one point, when his troops were minus onions, he warned the War Department at Washington: "I will not move my army without onions."

ONIONS WERE NOT ONLY IN DEMAND AS FOOD AND FLAVORING, BUT PLAYED A GREAT ROLE IN MEDICINE AND MAGIC. Egyptians thought the onion sacred, a symbol of the universe. When necessary to take an oath, the ancient Egyptian would rest his hand on an onion. Among the Greeks, the onion was supposed to contribute to wedded bliss. So, wedding gifts would include a jar of snow, a jar of lentils, a jar of onions.

ENGLISH GIRLS ONCE THOUGHT IT POSSIBLE TO TELL FORTUNES WITH ONIONS. Also, when buying onions, they used to think it bad luck to enter and exit from the same door; it was wise to shop in a market with two doors. While young girls tucked an onion under their pillows to dream of future husbands, once they had married it was considered bad luck to dream of **eating onions.** This was sure to bring on a family fight.

AS A PRACTICAL BIT OF ADVICE TO WIVES, IF AN ARGUMENT WITH FRIEND HUSBAND SEEMS IN THE OFFING, cook something very good, with lots of dehydrated onion in it. This will get him in a darling mood, one might hope.

For inspiration, do try this recipe.

RECIPE

1 medium-size ripe avocado	1/2 teaspoon salt
1 tablespoon lemon juice	1/16 teaspoon ground black pepper
1/4 cup finely chopped tomato	
1 teaspoon instant minced onion	1/16 teaspoon instant garlic powder

Cut avocado in half, remove seed and skin. Dice and combine with lemon juice. Mash and put through sieve or blend in electric blender. Add tomato, instant onion, salt, pepper and garlic powder. Chill until ready to serve. Serve over cooked or raw vegetable salads.

YIELD: 1 cup

Heavenly Fruit Dessert

Coriander seed rates among the most venerable of spices. It grew in the hanging gardens of Babylon, resembling the manna which sustained the children of Israel on their long trek across the desert. It was known and loved by Romans and is still used in some of the world's most famous dishes.

While 2,742,000 pounds of coriander were imported last year, principally from Morocco and Rumania, most of this was used in mixed pickling spices, curry powder or in the zillions of frankfurters consumed in the United States.

Coriander can be grown in this country easily enough, but it is hard to harvest, for it must be completely ripe to taste good and then the seeds fall to the ground at the slightest touch. Most of the coriander grown domestically ends up in gin bottles or other liquors as a flavoring.

Incidentally, green leaves of **Coriandrum sativum L.** are widely used in Latin-American cookery and are called "cilantro." They are also called "Chinese parsley."

Coriander is a fragrant but mild spice with a hint of orange about it. You would use several times as much coriander as of most sweet spices. An old-fashioned coriander cookie made with two cups flour requires four or five teaspoons ground coriander.

Coriander is available whole or ground. Use it only in breads, cakes, candies and cookies, but try it also in pea or mushroom soup. Ground coriander butter is excellent with artichokes or mushrooms. Or, use coriander in this recipe for a simple but great dessert.

RECIPE

1 can (8 1/4 oz.) crushed pineapple
1 package (3 3/4 oz.) deluxe whipped vanilla dessert mix
2 1/2 teaspoons ground coriander
1 teaspoon pure vanilla extract
1/2 cup diced maraschino cherries

Drain pineapple, reserving liquid; set aside. Prepare dessert mix according to package directions using reserved pineapple liquid in place of water called for in directions. Stir in coriander and vanilla extract. Fold in reserved crushed pineapple and cherries. Turn into a 2-cup mold or 6 individual dessert dishes. Garnish with whipped cream, if desired.

YIELD: 6 portions

Hunters' Sauteed Quail

The skies of our country were once darkened with immense flocks of wild birds. Then came the hunter with his taste for game and his need to supply his family table. With his arrows, guns, and dogs, birds were killed and soon whole species had all but vanished. The farmer came and, with his plow, ripped up vast natural breeding grounds. Since that time we have launched an intelligent conservation policy and the adaptability of these wild birds themselves have re-stocked the skies. During any normal hunting season, hunters can now bring home millions of assorted fowl.

All game birds have a special intrinsic flavor, something apart from the natural taste of their flesh. For any sportsman, a bite of a bird that he has bagged will bring back fond moments he likes to remember—the sudden flush of a grouse from cover, the hoarse whistle of ducks coming in, the shuffling flight of a woodcock, the faint taste of gaminess will, for a moment, transport anyone to the hills, fields, and marshes, and the days when men hunted to live.

The flavor of game birds varies considerably, much more than domestic fowl. Some birds, like woodcock and rail, possess a cogent wild flavor. Other white meat species such as pheasant, quail and grouse, have a more sanguine taste factor. Wild ducks vary considerably in taste, depending on the time of the year and the area from which they come. Their taste depends, for the most part, on what they have been eating. An esculent mallard bagged in the Midwest where it has been eating grain, might be most undesirable in the deep South where it has been feeding in the swamps.

During each hunting season I receive hundreds of phone calls and letters requesting recipes and kudos for the proper presentation of game birds. The trenchant gourmet prefers the natural game flavor while the average homemaker, shackled with the chore of cooking husband's bag, desires a more subtle approach. I have observed, through experience, that the length of time the birds are hung is an important factor in their taste. Quail, for example, needs little or no hanging and can be eaten the day they are shot. Other birds, like pheasant, improve in flavor if they are hung for awhile in a cool, airy place. Depending, of course, on the weather, a pheasant may be hung from two days to two weeks.

I have found, likewise, that the cardinal rule of not roasting older birds is one to follow. An old bird should be cut up and braised or prepared casserole style. Some game birds, including pheasant and partridge, have a dry flesh and should be larded or cooked covered with strips of bacon. A goose or a duck, on the other hand, normally has excess fat and does not require this attention. I suggest, also, that when cooking wild game birds that fresh or canned juniper berries be added to the container. This trapping removes a large percentage of the wild taste. The following recipe is my favorite for quail.

RECIPE

6 quail, split	1 teaspoon salt
6 club rolls	Freshly ground black pepper
3/4 cup butter	Fruit sauce

Split rolls in half and hollow out centers. Toast in a low oven (325 degrees) until brown. Melt 1/4 butter and brush the rolls with the butter. Saute the quail over high heat in the remaining 1/2 cup of butter for 10 minutes or until golden brown. Sprinkle them with salt and pepper. Arrange quail on rolls and serve with fruit sauce.

Serves 6.

Fruit Sauce

1 cup seedless white grapes	2 tablespoons finely chopped mushrooms
4 tablespoons butter	
1/2 cup port wine	1/2 cup finely chopped hazelnuts
1/8 teaspoon ground cloves	
1/2 teaspoon ginger	

Bring grapes and 1 cup of water to a boil. Cover, reduce heat and simmer for 5 minutes. Drain off water. Add butter, wine, cloves, and ginger. Cover and simmer for 5 minutes. Stir in mushrooms and simmer for 5 minutes. Add hazelnuts and serve immediately. Makes about 2 1/2 cups.

King Crab

One of the best seafood treats of all is the deliciously different, delicately flavored meat of the king crab. Full of protein, vitamins, and minerals, this is truly a dish fit for a king.

King crab are caught in the Bering Sea off the coast of Alaska in huge crab pots lowered to an ocean depth of around 300 feet, from the sides of fishing vessels. Females and small males are returned to the sea for the preservation of the species, and the average size of the big male crabs which are kept is around 11 pounds. However, occasionally huge 6 foot king crabs big, barnacled, and ferocious looking, are caught and it is estimated that these giants may have crawled great distances along the ocean floor for over thirty years. The crabs are kept alive and healthy in a "live" tank of circulating sea water until ready for the processing plant.

Prime meat of the king crabs is in the claws, legs and shoulders and this is the only part used. These parts are cooked in boiling water in stainless steel tanks for 18 to 25 minutes, then chilled and washed again before being trimmed, processed, inspected, packaged and quick frozen, ready for marketing. King crab is available either fresh packed or frozen and also canned, usually in 5, 6 1/2, and 13 ounce cans.

King Crab Salad Bowl

1 pound king crab meat or other crab meat, fresh or frozen or

3 cans (6 1/2 or 7 1/2 oz. ea.) crab meat

1 quart mixed salad greens

2 tomatoes, cut into wedges

1 cup corn chips

1/2 cup sliced pitted ripe olives

1/4 cup chopped green onions

Avocado Cream Dressing

1/2 cup shredded natural cheddar cheese

Whole pitted ripe olives

Thaw frozen crab meat. Drain crab meat. Remove any remaining shell or cartilage from crab meat. Break crab meat into large pieces. Combine salad greens, tomatoes, corn chips, olives, onion, and crab meat. Add dressing and toss lightly. Sprinkle with cheese and garnish with olives. Serve immediately. Serves 6

Avocado Cream Dressing

1/2 cup mashed avocado

1/3 cup sour cream

2 tablespoons lemon juice

1/2 teaspoon sugar

1/4 teaspoon chili powder

1/4 teaspoon salt

1/4 teaspoon liquid hot pepper sauce

1 clove garlic, crushed

Combine all ingredients and mix until smooth. Chill. Makes 1 cup dressing.

Lamb Chops Durban

Next stop, the Union of South Africa. The scene by jet arrival is not different from your arrival in any metropolis in any country. A large, modern airport, located between Johannesburg and Praetoria, cars, taxis, luggage check out, well-dressed travelers and meeters-of planes. If you were brought up on Tarzan and the late-night movie safari, your initial impulse may be a twinge of disappointment. No great white hunter bedecked in his safari best to greet you; not even a slithering snake outside your hotel; nor chattering monkeys in the trees. But just a few miles away . . .

Arriving by ship at Cape Town you are eye-witness to the same point of entry the very first Europeans gazed upon when they penetrated the little-known and primitive Dark Continent. That is, this is the same spot. More modern, more populated, more citified, more sophisticated. Charming, but much like other ports of entry in other countries. Again, that twinge of disappointment. Where are the sailors of those old sealore dramas, the beat of the native drums, the trumpeting of elephants? Not here, but just a few miles away . . .

The food of South Africa and the country itself are much alike. Just as your arrival did not reveal the real Africa, you will not get the authentic food of Africa in the city hotels and restaurants which are popularly frequented. In these fine establishments you will order "Continental" dishes which are the same the world over. But just a few miles away . . .

In the city cafes the magnificent South African Rock Lobster Tails are featured, the most desired seafood delicacy on the planet, along with oysters, and salmon, of highest quality. Steaks, Americans will be glad to learn, are good, popular and plentiful. Afrikaners are a meat-producing and meat-eating people. Cattle and sheep are raised on the plains in fatuous abundance. The opulence of the table includes taste-pleasing tropical fruits—pineapples, apples, peaches, tangerines, pawpaw, melons, lemons and pears.

If however, you like to adventure palate-wise in your traveling, as well as by sight and sound, then investigate the food world of the Afrikaner. Ask for bredee (meat stew), and maika (fish stew), ask for boerewors (sausage), and Kaffir (home-brew beer), and braaivleis (barbecues) and melksynsels (milk soup). There is absolutely no need to worry about the purity of either water, milk, or fruit. All are safe.

I'm sure there is no food in South Africa which can over-shadow the sight of the awesome animals (nor anywhere else in the world) but while you search out the King of the Beasts (you can't go home without seeing him) in that last Eden of the world, search out the national dishes of the Afrikaners. (Don't go home without trying some of these either). You may have to wangle an invitation from an Afrikaner to get the full, real taste of the authentic, but it will be worth it.

Here is a good example of Afrikaner cuisine:

RECIPE

2/3 cup tomato sauce	1 onion, grated
2/3 cup vinegar	1 teaspoon dry mustard
2 tablespoons David Wade Worcestershire Powder	1 teaspoon salt
	12 lamb chops

Combine the tomato sauce, vinegar, Worcestershire Powder, onion, mustard, and salt in a bowl. Mix well. Marinate the chops at room temperature for one hour. Drain. Take the sauce and put it in a saucepan. Meanwhile, pan-fry the chops, turning them over and over until well done. Now heat the sauce until hot. Pour over the lamb chops and serve hot.

Land of Mystery — Food of Mystery

India. Continent of mystery and intrigue. In a small village just outside Calcutta, an Englishman strolls through the bazaar stalls examining brass, jewelry, fine cloth. He stops at one stall, and the Indian merchant hands him a small piece of paper. It is a secret formula—never intended to reach alien hands. The Englishman leaves the pay-off under a piece of fine cloth, glances furtively around, then quickly, silently, disappears into the crowd.

The paper is passed along, through top secret channels, to the Home Office in London. The Chief rings for his assistant, hands him the formula. Puzzled, the assistant comments, "It looks like a—recipe?" "Of course, it's a recipe, old man," replies the Chief. "Paid dearly for it, too—from the Maharajah's own palace householder. It's for the Commonwealth dinner. We could not possibly offend the government of India by serving an inferior curry. Tell the chef it must be perfect, exactly like this secret formula."

Well, perhaps, this is somewhat far-fetched, even in the world of Agent 007's and spies around every corner, but in India curry is as important as any national secret they possess. Maybe you have known a few people yourself who were just about this secretive with their recipes. Through the ages, many recipes have been regarded as family treasure and passed from one generation to another. Sometimes (but not as often as imagined) a big price is paid for a recipe. Amusingly, some people—women seem to delight in this—will give you a recipe but leave out the really important ingredient or method. It would take a spy, and possibly even torture, to pry the secret from them. Come to think of it, our spy story is not so far-fetched after all.

Seriously, Indian curry is a serious, even sacred, dish in every household, be it ever so poor and humble, or royal and affluent. The poorest home in India will have at least three or four curry blends which they use for different types of foods. The more regal palaces parade anywhere from fifteen to twenty-five different curry mixtures.

You see, curry is a blend of many spices. It is not itself a spice, but the recipe for other spices in infinite combinations. Curry shouts its presence, or subtly undertones a food. A real curry fancier will fancy only one blend for vegetables, and an entirely different one for rice, or fish, or fowl. The blends can be very simple, consisting of only 7 or 8 spices, or very intricate, with as many as 27 different condiments. This is the great mystery of curry, and why "secret" blends so often exist. Yes, really. The balance of the different measurements would not be easy to duplicate even if the exact number and names of the spices were known.

The reason so many Americans think that curry is a spice like, say, nutmeg, is that curry powder is sold commercially. Many of these are excellent curry blends, and you won't have the bother of grinding and mixing. But, likewise, you won't have the fun of experimentation, and perhaps, discovering your own curry, your own "secret formula." If you are a food chemist at heart curry is probably the most fascinating experiment you can conduct. You'll learn volumes about most other spices too, for curry often contains a long list of the familiar and unfamiliar: Paprika, cinnamon, cloves, cayenne pepper, mustard, allspice, mace, ginger, garlic—among the familiar items; Fenugreek, cumin, coriander, poppy seeds, saffron, turmeric, fennel, anise—among the not so familiar. Still others are: white pepper, dill, nutmeg, sage, bay leaf, chilies, caraway, mint, and juniper berries.

If you are not so adventurous as to create your own blend, often a curry powder, commercially bought, is used as a base for the curry flavor, then heightened by a few choice condiments of your own choosing. This makes curry blending easier, but still offers a little individuality to your curried dishes. This is the case with Maharajah Chicken Curry which I am showcasing for you now.

I know you are wondering if **this** is the secret formula recipe the spy in our opening story was after, but I don't tell you that. We spies in the gourmet department must protect our sources. I will say that it is "just as good as" and so I have named it after the Maharajah.

Maharajah Chicken Curry

1/2 cup chopped onion
1 clove garlic, minced
1/4 cup salad oil
1 medium tomato, chopped
1 small bay leaf
1/2 teaspoon cinnamon
3 whole cloves
5 cups cubed, uncooked chicken (2 1/2 pounds, boned)

1 1/2 teaspoons salt
1 tablespoon curry powder
1/2 teaspoon cumin
1/2 teaspoon coriander
1 teaspoon David Wade Worcestershire Powder
Dash pepper
Pinch powdered saffron
1 1/2 cups water
1/4 cup fresh coconut milk

In a large skillet cook onions and garlic in oil until tender, but not brown. Add tomato, bay leaf, cinnamon, and cloves; cover and cook 5 minutes. Add cubed chicken; simmer slowly uncovered till juice of chicken has steamed off (about 30 minutes). Stir in salt, curry powder, cumin, coriander, Worcestershire Powder, pepper, saffron, and water. Cook slowly for 35 to 40 minutes, or until chicken is tender. Blend in coconut milk. Serve over hot Saffron Rice. Makes 6 to 8 servings.

Note: If you cannot obtain fresh coconut milk you can make a substitute by using the vacuum-packed shredded coconut. To make 1/4 cup (as called for in this recipe) of coconut milk take 1/4 cup of the dried coconut and let it stand in 1/2 cup cold water until it is soaked well—about 20 minutes. Then squeeze the juice through muslin cloth. Repeat the process two or three times as each time the milk becomes richer, thicker.

Saffron Rice

Dash powdered saffron

1/2 cup hot water

1/4 cup butter or margarine, melted

1 1/2 cups uncooked rice

1/4 cup chopped onion

1/2 teaspoon salt

2 1/2 cups hot water

Dissolve saffron in 1/2 cup hot water. Combine the dissolved saffron, butter, rice, onion, salt, and 1 cup of the water in a 1 1/2 quart casserole. Bake uncovered in hot oven (450 degrees) for 20 minutes or until rice is very dry, stirring at the end of 10 minutes. Stir in remaining 1 1/2 cups hot water; cover and return to hot oven for 15 minutes. Uncover and cook 5 minutes longer. Fluff with fork before serving. Makes 8 to 12 servings.

You may not be entertaining a Maharajah, but curry can be an intriguing new food adventure for you into the world of spices, new taste thrills, enjoyment, and new cooking knowledge.

Menudos De Gallina Con Arroz

(Chicken Livers with Rice)

The "rains in Spain" stay mainly on the coastal plains, yielding the grains, olives, grapes, oranges, lemons and other fruit which figure importantly in the Spanish diet. Herbs and aromatic plants thrive there, too, enough not only for spaniards, but for export as well. Spain is one of our important suppliers of anise, paprika, thyme, rosemary, saffron and savory. Onions and garlic grow on these same plains and are two of Spain's essential seasoners.

In past centuries, Spain was invaded numerous times, but each newcomer added something to what was eventually to become the modern Spanish cuisine. Three thousand years ago the Phoenicians brought to the southern coast of Spain the chick pea, the grape vine and olive tree. Since the Phoenicians were great spice traders, they would have brought some early knowledge of some of the spices of the Orient.

Early in the eighth century came the Islamic invasion and with them some of the foods of the lands to the east: rice, sugar, lemons, bitter oranges. The Moors brought saffron bulbs and cumin seeds and exotic spices such as cinnamon and cloves. The world-famous **paella** is an adaptation of **pilaff,** a spiced and seasoned rice dish which originated east of the Mediterranean.

The cuisine of Spain as well as most of the world profited enormously from the discovery of the New World. Columbus and his successors never found the spices of the Indies, but they brought back to Spain tomatoes, potatoes, sweet potatoes, corn, squash, chocolate, vanilla, allspice and the pod peppers, which were to change the world's cooking forever.

Today, while there are variations of the basic Spanish cuisine in various parts of the country, about a dozen staples and spices give Spanish food its characteristic taste and aroma. On this list I suggest saffron, paprika, garlic, onion, bay leaf, parsley, cloves, nutmeg, pine nuts, almonds and olive oil.

RECIPE

Combine and let stand 10 minutes to soften:

1/2 cup instant minced onion

3/4 teaspoon instant minced garlic

1/2 cup water

Meanwhile, heat in a large saucepan:

3 tablespoons olive oil

Add and fry until brown:

6 (1/2 lb.) chicken livers, halved

3/4 cup (1/4 lb.) diced cooked ham

Remove from saucepan; set aside. In same saucepan (adding more oil, if needed) brown:

Softened onion and garlic

1 1/2 cups raw regular cooking rice

Return livers and ham to the saucepan and add:

1 cup diced tomato

1 teaspoon David Wade Worcestershire Powder

1 1/2 teaspoons ground black pepper

3 cups water

Bring to boiling point. Reduce heat, cover and simmer until rice is tender, about 18 to 20 minutes. Garnish with parsley flakes, if desired. Serve as an appetizer or meat accompaniment.

Yield: 6 to 8 portions

Minted Strawberry-Rhubarb Pie

Many of the older herbs and spices have acquired myths and superstitions over the years. Take mint for example. The story of its origin is a dramatic one: The gods and goddesses of ancient Greece all seem to have had roving eyes. Pluto, god of the underworld, was no exception. He was much taken by the nymph, Mentha. But he had a jealous wife who put a sudden stop to this romantic trifling. She turned Mentha into a mint plant and then began jumping up and down on her. Mentha's happy ending is that she became everybody's favorite herb.

Mint has been mentioned variously in ancient writings. The Bible, for instance, states that the Pharisees paid tithes of mint, anise and cumin. The Roman naturalist Pliny found medical uses for mint: "It will not suffer milk to curdle in the stomach." It was also considered a remedy for watering eyes and for the bites of sea serpents, mad dogs, wasps and bees. It was also to be sniffed as a refresher of the head and memory. The two varieties of mint which are sold in dried form for culinary use are spearmint and peppermint. Spearmint was known in ancient Greece and Rome. Peppermint came to the attention of herbalists in England toward the end of the 17th century. Both varieties reached America soon after its discovery. Some mint escaped from gardens and grew wild.

Mint has always been a beloved herb in America as throughout much of the world. In Morocco mint is added to green tea and is sipped every hour. In England they like mint on apples. Italian cooks sometimes use mint and basil in their famous minestrone soup. The Spanish make a marvelous cold drink, sangria, using red wine, mint, cinnamon and chopped fruit. It is widely used with meats—especially lamb—in the lands east of the Mediterranean.

In this country mint is a very popular flavor for candies and frozen desserts of many kinds. It teams deliciously with chocolate and fruits such as pineapple and pears. Add a few mint flakes to the dressing for a tossed green salad; this is a seasoning hint from the Near East. Plain strawberry rhubarb pie is a fine dessert, but a teaspoon of mint flakes makes it even better!

RECIPE

Prepare 1 package (10 oz) pie crust mix following package directions. Roll half of the dough 1/8 inch thick and fit into an 8-inch pie plate. Roll remaining dough 1/8 inch thick and cut into 1/2 inch wide strips; set aside. Combine 1 can (1 lb. 6 oz) strawberry-rhubarb pie filling with 1 teaspoon mint flakes, crumbled; mix well and pour into prepared pie shell. Arrange reserved strips in lattice fashion over filling. Crimp edge of pie shell. Bake in preheated hot oven (425 degrees) for 30 to 35 minutes. Cool. Yield: 6 portions

Mushroom Cheese Casserole

There are certain eras of history when the very rich and privileged really lived it up. Wealthy Romans of Caesar's day made the banquet table famous. Centuries later, in France, Louis the Fourteenth, Fifteenth and Sixteenth, lived off the fat of the land, feasting on the choicest viands.

The mushroom serves as a symbol of the fabulous foods set before these privileged people. At one point in Ancient Rome, a reform government decided people were living too richly, eating too much meat and fish. They must eat more vegetables and a law was passed to that effect. It didn't take some of the smarter Romans long to remember that mushrooms are vegetables. Ingenious cooks discovered more and more delicious ways of preparing mushrooms.

This passion for mushrooms was noted by the Roman orator, Cicero, who declared "These elegant eaters prepare their fungi (that is, mushrooms) and all their vegetables with such highly-seasoned condiments that it is impossible to conceive anything more delicious . . . "

Historian Pliny noted that mushrooms were the only food which the "dainty voluptuaries" prepared with their own hands, using knives and silver service. The Romans went so far as to fashion sets of cooking utensils to be used only for mushrooms, never to be used for lesser foods.

Today's cultivated mushrooms are so delicately good that they can be prepared very simply. Broil or saute in a little butter or margarine and serve them on buttered toast. Spoon sliced fresh or canned mushrooms on half an omelet before folding it. Marinate sliced mushrooms in French dressing and toss with mixed greens or add to a macaroni salad flavored with onion and oregano.

Mushrooms are a real convenience vegetable, whether fresh, canned or frozen. Wash fresh mushrooms briefly, jiggling them in clear water. Do not peel. Saute for three to five minutes in hot fat.

Canned mushrooms should be drained carefully before sauteeing. (Save the canning liquid for a soup or sauce.)

Mushroom flavor can be varied deliciously with herbs such as thyme, tarragon or garlic powder. Oregano is so compatible with mushrooms that Italians call this "the mushroom herb."

This is one mushroom recipe that I often enjoy.

RECIPE

Saute 1/2 pound sliced fresh mushrooms, or 1 can (6 or 8 oz.) mushrooms, drained, in 2 tablespoons melted butter or margarine 3 to 5 minutes. Cook 1 package (10 oz.) Brussels sprouts in 1/2 cup water 5 minutes. Place mushrooms, Brussels sprouts and 1/2 pound cooked, diced ham in layers in 1 1/2 quart casserole. Prepare 1 package (1 1/2 oz.) cheese sauce mix according to package directions and pour over ingredients in casserole. Mix together 1/4 cup dry bread crumbs, 1/4 teaspoon paprika and 1 tablespoon melted butter or margarine. Sprinkle over casserole. Bake in preheated hot oven (400 F.) 10 to 12 minutes.

YIELD: 4 portions.

New South Venison Steak

In many of our rural areas, sportsmen still go a-hunting for the makings of a brunswick stew or a rabbit roast. Most game, for gourmets however, comes from the market man. He selects it at a game farm, where animals and birds are raised in conditions closely approximating the wild state. From time to time these game farms release surplus stocks to the countryside and thus do a double service, supplying the gourmet's table and replenishing the wild species for their own sake and the sportsman's. The most popular game meat in America today is venison. Any antlered animal is venison. The most often eaten venison is deer, with elk coming in a tardy second. I have found that to insure tenderness, venison should hang from two to four weeks. Chops and steaks from a reasonably young animal may not require marinating, but they should be cooked in a generous amount of fat. Roasting cuts of venison are usually very lean and should be larded through with fat pork or some other lubricity.

Whether a sportsman bags his game or buys it, the initial preparation will probably be left to the sharp knives, skilled hands, and experience of a professional. Let him bleed the deer, skin the rabbit, and pluck the pheasant. After the proper preparation of the meat and hanging, large game, generally speaking, can be cooked like corresponding cuts of meat, and small game and game birds like poultry.

There are numerous compatible uncooked marinades for venison but the one I prefer is a blending of olive oil, vinegar, and dry white wine, seasoned with onion, carrots, parsley, salt, braised peppercorns, juniper berries, and a little thyme. The olive oil in this mixture coats the meat and prevents it from discoloring, and aids in retaining the marinade flavor. For the best flavor effect, coat the venison with this marinade in a bowl and place into the refrigerator. Allow the meat to marinate for two or three days, turning the selection once a day. When the meat is ready to cook, wipe clean with a cloth but reserve the marinade, which is often used for basting during the cooking time. The following recipe will excite any hunter's discriminating propensity for venison.

RECIPE

1/4 cup flour

3/4 teaspoon salt

Cayenne

Dash of thyme

Dash of nutmeg

Dash of clove

3-pound steak cut from rump of venison

2 tablespoons melted beef suet

3 large onions, thinly sliced

2 cups fresh tomatoes, peeled & quartered, or 2 cups stewed tomatoes

1 tablespoon David Wade Worcestershire Powder

4 drops Tabasco

1 1/2 cups red Burgundy

1 clove

1/2 small clove garlic

Bouquet garni

Salt and pepper to taste

1 scant cup sauteed mushroom caps

Sift flour with salt, a few grains of cayenne, thyme, nutmeg, and clove. Vigorously pound this seasoned flour into venison steak. Cut the steak into 1-inch cubes.

Heat melted beef suet in a heavy stew pot or Dutch oven and sear venison on both sides, adding thinly sliced onions to the pot. When meat and onions are well browned, add peeled and quartered fresh tomatoes or stewed tomatoes, Worcestershire Powder, Tabasco, Burgundy, clove, garlic, and bouquet garni.

Cover pot closely, set in a moderate oven, and cook 2 1/2 hours or until meat is tender. Add salt and pepper to taste and bring to boil over direct heat. Stir in sautéed mushroom caps and serve with wild rice and red currant jelly.

As a variation, port may be substituted for part of the Burgundy, or 2 tablespoons red currant jelly may be stirred into the sauce.

Omelet Parisienne

A volume of words has been written about the temperamental nature of the classic omelet. So much so, in fact, that otherwise daring kitchen technicians often refuse to attempt it. I find that it is much easier to actualize an omelet than it is to blueprint the production techniques.

Omelets can be infinitely varied in flavor, for no other dish so lends itself to the imagination of the cook. Once you learn to negotiate the basic omelet, its countless variations become a simple matter of inventiveness. While an omelet is simple to produce, one false move and the dish is ruined. It requires diligence to stage it properly as you must be on the job every moment during its preparation, for speed and efficiency count above all. Each omelet must be prepared to measure; allow your guests to wait for the omelet, never allow the omelet to wait for your guests.

Contrary to popular belief, small omelets are more easily accomplished than the larger ones. A four-egg omelet is the easiest to manipulate and will usually serve two or three persons. If your guest list is larger than three, I suggest that you make several omelets, for they are presented hotter at the table with a nicer consistency.

For each small omelet, break four eggs into a bowl and season according to the dictates of your own particular taste with salt and pepper. Add one tablespoon of heavy cream to this mixture.

Heat the omelet pan gradually over a medium flame until it is hot enough to force butter to sizzle on contact. Beat the eggs with a fork or wire whisk just enough to mix yolks and whites. (About 30 seconds). Add two tablespoons of butter to the heated pan and shake so that butter will coat the bottom of the pan evenly. When the butter starts to sizzle, but before it has changed in color, pour in the beaten eggs, all at once. Next quickly stir the eggs for a second or two in the pan to assure even browning as you would for scrambled eggs. Then, as the eggs start to set, lift the edges of the omelet with your fork so that the liquid on top can run under. Repeat this procedure until all of the liquid is used but the eggs are still moist and soft. You can always keep your omelet "slipping-free" by shaking the pan during the above operation. Now remove the eggs from the flame and with one movement press the handle of the pan downwards and slide the omelet towards the handle. When about one-third of the omelet has slid up the rounded edge of the pan, quickly fold this amount of the recipe toward the center with a knife. Then, very quickly, raise the handle of the pan, and slide the opposite edge of the omelet one-third up the side farthest away from the handle. Hold a heated serving dish under it and, as the rim of the omelet touches the dish, raise the handle more and more until the pan is turned upside down and your oval-shaped, lightly browned omelet rests on the dish. Rapidly "finish" the omelet by impaling a piece of butter with the tip of a knife and brushing the surface of the omelet lightly to leave a glistening finish. Garnish your omelet with fresh mint snippets of parsley and serve at once.

Although many expert cooks contend that an omelet can be produced in any pan, I champion the practice of reserving a special pan exclusively for these egg recipes. There are pans expressly designed for cooking omelets but I have found the french skillet with slanted sides so the eggs can slide easily onto the plate when cooked to be effective. To prevent your omelet from sticking, never wash your special pan. Instead, just rub it clean with a paper towel coated with a few drops of cooking oil.

RECIPE

8 eggs	Orange or banana slices or diced pineapple
Sugar	
3 tablespoons butter	Butter
1 tablespoon peanut oil	2 teaspoons sugar
3 tablespoons Cointreau or Grand Marnier	4 tablespoons Cognac, Armagnac or Rum

Separate eggs; whisk yolks until frothy; whisk whites until very stiff. Fold yolks into beaten whites and add sugar to taste. Heat butter and oil in an omelet pan, and, when very hot, pour in omelet mixture. Spoon over Cointreau or Grand Marnier and cook until omelet is done but still moist. Place slices of orange, banana, or pineapple, which you have heated in a little butter, in the center of the egg mixture. Fold over. Place on a hot platter. Sprinkle with sugar and glaze under a hot grill. Flame with Cognac, Armagnac or Rum and serve immediately. Recipe serves 6.

Paprika Potatoes

Don't you wonder sometimes, how certain words came into existence? Many seem to have reached us in the most round-about way. Take an everyday word like "garnish." Who'd think this started as an Old French word meaning "to give warning?" Once warned, men would put on armor which was usually beautifully adorned or "garnitured." In the course of time, garniture or garnishing came to mean anything handsomely decked out that included things to eat. Foods were "garnished" or beautified just before they were sent to the table. Today, paprika is a favorite American garnish—that dash of brilliant red on broiled fish, scrambled eggs, a molded salad or over a pale sauce which makes these foods more appetizing.

PAPRIKA, INCIDENTALLY, IS KNOWN AS THE "COSMETIC SPICE." It does for many foods what rouge does to a woman's cheeks—they say, it makes a "tasty-looking dish."

GETTING BACK TO THE ORIGIN OF WORDS, HOW DID PAPRIKA GET THAT NAME? Looking in the dictionary, we find that "paprika" is a Hungarian word meaning "Turkish pepper." As it happened, paprika didn't originate in Turkey—any more than our Thanksgiving bird, the turkey was first found there. Both, however, were among the many marvelous new foods found in the New World by Columbus and his successors and taken back to the Old World. Eventually paprika reached Hungary and parts of eastern Europe.

DURING THIS SAME PERIOD IN HISTORY, the Turks were invading from the east, bringing with them Turkish foods and eating habits. Soon people weren't sure which foods had come from where and the shiny red pod peppers from the New World became known as "paprika" or "Turkish pepper."

Ever since that time the "paprikash" has been Hungary's most famous kind of dish. Whether paprikash starts with meat, fowl or a vegetable like mushrooms, it is simmered in a paprika-rich sauce. Incidentally, Hungarian cooks are very likely to use paprika lavishly. "Use enough to make everything good and red" is apparently their motto.

MOST OF THE PAPRIKA USED IN THE UNITED STATES IS OF THE SWEET, MILK VARIETY—AND QUITE RED. This is the kind we prefer. Some foreign dishes require a nippy paprika. In that case you can "hop-up" paprika with a pinch of cayenne—about one-sixteenth to one-eighth teaspoon cayenne per tablespoon of mild paprika.

BECAUSE OUR PAPRIKA DOES HAVE A MILD FLAVOR DON'T HESITATE TO USE IT WITH OTHER SPICES AND FLAVORING INGREDIENTS. This familiar "garnish spice" can be used liberally to give an appetizing appearance to a wide variety of dishes, including salads and salad dressings, fish, meat and chicken, soups, eggs and vegetables. Naturally, it is most effective on light-colored foods. Commercially, great quantities of paprika are used in the manufacture of sausages and other meat products, salad dressings, condiments and ready-prepared foods.

RECIPE

Melt 2 tablespoons butter or margarine in large skillet. Add 18 small new potatoes, 1 tablespoon instant minced onion, 1 cup water, 1 tablespoon paprika, 1 teaspoon salt and 1 bay leaf. Cover and cook over moderate heat until potatoes are tender. Remove bay leaf. Add 1 tablespoon cider vinegar and bring to boiling point. Boil 1 minute. Drain, if necessary. Add 1/2 cup sour cream. Heat, but do not boil.

YIELD: 6 portions.

Pennsylvania Dutch Hash

In the late 1600's a remarkable group of immigrants settled in and around Lancaster County, Pennsylvania. From the Rhineland of Germany, they brought with them a deeply ingrained love for fine food. Although they do not participate in sophisticated, worldly pleasures, they do believe in the fullest enjoyment of the twin necessities of cooking and eating, and with a passion. So great is their cooking of good vittles, they have created gourmet masterpieces which have achieved the heights of epicurean praise. Yet many of these hausfraus have never been farther than 50 miles from their homes. Countless dishes have been created and made famous right where they are, proving the old saying that "if you build a better mousetrap. . . ." In this case, if you cook a better casserole, or pudding, or even hash, "the world will beat a path to your door." At the door of the Pennsylvania Dutch every gourmet winds up sooner or later. Let's hope it won't be late for you. What a shame to miss this kind of down-to-earth gourmetmanship when you could be, as the Pennsylvania Dutch say, "eating yourself full."

In spite of the quality, the hausfraus' recipes are economy cooking, as the Dutch are thrifty people. Their recipes consist of no fancy ingredients, only wholesome good food put together with loving care. The responsibility for "making-do" with what is available and making it into great tasting fare is the hausfraus'. They have a proverb to this effect: "A woman can throw away more with a spoon than her man can bring in with his shovel."

Many Pennsylvania Dutch people speak the language of their homeland, though the dialects vary here and there depending on the county you are in. It makes a delightfully happy and descriptive language as they translate it into a kind of Dutch English. Coming out half and half, the idiom provides such as this: "It makes somesing down like a drizzle," or another favorite expression about the weather, "Look the door out and see if it's puttin' down somesing still". Surely we can all sympathize with the Pennsylvania Dutch woman who told me, "buying so much food reaches me so much in the pocketbook, I bought myself poor." Doesn't it to all the pocketbooks, ain't? But on the other hand, they believe that "them that works hard eats hearty", so no problem, because they are very very industrious people.

On a Pennsylvania Dutch table this recipe would not be the main dish, but only one of the dishes to choose from. Their tables are heavy with every kind of food. A Dutch hausfrau doesn't think she can live up to her true potential as a cook unless she has at least ten to cook for. Meals prepared for any less than that would be considered a mere snack, not a meal. And "to sit down mit yourself alone to eat" is true rejection, an unhappy Pennsylvania Dutchman indeed. It's happy the hausfrau is when "she's wonderful busy cookin' wonderful good it eats."

RECIPE

2 tablespoons shortening	2 cups coarsely crushed pretzel crumbs
1 pound ground beef	
2 large onions, sliced	1 tablespoon minced parsley
2 green peppers	1 teaspoon David Wade Worcestershire Powder
2 cups canned tomatoes	Dash of pepper

Melt shortening in a heavy skillet over medium heat. Add ground beef and cook until pink color disappears, stirring with a fork to break up meat into small pieces. Add and saute the onions and peppers for about 10 minutes, stirring occasionally. Stir in tomatoes, pretzel crumbs, parsley, Worcestershire Powder, and pepper to taste.

Serve this hash with Dutch Potato Pancakes which are easy to accomplish in the following manner:

Dutch Potato Pancakes

4 tablespoons bacon fat	2 eggs
2 cups grated raw potatoes	1 teaspoon salt
1 tablespoon onion, minced	2 tablespoons flour

Beat eggs until fluffy. Add potatoes, onion and salt. Mix together thoroughly. Stir in flour and drop from a tablespoon into hot bacon fat. Brown, turn, and brown other side. Serve hot.

Pineapple Glazed Chicken

When in the course of social events it becomes necessary to entertain, are you pulling out pans, pots, recipes and guest lists with a big smile? Or is that you over there in the corner, slumped in your chef's chair, biting your nails, groaning, but vowing to make the best of it?

The host and hostess to whom happiness is giving a dinner party are the ones whose parties are worth attending, and whose hospitality is even courted.

Party giving is one of the most delightful of social events—or else a disaster. What makes the difference? It is not only food that takes a party out of the ordinary into the sublime class, even though well-chosen, savory, served-just-right food is a very big essential. Actually, a dinner party should be a packaged deal—a group of elements adding up to harmony for an entertaining evening. This kind of a memorable dinner party, happily memorable, that is, is never achieved without a very thoughtful plan, and even more thoughtful preparation to carry out your plan.

In my opinion what most dinner parties lack is an interesting **theme.** A central idea which is unique—not just for the sake of being unique—but one which creates an atmosphere.

I like to compare party giving with a stage production, which it really is. If you will think about your dinner party this way, you'll find it makes all the difference. Focus your thought on your theme and bring everything into harmony with it. Let me suggest a luau as the perfect theme to begin your career as a dinner-play producer. A luau isn't as complicated as you may think. Neither is it very costly. You will need some special props, but many can be improvised from things you have in your home; others you can beg or borrow.

To get back to the analogies between drama production and party giving, we'll appoint you the producer-director of your play—"The Luau". First you choose sets, stage props, costumes, music; your food will be the stars of the show, and you choose your own audience (guests). In this respect you are much more fortunate than the Broadway producer!

Plan your Hawaiian decor to set the mood. Begin with the luau table. You can make your own by placing several bricks or boxes to an elevation of about one foot above floor level. A top can be made of planks, or a large piece of plywood. (These tables are narrow and long —2 ft. by 6 ft. or 3 ft. by 8 ft. are about the right proportions.) Cover the top with leaves, straw matting, or colorful fish netting. Provide floor cushions for the comfort of your seated-on-the-floor diners. Before we leave the table, let's make a centerpiece of tropical fruits—pineapples, bananas, melons and grapes—just pile them up in middle of the table with artistic naturalness.

Hawaiian paper leis can be purchased at the variety store and each guest is greeted with one upon arrival. (Be sure to spread the word that this is a luau so women may wear full skirts for seated comfort and the men can sport their flowered, short-sleeved shirts).

Island music can be piped in by means of a stereo system. Bring in plants from your garden—any kind of greenery you have will give a tropical effect. Indoor potted plants of large variety will give the same atmosphere. A screen can be used as a background. Cut out travel pictures, tropical scenes, or Polynesian art objects from magazines and tape them to the screen. Now your scene is set. Your audience has arrived. It is time for the curtain to rise. Enter the stars, the food, front and center stage!

RECIPE

Large fryer size chicken, cut up

Milk

Flour

Salt and pepper

Shortening

Coat pieces of chicken with milk and flour, and salt and pepper to taste. Deep-fat-fry in shortening until a golden brown. Remove chicken from skillet and place into a greased kettle with cover or a baking dish with cover. Cover the chicken with the following Pineapple Almond Sauce and cover, then place into pre-heated oven at 375 degrees and bake for 45 minutes to one hour, until chicken is very tender. Remove and serve over a bed of cooked rice. Add some make-up to your stars with a garnish of pineapple slices and endive.

Pineapple Almond Sauce

1/4 pound butter

1/2 bell pepper, diced fine

1 cup chopped blanched almonds

1/4 cup soy sauce

2 tablespoons David Wade Worcestershire Powder

5 drops Tabasco

1 teaspoon garlic salt

1 teaspoon M.S.G. powder

1 No. 1 can chunk pineapple and juice

1/2 cup white corn syrup

1/2 cup white vinegar

Melt butter in a skillet and saute bell pepper and almonds until soft, then stir in other ingredients. Simmer for a few minutes until mixture becomes rather thick. Serves 4.

Islanders are surrounded by every luscious fruit that grows in tropical climates. They naturally make use of fruit in everything, and the most typical dessert you could serve with your luau would just have to be fruit.

Plum Chiffon Pie

A century ago, if an American sailor hadn't been adventurous enough to taste the gorgeous plums he had seen growing in Japan—if he hadn't included this gastronomic experience in his notes—if Luther Burbank hadn't worked up a yen for ripe plums while reading this account, we might never have known the succulent plums we enjoy today.

"I came across a book written by an American sailor about his wanderings in Japan," Burbank recalled in his writings. "In it there was a description of a blood-red plum; he described the plum so that it made my mouth water to read about it." Luther Burbank, world-famous plant breeder, then sent to Japan for seedlings which would bear such plums. He was lucky to receive one seedling of the variety the sailor had described so lovingly. The seedling grew, and bore fruit in Burbank's Santa Rosa, California orchard. Ten years later, this very fruit had attained perfection. Burbank had developed all the possibilities latent in its ancestry.

Our annual plum supply is mostly from California but also from the Northwest. Plums for the fresh market are almost exclusively a California product. The shipping varieties are classified in two general groups, Japanese and European, the former usually for the early markets, and the latter for the mid-season and late markets. The Japanese varieties are characterized by their large size, heart shape, and bright red or yellow color. Japanese varieties are never of blue color. The European varieties are usually blue and oval.

Of all the stone fruits, plums have the largest number and greatest diversity of kinds and species; there are more than 2,000 varieties. Some are of European origin, some Japanese. Plum pits from Europe were probably brought to America by the early colonists. It is reported plums were planted by the pilgrims in Massachusetts and that the French brought them to Canada.

The Santa Rosa plum is the leading variety shipped from California. It is large, conical, purplish-crimson—never blue. The flesh color ranges from yellow to dark red near the skin. It is rich and juicy with a pleasing, somewhat tart flavor.

The small Damson came to America by way of Europe. It is oval, dark purple to black, and is particularly good for making jams and jellies.

The green gage plum stands for a group rather than a single variety. These are small, roundish-oval, green and yellow-green. The flesh is greenish-yellow or golden-yellow. It is juicy, firm, sweet, and mild.

The Italian prune plum is a European variety which will start coming from the Northwest late in the season. It is medium to large, with dark purple skin. The flavor is tart and pleasing.

Another variety of plum is the prune which can be dried without fermenting when the pit is left in it. Most plums would ferment in the process. Fresh prunes, as compared with plums, have a firmer flesh, higher sugar content and frequently a higher acid content. A fresh ripe prune can be separated from the pit but a plum cannot be opened this way.

When shopping for plums, look for plump, clean fruit with fresh appearance, full color, and soft enough to yield to slight pressure. Color alone cannot be relied upon as an indication of ripeness. Softening at the tip is a good indication of maturity.

Plums are low calorie, low sodium, and low fat. Both plums and prunes contribute useful amounts of Vitamins A and C, as well as other vitamins and minerals. The following recipe is one that I am certain you will enjoy when fresh plums are in season.

RECIPE

1 envelope unflavored gelatin	1 teaspoon pure vanilla extract
1/3 cup cold water	1 1/2 cups sliced fresh plums (when in season)
3 eggs, separated	
3/4 cup sugar	1/4 cup sugar
1/4 teaspoon salt	1 9-inch baked pie crust
3/4 cup milk	

Soften gelatin in water. Combine egg yolks and 1/2 cup of the sugar in top part of a double boiler. Stir in salt and milk. Cook over hot water (not boiling), stirring constantly, until mixture coats a metal spoon. Remove from heat. Add softened gelatin and vanilla. Beat egg whites until they stand in soft peaks, gradually beat in remaining 1/4 cup sugar. Fold into gelatin mixture. Turn into chilled baked pie crust. Chill several hours before serving. Recipe yields 6 servings.

Pork Chops Modena Style

Many Americans will be returning from trips to Italy this year with the happiest memories of some of the great dishes they enjoyed in that country. In the United States we are so fond of spaghetti, ravioli and pizza that we don't realize that these savory dishes are typical of Naples, representing only one region of Italy. The Italian boot has roughly eight cuisines, according to region, with Sicily and Sardinia making the ninth. These have been divided into butter cooking in northern Italy; olive oil in the South. The Bologna cuisine is typical of the North, while the dishes of Naples typify the pasta-garlic-tomato-olive-oil cuisine of southern Italy. All of Italy loves spicy aroma: rosemary, basil, oregano, bay leaf, parsley, sage, mint, coriander and saffron. Garlic and onion, of course. Anise speaks Italian and the spices of the Orient have been in demand since Roman times.

Looking at the recipes of various regions is like a lesson in the art of seasoning. The famous Roman veal and ham dish called Jump-in-the-Mouth, requires sage and pepper. Florentine Deviled Chicken gives off the intriguing aroma of garlic, onion, parsley, and red pepper. In Bologna, where they use more milk and cream in cooking than in southern Italy, they add a bit of nutmeg to some of their best meat concoctions. Venice, once the greatest of ports for incoming spice ships, has a high regard for seasoning. A favorite fish soup served there for-instance, is sparked with parsley, bay leaf, thyme, oregano, saffron, pepper, garlic and onion.

From Genoa and northern Italy we would surely select **pesto** which is a richly scented paste of basil, lemon, garlic, Parmesan cheese, pine nuts and olive oil. A dab of this is used in soup or pasta sauce or anything which demands such lusty seasoning.

Osso Buco—braised veal shanks—is very much a man's favorite. As prepared in Milan it requires basil, thyme, parsley, bay leaf, black pepper and garlic.

Sicily specializes in fruit preserves, nougats, ice creams and sherbets, as well as the fruit-filled **Cassata.**

All in all, Italian food is excellent and most savory. There can be little doubt that the Italians have given us some of their best culinary hints especially where seasoning is concerned.

RECIPE

Combine:

1 teaspoon rosemary leaves, crumbled

1 teaspoon sage leaves, crumbled

1/2 teaspoon salt

1/4 teaspoon instant garlic powder

1/8 teaspoon ground black pepper

Pat mixture into both sides of 6 (1/2 inch thick) pork chops

Place chops in a large skillet

Add:

1/4 cup water

Cover and simmer 1/2 hour. Remove and cook until almost all of the liquid has evaporated and chops begin to brown, about 1/2 hour longer, turning occasionally. Remove chops to warm platter. Add to pan gravy:

1/2 cup dry white wine

Cook, stirring, until hot, about 2 minutes.

Yield: 6 portions

Pot Luck Potato Salad

Throughout history, it has been said, the country that controls the spice trade is also the richest and most powerful in the world. It must still be true because the United States is now the prime figure in world spice buying and New York is its center. Some five to six hundred ships dock in U. S. ports each year bearing spices from all parts of the world.

In 1967, we imported 244 and one-third million pounds of spices from the four corners of the earth and produced about another hundred million pounds of onions, garlic, paprika, sesame and mustard seeds in this country. This means that for every baby, child and grown-up we had an average one and three-fourths pounds of true spices, herbs, dehydrated vegetables such as onion and garlic and aromatic seeds such as poppy, anise, caraway and others.

Part of this zooming demand stems from the post-war travel, which brought millions of tourists back from Europe and the Far East with an appreciation of spicing hitherto untasted. Cooking has become one of the fine arts with hobby cooks buying the shelves full of new cookbooks. In earlier days there might be eight or ten spices in the average home. Now shoppers are tempted by supermarket displays of spices in a hundred different forms.

We Americans are descendants of immigrants from all the countries of the world and have lingering memories of spice use in the native lands of our ancestors.

Spices and herbs were important in colonial times. They were precious commodities, vital to food preparation, essential as preservatives and highly regarded as medicines. With the "Spice Islands" under a tight Dutch monopoly, the price of most aromatic spices was high and colonials regarded them almost on a par with jewels. Spices then were always bought in their whole form and ground at home, because factory ground spices would have lost most of their flavor by the time they reached the home.

The Pennsylvania Dutch loved nicely spiced dishes, such as their famous "seven sweets and seven sours", which appeared on well-set tables.

In Louisiana, French cooking has been most influential so that we find a skilled use of many spices, but especially of herbs.

Scandinavian baking in Minnesota smells deliciously of cardamom as well as other sweet spices. The Mexican-type dishes of the Southwest need chili powder, onions and garlic above all. California owes some of its spicing to immigrants from Spain, Mexico, Italy and the Orient.

With a country as large and representative of the cuisines of the world, who's to say which are "typical" American dishes? I suggest a potato salad dish that is highly regarded everywhere.

RECIPE

Cook until done in boiling salted water to cover:

2 1/2 pounds (6 medium) potatoes

Cool slightly; peel and dice into 1-inch cubes. Place in a medium mixing bowl.

Combine and mix well:

1 cup dairy sour cream

2 tablespoons instant minced onion

2 tablespoons white vinegar

1 tablespoon salad oil

1 3/4 teaspoons salt

1 teaspoon celery seed

1/4 teaspoon ground black pepper

Spoon over potatoes. Toss gently and chill thoroughly.

Just before serving toss in:

1/2 cup sliced radishes

Yield: 8 to 10 portions.

Quick Tuna Pie

We came across such a promising word the other day: ONIO-MANIA. Now doesn't it seem that this should mean a mad passion for onions in any form? But it doesn't. It comes from a Greek word meaning an uncontrollable love of shopping, or buying things just to be buying. Considering the fact that there are now more than three billion people on earth and practically everybody loves the flavor of onion, there certainly ought to be a word for "onion-lover". We can easily make one, right here and now: **Allium** (Al-ee-yum) is the genus name for onions. **Philos** (Fi-Los) is the Greek word for loving. So we put them together and make **alliophile,** or onion-lover.

OF GREAT INTEREST TO ALLIOPHILES ALL OVER THE COUNTRY is the fact that dehydrated onion products are now available for various seasoning uses. One of the most popular of these is the one called instant minced onion. (This is also labelled "chopped onion" by some packers). As the name implies, it provides a convenient way of adding the flavor of finely minced onion to dishes. Instant onion powder, and onion salt and flakes are other dehydrated onion seasoning on the spice shelf.

PEOPLE HAVE BEEN USING ONION FLAVOR IN THEIR FOOD FOR SO MANY THOUSANDS OF YEARS archeologists have lost track of the early history. The native land of this seasoning isn't known, although plant historians suppose it may have been western Asia, around the eastern Mediterranean. That's the part of the world known to students of history as "the Fertile Crescent".

AS WITH ALL PLANTS WHICH HAVE A LONG HISTORY, THERE ARE MANY SUPERSTITIOUS BELIEFS IN CONNECTION WITH THE ONION. Young girls eager to know names of future husbands, used to set a row of onions on the mantelpiece. Each onion was named for an eligible young man, a possible husband. Tom, Dick, or Harry Onion. Whichever started growing first, represented the future bridegroom.

ANOTHER WAY TO FIND OUT: On St. Thomas's Eve — that's December 21 — tuck an onion — or scatter some instant minced onion — under your pillow. Drift off to sleep and ere the arrival of the rosy-fingered dawn you will have dreamed vividly of your husband-to-be.

LIFE IS NEVER SIMPLE, HOWEVER. THERE'S ANOTHER SIDE TO THIS COIN: According to some astrologers, onions are under the dominion of Mars, and Mars means battle. Or, as an old rhyme went:

"To dream of eating Onions means
Much strife in thy domestic scenes . . ."

ONE THING WHICH COULD LEAD TO A GOOD DEAL OF GRUMBLING BY FATHER IS TO FORGET TO ADD THE TANTALIZING FLAVOR OF ONION TO HIS FAVORITE POT ROAST OR STEW. You might as well try cooking without salt and pepper as to forget this versatile seasoning.

Add instant minced onion, just as is, to any cooking mixture which has plenty of liquid — a stew, a soup, a sauce. It takes about two or three minutes of cooking time to release the appetizing flavor. If the instant minced onion is to be sauteed, soak it for a few minutes in an equal amount of water. (Onion flakes need just a bit less water — four parts flakes to three of water). Whether to soak instant minced onion in water before adding to salad dressings is optional. Instant onion powder and onion salt need no reconstituting at all. Just dash them over or stir them in. Do cut down slightly on regular salt when using onion salt, however, for this seasoning is a mixture of onion powder and regular salt.

RECIPE

2 cans (7 oz. ea.) tuna fish

1/2 can of a 10-1/2 oz. can cream of celery soup

1/8 teaspoon ground black pepper

1/4 teaspoon poultry seasoning

1 tablespoon instant minced onion

1 envelope instant mashed potatoes

1/2 cup finely shredded American cheese

1. Flake tuna fish and mix with soup, black pepper, poultry seasoning and instant minced onion. Heat 2 to 3 minutes.
2. Turn into a 10-inch pie plate.
3. Prepare potatoes as directed on the package.
4. Place in a ring around the top of the pie.
5. Sprinkle cheese over the potatoes.
6. Bake in a preheated hot oven (425 degrees) until cheese has melted and browned.
7. Serve hot as the main dish.

Yield: 6 servings.

Roast Pheasant

Many years ago, I received a letter from a lady in California asking me to settle an argument. "What is the difference", she asked, "between baking and roasting?" My first reaction was one of surprise. Meat is roasted while baking refers to cakes and breads! But then I realized that this was not strictly true. A ham is baked and chestnuts are roasted. A turkey is sometimes baked and at other times roasted, depending on the background of the cook.

But for the present, I think I will just duck the finer points of the argument and consider roasting to be that method of cooking meat by dry heat in an enclosed oven. The old-fashioned covered "roaster" notwithstanding, if meat is covered, it is not roasted, it is braised— even if it is cooked in the oven.

Most of the time I prefer to do my own experimenting and come to my own conclusions about cooking. But when it comes to cooking hundreds of roasts at different temperatures to determine the right one, I am perfectly willing to profit by the experience of the U.S. Department of Agriculture. For that is exactly what they, as well as other experimenters, have done.

Meats have been measured before and after cooking to determine the amount of shrinkage, and the taste preferences of thousands of people have been polled. In experiment after experiment, the results have been in favor of long, slow cooking.

Not only does this method produce the tenderest, juiciest and most flavorful meat, but it has been found that a roast cooked at very low temperatures will shrink only about 15% while the same type roast will shrink as much as 50% if cooked at a very high heat. How is that for an economy measure!

Every housewife knows this simple fact—that high temperature causes protein to become tough. This is the reason that a bloodstain is easily removed in cold water but becomes hopelessly set by hot water. Milk glasses wash more easily if rinsed in cold water and eggs cooked at a high temperature have the delicacy of an old innertube.

Your first step is to make sure you have set your oven thermostat at the right temperature. But a more important step is to make sure the oven temperature is the one you have selected. Few oven thermostats are really accurate (don't blame your oven, it would take a scientific instrument for real accuracy) and the temperature varies in different parts of the oven. It is best to use an oven thermometer, at least occasionally, so you will know where you stand.

If you do not already own a good meat thermometer, I insist that you not let another week go by without one. It is the only way to be sure of properly cooked meats. Time and temperature guides are merely to help plan your time. Size and shapes, as well as fat and bone content, affect cooking time.

When you are roasting a pheasant, you don't have to worry a great deal about shape as most pheasants are pretty much the same shape. With lamb, pork and beef, however, you should remember that in terms of minutes per pound a flat roast will cook faster than a chunky one and a large roast will require fewer minutes per pound than a small one. Bones conduct heat readily but fat does not. A crown roast may cook in half the time required for a rolled roast of the same weight. A well-marbled roast will take considerably longer to cook than a lean roast. When calculating cooking time, remember to allow for about 20 minutes for the roast to "repose" before carving. Not only will it carve more easily, but the juices will gelatinize and less will be lost.

When choosing a roast, bear in mind that a rolled roast is easier to carve, but the slices are less attractive than those of a bone-in roast. And don't be afraid to choose a large roast, it is more economical for several reasons. One being that a roast under 3 and 1/2 pounds or so will shrink excessively. Remember, with a good roast, there are no leftovers, only planned-overs.

RECIPE

1 two to three pound pheasant	**Few celery leaves**
Salt and freshly ground black pepper to taste	**1 slice lemon**
	4 slices bacon
1 bay leaf	**Melted butter**
1 clove garlic	**Madeira Sauce**

Preheat oven to 350°. Sprinkle the pheasant inside and out with salt and pepper. Place the bay leaf, garlic, celery leaves and lemon in the cavity. Tie the legs together with string and turn the wings under.

Cover the breast with bacon and a piece of cheesecloth soaked in melted butter. Place the pheasant, breast up, on a rack in a baking pan and roast until tender (about thirty minutes per pound), basting frequently with melted butter. Remove the cheesecloth and string.

Serve the pheasant on a bed of rice accompanied by Madeira Sauce.

Madeira Sauce

Remove the pheasant to a warm serving platter and add one cup consomme to the pan. Stir over moderate heat, scraping loose the browned particles. Blend two tablespoons flour with two tablespoons butter and stir into the gravy bit by bit. When the gravy is thickened and smooth, add two to three tablespoons Madeira wine and the cooked pheasant liver, finely chopped.

Round-Up Beans
and Hominy Casserole

During round-up time from early in the autumn to late in the spring a few big ranches still send out mule-drawn chuck wagons. But gradually the tradition of the chuck wagon is dying out of the Southwestern cowboy culture. Most ranches send a truck now to pick up the riders and bring them into the ranch house for meals.

However, one of the reasons the familiar chuck wagon doesn't go out on the range often is not mechanization, but because ranches can't find experienced cooks to man the range kitchens. The life of a ranch cook is both difficult and rewarding. The number one difficulty is getting up before 5 a.m. to begin breakfast and packing up supplies for lunch, moving out to another location, setting up the kitchen again. Sundown finds the camp cooks still serving late riders into camp, and then preparing the night before for a 5 a.m. rising the next morning.

On the favorable side though he has time for a cat-nap during the day while the boys are out working, but more than anything else his reward is respect—the better cook he is the more respect he gets. In the last few years chuck wagon cooks have been highly regarded indeed because they are a vanishing breed. Some cooks of the range have taken lately to store-bought foods—instants, canned and boxed food stuffs. The old veteran cook would wince with shame. Always in the recipe files of the cowboy chef was a version of at least four specialties that the cowboy loves: Biscuits, preferably sour dough, chili, son-of-a-gun stew, and beans. Beans cooked that way and this way, and any way, because beans were the easiest to transport and cook of any of the staples available to the ranch cook. Gradually different bean recipes were developed for variety. The following Round-Up Bean and Hominy recipe was sent to me by a retired chuck wagon cook. He used to bake it in a Dutch oven set down in a hole pit. Unless you have a hankering to perfect the craft of ranch cook you may as well take the easy way and bake the recipe in your kitchen oven. On the other hand, someone reading this may yearn for a home on the range and cooking in the wide open spaces. If so, this recipe will get you a job on any ranch you care to cook for. Some ingredients are canned, but with such a recipe no one will ever know, or care!

217

RECIPE

2 tablespoons butter or margarine

1 medium onion

1 clove garlic, minced or mashed

1 can (1 pound) red kidney beans

1 can (1 pound) hominy

1 can (1 pound) tomatoes, broken with a fork

1/2 cup chopped green pepper

3 teaspoons chili powder

1/2 teaspoon salt

3 slices bacon

4 tortillas, cut in thin strips

2/3 cup shredded cheddar cheese

Melt butter in a large skillet over medium heat. Brown onion and garlic in the butter. Add beans, hominy, tomatoes, green pepper, chili powder, and salt. Remove from heat after mixed together thoroughly and heated completely, and turn into a 2 quart casserole. Set casserole aside and fry bacon in a skillet over medium heat until crisp. Remove bacon from the skillet and drain. Add to the hot bacon fat, tossing until lightly browned and crisp (about 2 minutes) the tortilla strips. Remove and drain.

Add crumbled bacon to Cheddar cheese. Combine 1/2 of the bacon-cheese mixture with the bean-hominy mixture in the casserole. Sprinkle tortilla strips over the top. Bake in (350 degree) moderate oven for 30 minutes or until thoroughly hot. Do not cover. Makes 6 to 8 servings.

Runderlappen

(Stewed Beef Cubes)

We sometimes think of the Netherlands as a small and not very adventurous country. Yet in times past its influence was global because of leadership in the spice trade. Many of the sons of the Netherlands spent their lives sailing to the rich spice markets of Indonesia, then called Netherlands East Indies.

About the beginning of the seventeenth century the Dutch East Indies Company was formed and the Dutch made trips of some twenty six thousand miles to Java and nearby islands to fill their ships with cloves, nutmegs, mace, cinnamon, pepper and ginger.

After a century of spice trading the Dutch had a monopoly on the clove and nutmeg supply of the world. A contemporary wrote, "No lover ever guarded his beloved more jealously than did the Dutch the Island of Amboina where the clove trees grow".

As we might expect, Dutch sailors brought back to their homeland an appreciation of East Indian spicing so that today there are Indonesian restaurants in Holland, ready and waiting for any Dutch guests who've worked up an appetite for the exotic.

Two world-famous spices—caraway and poppy seeds—are grown right on Dutch soil—on some of the half million acres that have been made by pushing back the North Sea with dikes.

In general, the food of the Netherlands is substantial and world-famous for its freshness. One of the freshest things going is a catch of young herring, still dripping sea water. The Dutch love to munch freshly dressed herring raw, head to tail.

The Dutch use pepper with abandon, four or five times as much as Americans might use in a comparable dish. Nutmeg is a favorite spice, as might be expected, and they like it especially in seasoning vegetables such as asparagus, carrots, red beets and endive.

The housewives of Holland are great bakers of breads and cakes, cookies, puddings and **torten**—a pastry which is very rich, fine-grained, elaborately topped. Cinnamon and poppy seeds are in great demand on baking day. On special days this recipe is served.

RECIPE

Mix together and let stand 10 minutes to rehydrate:

1/4 cup onion flakes

3 tablespoons water

Heat in a large skillet:

2 tablespoons oil

Add and brown well on all sides:

1 1/2 pounds beef chuck, cut into 1-inch cubes

Add and saute 2 minutes:

Rehydrated onion

Add, stirring to mix well:

1 small bay leaf	**1/4 teaspoon ground nutmeg**
1 teaspoon salt	**1/16 teaspoon ground black pepper**
1 teaspoon David Wade Worcestershire Powder	**1 teaspoon white vinegar**

Pour over all:

1/4 cup water

Bring to boiling; cover; reduce heat and simmer 45 minutes to 1 hour or until meat is tender.

Yield: 4 portions

Sauerbraten

During midsummer and at evening concerts and music festivals across the country we may hear Mendelssohn's enchanted "Midsummer Night's Dream." This was inspired by Shakespeare's play of the same name and the shimmering music of the violin should remind us of the lovely verse which begins:

"I know a bank whereon the Wild Thyme blows,
Where Oxlips and the woody Violet grows. . . "

In olden times it was thought that "the little people"—the elves and fairies—were particularly fond of thyme. Thyme is a truly venerable herb, known and loved way back in ancient Greece. Among the Greeks thyme was a symbol of elegance. It grew all over Mt. Hymettus which is within sight of Athens.

THYME GROWS CHEERFULLY in some of the poorest, driest soil that can be found. It is native to the greatest part of the dry land of Europe, not only the mountains of Greece, but in the lower meadows of the Alps, the highest crags of the Pyrenees and, of course, in England. Thyme was commonly cultivated in parts of England before the 16th century. Long before the people of England had access to spices from the Orient, they could grow thyme in their little gardens.

THYME WAS NOT ONLY GOOD, BUT HERBALISTS OF THOSE DAYS SAID THYME WAS VERY GOOD FOR PEOPLE. John Parkinson was one of those 17th century herbalists. He wrote "There is no herb almost of more use in the houses both of high and low, rich and poor, both for inward and outward occasions; outwardly for bathings among other hot herbs and among other sweet herbs for strewings: inwardly in most sorts of broths with Rosemary, as also with other herbs, and to make sauce for diverse sorts of both fish and flesh. It is held by diverse to be a speedy remedy against the sting of a bee, being bruised and laid thereon." Modern medicine has upheld their thinking for the oil from thyme, know as **thymol** is an effective ingredient in many brands of modern cough drops.

TO GET BACK HOME TO THE RANGE AND THE SPICE SHELF. Thyme has always been one of the favorite herbs in the American cuisine. This love of thyme goes back to the days of the first settlers who brought all kinds of seeds and roots with them for wilderness gardens. Thyme is one of the moderately potent herbs. For a very elusive aroma of thyme, we might use between one-fourth to one-half teaspoon ground whole thyme in a dish to serve six. For a more pronounced taste, use at least a teaspoonful. In the stuffing for a three-pound fish, for instance, we would want about 1/2 teaspoonful of thyme. In the very delicate oyster stew a quarter teaspoonful is just about right. It's all a matter of taste: that's what makes seasoning and cooking one of the fine arts. Nothing beats frequent use of the tasting spoon.

THYME CAN BE HAD EITHER GROUND OR AS WHOLE LEAVES. This depends on how it is to be used. Ground thyme is a bit more convenient, especially when seasoning heat-to-eat foods. Whole thyme, however, keeps its delectable aroma somewhat longer than the ground product. Whenever possible, delay adding any herbs to a long-cooking mixture until within ten minutes of the end of the cooking period.

THYME IS A FAMOUS SEASONER OF ALL KINDS OF SEA-FOOD, but do use it also with meats, stuffings, croquettes, fricassees and egg and cheese dishes. For inspiration, try this thyme-scented recipe.

RECIPE

4 pounds rump or bottom round of beef

2 teaspoons powdered mustard

2 tablespoons parsley flakes

2 tablespoons grated lemon peel

1 teaspoon salt

1/2 teaspoon ground thyme

1/2 teaspoon whole black pepper

1 teaspoon David Wade Worcestershire Powder

1/4 teaspoon ground sage

6 whole cloves

2 beef bouillon cubes

1/2 cup onion flakes

1/2 cup cider vinegar

2 to 3 tablespoons shortening

Flour

Place beef in close-fitting pan. Combine mustard and 1 tablespoon water; let stand 10 minutes for flavor to develop. Combine mustard with parsley flakes, lemon peel, salt, thyme, black pepper, Worcestershire Powder, sage, cloves, bouillon cubes, 2 cups boiling water, onion flakes, and vinegar; pour over meat. Cool. Place in refrigerator to marinate 24 hours, turning several times. Remove meat from marinade. Brown on all sides in shortening. Add marinade. Cover and simmer until tender, about 2 1/2 to 3 hours. Remove meat and make gravy, using 1 1/2 tablespoons flour to each cup liquid left in pan.

Yield: 8 to 10 servings.

Shrimp Fricassee

I am frequently asked what qualities differentiate excellent kitchen technicians from the ordinary ones. This question naturally has a multiplicity of answers, however, the premier characteristic is imagination. Contrary to popular thinking, fatness of purse does not make a good cook. Imagination teamed with experience in spicemanship is a wedding that usually produces the best marriages in flavor. I have always advised new cooks to start with a command of their spice shelves. This can best be accomplished by a study of the fascinating historical backgrounds of individual spices and herbs.

For example, see if you can guess the name of this truly romantic spice. To begin with, it has been used in southern cookery for many, many years. Every great cook knows it. It has two names. One is most commonly used in cookbooks, the other used more often in mythology. This evergreen tree was once a beautiful nymph of Greek legend. She was turned into a tree to escape the unwelcome advances of the God of the Sun, Apollo. Incidentally, this transformation is shown in a famous marble sculptured by Bernini.

Because this tree was beloved by Apollo, no harm could ever come to it, or to those who stayed near it. It was a great old lightning-arrester for one thing. Tiberius Caesar, afraid of Roman thunderstorms, clung to a branch of this fragrant tree. (In addition, he's also said to have crawled under his bed).

Julius Caesar wore a wreath of these leaves. This was not only the symbol of triumph but very nicely hid his baldness. It was called the plant of prophecy. Soothsayers wore wreaths of it. One of its leaves, under a pillow, could produce prophetic dreams. It was also used in incense.

This spice has been credited with all kinds of magical effects. One of the great herbalists of another day said this about it, "It resists witchcraft very potently, as also all the evils Old Saturn can do the body of man." "And these," continued Culpepper, "are not a few. The berries are very effectual against all poisons of venomous creatures, as also against the pestilence and other infectious diseases."

If you haven't guessed the identity of this spice, this should surely tell all; this tree and its small black berries have given us the word "baccalaureate". "Bacca" means berries and "Laureate" refers to the laurel or bay tree. Centuries ago, Laurel or bay was the symbol of scholarship and the arts. Success was crowned with laurel leaves. Today, we say that a college student who acquires the necessary credits wins his laurels. He becomes a "bachelor" of arts or science.

The culinary uses of bay leaves are numerous. They give excellent flavor to meats, potatoes, stews, soups, sauces and fish. Bay leaves are indispensable in pickling, and in the manufacture of vinegar. Like all seasoning agents, they must be used in correct amounts.

Bay leaves, like many other natural products, can vary in size from one to three inches. Whenever a recipe calls for a bay leaf, choose a medium-sized one, a leaf about two inches long, or use one and one-half small leaves, or half a large one. This amount of bay leaf should be used for about six servings of food. Five to ten minutes simmering should release the flavor and give just that teasing bit of aroma to all kinds of good dishes.

Bay or laurel leaves, come from the evergreen sweet bay or Laurus Nobilis tree. They are available in whole form. These fragrant leaves reach us from Turkey, Greece, Portugal, and Yugoslavia. A nineteenth century food writer once rhymed: "To win a laurel wreath for your brow, put a laurel leaf in the stew pot now."

Years of experience have demonstrated to me that the bay leaf adds incomparable accent to recipes, however, I always suggest to the novice cook that this flavor jewel should always be used in whole form or in a bouquet garni. The bay leaf should never be crushed into a recipe since this action creates an obtrusive texture contrast to a diner. This laurel leaf should always be removed from the table presentation prior to serving.

The following recipe combines an aggregate of other spices with the bay leaf to effect an optimum of flavor:

RECIPE

2 tablespoons butter or margarine

2 tablespoons flour

1 1/2 cups canned tomatoes and juice

2 tablespoons instant minced onion

2 tablespoons sweet pepper flakes

1/4 teaspoon garlic salt

1/8 teaspoon ground thyme

1/2 teaspoon parsley flakes

1 bay leaf

1/2 teaspoon celery salt

1/8 teaspoon ground black pepper

1 pound shrimp, cooked and deveined

2 cups cooked rice

Melt butter in a frying pan. Add flour and heat, stirring constantly, until slightly brown. Add tomatoes, onion, sweet pepper flakes and seasonings and stir until blended. Add shrimp. Cover and simmer gently 15 to 20 minutes. Pack cooked rice into greased cups and place in preheated moderate oven at 350 degrees for about 5 minutes, unmold onto platter and pour shrimp mixture over them. Remove the bay leaf. Recipe serves 4.

Shrimp Pie

Twenty years ago there were arguments on how to pronounce the name of the "new" herb, O R E G A N O. Since then we've all learned to call it "or-REG-a-noh". Oregano has zoomed to fame sprinkled on the coast-to-coast favorite, pizza. Often you hear it called "pizza pie" but "pizza" is the Italian word for "pie" so "pizza pie" is redundant.

At any rate the highways of America are lined with pizzerias and the parking lots in front of the **pizzerias** are lined with cars of pizza-eaters indulging themselves. Pizza ranked way ahead of many other American favorites in a restaurant survey made on the West Coast **not** long ago.

What makes this dish so irresistible is the aroma of the oregano which rises from a hot pizza, mingled with the redolence of cheese, anchovy or sliced sausage! It's the teen-agers "way-out" treat, too, and the only thing to serve at a party.

That's not all: Another great favorite, chili con carne, is that much more tempting for the oregano it contains. Did you know that oregano is one of the basic ingredients of chili powder? Many of the most appetizing Mexican dishes have that same whiff of oregano.

Oregano's flavor is strong and aromatic. It's similar to marjoram. That's why our word "oregano" is the Spanish for marjoram.

After cooks had discovered what oregano would do for pizza and chili con carne they began trying it with roast lamb, omelets, beef stew, soups, boiled eggs, tossed green salads. It's great on steaks and lamb chops, too. And, of course, any tomato dish tastes twice as good for a sly pinch of this herb.

Here is one of my savory oregano recipes.

RECIPE

3/4 pound cooked, peeled and cleaned shrimp fresh or frozen

—or—

3 cans (4 1/2 ounces each) shrimp

1 cup onion rings

1/8 teaspoon oregano

2 tablespoons melted fat or oil

1 can (10 1/2 ounces) condensed cream of celery soup

1 can (4 ounces) mushrooms, stems and pieces, drained

1 teaspoon David Wade Worcestershire Powder

Dash pepper

2 cups seasoned mashed potatoes

1 tablespoon chopped parsley

Paprika

Thaw frozen shrimp or drain canned shrimp. Rinse canned shrimp with cold water. Cook onions and oregano in fat until tender. Combine all ingredients except potatoes, parsley and paprika. Combine potatoes and parsley. Pour shrimp mixture into a well-greased pie pan, 10 x 1 1/2 inches. Top with a border of potatoes. Sprinkle with paprika. Bake in a very hot oven, 450° F., for 15 to 20 minutes or until lightly borwned. Serves 6.

Sour-Cream Cabbage

The lowly cabbage, the unpretentious, inexpensive, always available head of cabbage—can anyone find romance there? Well, man has for centuries and the legends that have sprung up all over the world about the cabbage surely attest to its popularity.

Babies have been found in cabbage patches all over the world. In Scotland, blindfolded young ladies draw cabbages on Halloween night to learn about their future husbands and the man in the moon was sent there by a child who caught him stealing cabbage on Christmas night.

Cabbage was eaten in Europe, Africa and China thousands of years ago. Egyptians, Greeks and Romans adored it and the great Roman statesman, Marcus Porcius Cato admired it so much that he wrote five pages on it. He gave us the first recipe for coleslaw, which he recommended as a remedy excellent for drunkenness, suggesting that one eat as much as possible before and after a feast. Cato was full of praise, also, for the virtues of cabbage as a medicine (today's health food advocates agree) and he gave a good many details as to its uses in promoting good health.

Cabbages come with loose heads and with firm heads, with flat, conical, or egg-shaped heads. Cabbages are white, green, red; they have plain leaves or fancy leaves. To carry the montage even further, some have open leaf buds and some closed leaf buds. Kale, Brussel sprouts, savory cauliflower and broccoli are cabbages too and this is the way scientists designate their divisions.

Winter cabbage which has been stored is light green or white. Freshly harvested cabbage is a darker green and has more vitamins. When selecting cabbage, always look for the brightest, freshest looking colors. Avoid any heads with blemishes, or those where the leaves appear to be splitting away from the stem.

The following recipe, glamorizing one of our most inexpensive vegetables is one of my favorite examples to illustrate that good eating need not be expensive—that even young people on young budgets can enjoy gourmet eating!

RECIPE

3 tablespoons butter, margarine or salad oil

1/2 clove garlic, minced

8 cups finely shredded
cabbage firmly packed

1/4 cup boiling water

1/3 cup commercial sour
cream

1 tablespoon lemon juice

1 tablespoon sugar

1 tablespoon salt

1/2 teaspoon celery seeds

1 egg, beaten

In hot butter in large skillet, saute garlic over low heat 5 minutes.
Add cabbage, water. Simmer, covered 8 to 15 minutes or until tender.
Add rest of ingredients combined; toss. Makes 4 or 5 servings.

Sour Cream Cake

During my travels about the country, I have talked with many people about foods and cooking. I am constantly amazed by the numbers who tell me that they are good cooks, even creative cooks, yet are complete failures at baking. How can this be with all the wonderful fresh ingredients available and accurately tested recipes in every sack of flour?

That is the answer. Accurately tested recipes and creative cooks are apt to mix about as well as oil and water.

I know that this is the way grandma cooked—with a glib of this and a glop of that, but grandma had been serving an apprenticeship since she was knee high to an old iron stove and her glibs and glops were as accurate as your teaspoons and tablespoons.

I heartily approve of creative cookery. In its proper place, it can be one of the most rewarding of kitchen accomplishments. But start fooling around with kitchen chemistry, unless you know exactly what you are doing, and all you are likely to create is one great big mess!

For this is exactly what baking is—kitchen chemistry. An exact science. The chemical reactions involved call for accuracy in measuring, mixing and baking. Cakes and breads are leavened by various combinations of three gases—carbon dioxide, air and steam.

The leavening air is the air you put into the batter by beating. Too little beating and too little air in the mixture and there won't be enough leavening action. Too much beating and you will have a cake that is dry and full of holes and one that may even blow up like a balloon only to collapse completely.

The leavening steam is the water vapor produced by the heat of the oven. Oven temperature, length of baking time, and size of baking pan affect the amount of steam produced.

Carbon dioxide is produced when yeast ferments. It is also produced by the chemical reaction of $NaHCO_3$ (baking soda) and acid. When the acid content of your batter ingredients is high (such as when you use vinegar or buttermilk), the acid of the ingredients works in combination with the baking soda to produce the leavening action. With a low acid batter, you use a preparation that already has the acid combined with the baking soda—baking powder.

Baking powder is a combination of baking soda, an acid salt and a starch stabilizer. The chemical action begins as soon as the mixture is wet. This is why you should always mix the baking powder or baking soda with dry ingredients before adding liquid. When using a baking soda and acid ingredient mixture, the leavening gas is released as soon as the ingredients are combined. Therefore, the batter must be baked immediately otherwise the gas will escape and the product will not be leavened properly.

The leavening action of baking powder depends on the type of acid salt used. A batter containing tartrate baking powder should be baked without delay, as most of the carbon dioxide is released at room temperature. Phosphate is a little slower. About two-thirds of the gas is released at room temperature and the rest in the oven. SAS phosphate, or double-acting baking powder, releases most of its gas in the oven. You can refrigerate this dough for baking later.

The acid in baking soda ratio is critical and it is affected by the amount of protein in the recipe and by the amount of acid in the other ingredients, such as honey, sour cream, fruits, chocolate and even brown sugar. This is why you must measure so carefully and why it is so difficult to improvise in baking.

The proper baking temperature is important because so much leavening action goes on in the oven. So pay close attention to your oven temperature and if you have any doubts about your oven thermostat, be sure to have it checked.

The following recipe is an excellent example of the intricacies of kitchen chemistry.

RECIPE

Sift together onto a square of waxed paper:

1 1/4 cups sifted cake flour	**1/2 teaspoon baking soda**
1 1/2 teaspoons baking powder	**1/4 teaspoon salt**

Break into a medium-sized bowl and beat very well with a rotary egg beater:

2 eggs

Add gradually and beat until light:

3/4 cup sugar

Add alternately with flour mixture:

1/2 cup sour cream
  1 teaspoon vanilla

Beat together well with the egg beater and pour into a greased and floured (8-inch) layer pan. Bake in a moderately hot oven (375°) for 25 minutes. Remove from pan and cool on cake rack.

This cake may be split and served with a custard filling and topped with whipped cream or filled with softened ice cream and covered with lightly crushed berries.

South African Chicken Pie

South Africa has a unique cookery of its own, closely connected with the social history of the country. The roots of its gastronomic conditions go back to the 17th and 18th centuries and the most typical South African dishes date from those faraway days. The influence of the old established Malay community in the Cape is also to be noted, and especially in such well-known South African specialties as Bobotie and Sassaties, which have a distinctly Oriental flavor.

A popular way of entertaining in the summer months in this country of gloriously reliable weather is the so-called braaivleis, which is an al fresco "meat-and-beer party". The main ingredients are steak and sausages, and these are grilled over open air fires, in the style of the American barbecue. Mealies, or corn on the cob, are another unusual feature of the braaivleis.

When you glance through a group of South African recipes, you will realize that all of our labor saving devices are only substitutes compared with what the famous Cape cooks possess. First of all, they had all the foods fresh and home grown. Secondly, they had leisure and servants. To top all this, they had tremendous pride in their home cooking and jealously guarded their special recipes.

Another trait which gives South African cookery its very own character is the imprint made by the Dutch, French, English, and German settlers. The homely and substantial eating habits of the Dutch are perhaps the strongest influence in South Africa. All of their recipes have a rich and original flavor which is unique. South African cookery is a truly interesting and rewarding field for imaginative cooks to explore. If you are not familiar with South African cookery, the following recipe will introduce you to their resourceful ways.

RECIPE

1 3 1/2-lb. chicken

2 medium onions, each cut into 8 pieces

1 1/2 pints water

1/4 teaspoon allspice

1/4 pint white wine

1/4 teaspoon nutmeg

1 bay leaf

1/4 teaspoon cracked black pepper

1 teaspoon salt

1 teaspoon David Wade Worcestershire Powder

2 ounces butter

1 ounce tapioca

3 tablespoons lemon juice

1 egg yolk, beaten

2 hard-boiled eggs, sliced

4 ounces cooked ham, sliced

short-crust pastry

milk

egg

Cut the chicken into serving size pieces and place with water, wine, onion, allspice, nutmeg, bay leaf, pepper, salt, and Worcestershire Powder. Place these items into a covered saucepan and boil at a simmer for 30 minutes. Remove the bay leaf, then add butter and tapioca, recover and continue simmering for 20 minutes more or until the chicken is tender. Add lemon juice, egg yolk, hard-boiled eggs and ham. Mix the mixture by stirring, then allow to cool. Place this mixture into a deep casserole dish, and cover with pastry. Brush the top of the pastry with a little milk and egg mixed together, and bake in a 325 degree oven for 45 minutes. Recipe serves 4.

The French and Sauces

"The supreme triumph of the French cuisine consists of its sauces," a gastronomer of the late nineteenth century wrote, "nothing can so vary the routine of daily cookery as the different combinations of herbs and seasonings that may be utilized by a competent artist as an adjunct and a finish to a dish . . . As without flattery there were no society, so without sauces there were no gastronomy."

There are, quite literally, hundreds of sauces in the French cuisine. That's why Tallyrand could say, more than a century ago, "France has three religions and three hundred sauces; England has three sauces and three hundred religions."

One of the reasons the French are such great sauce-makers is their high regard for tarragon as a seasoning herb. This aromatic leaf with a hint of anise about it is best known in our country as we taste it in tarragon vinegar or tarragon salad dressings.

In France tarragon goes, quite naturally, into such sauces as tarragon mayonnaise or one of the several versions of tarragon sauce. Its delightful fragrance drifts up from many other French sauces: Bordelaise, Ravigote or Chasseur sauce; Sauce Verte, Verdurette Sauce, Sauce Italienne, Sauce Gribiche for cold seafood. We mustn't forget one of France's most famous sauces, Bearnaise for serving over grilled meats and fish. Just reading the recipe makes us hungry. In it tarragon is teamed with some of its best friends from the spice shelf: chervil, thyme, bay leaf and shallots. The new freeze-dried chives are an excellent addition to tarragon. For that matter, so is garlic. Tarragon is in some ways a "loner" in that it doesn't have to socialize with some other herbs and spices. The point is that tarragon is such a marvelous herb that we often prefer to use it "straight", without confusing its flavor with other aromatic products.

Tarragon is an herb of the aster family and seems to have come originally from Russia. It wasn't discovered until some time in the thirteenth century. Because it has a sort of serpentine root formation which suggested a small dragon it was given a name which meant "dragon". This name was spelled and re-spelled in various languages until today we call it "tarragon".

Tarragon is delicious with foods such as chicken; turkey; veal; fish and seafood; eggs and green salads . . . you name it.

The flavor is French, thanks to the touch of tarragon, and this Mock Gribiche sauce is not only delectable with fish, it is also excellent with cold cuts, cold roast beef or cheese.

Mock Gribiche Sauce

1 hard cooked egg, peeled

1/2 cup sweet mustard relish

2 tablespoons mayonnaise

1 1/2 teaspoons tarragon leaves, crumbled

1/4 teaspoon instant garlic powder

Mash or crumble egg yolk; finely chop white. Combine yolk and white with remaining ingredients; mix well. Let stand at least 1 hour before serving. Serve with fish.

YIELD: Approximately 2/3 cup.

Tarragon, parsley and garlic are frequently teamed in French cooking. Here they give delectable flavor to a good condensed cream of chicken sauce for serving with poultry, zucchini, green beans, asparagus or potatoes.

Quick Tarragon Chicken Sauce

1 can (10 1/2 oz) cream of chicken soup

1 tablespoon light cream or mix

1 teaspoon tarragon leaves, crumbled

1 teaspoon parsley flakes

1/4 teaspoon instant garlic powder

Combine all ingredients in a small sauce pan. Bring to boiling point, stirring constantly. Reduce heat and cook, stirring, 4 minutes. Serve as a sauce over chicken or turkey or over zucchini, green beans, asparagus or potatoes.

YIELD: Approximately 1 1/4 cups sauce

The Mystery and Romance of Wines

So many of us deprive ourselves of one of the finest gifts of nature. Since Biblical times the fruit of the vine has been one of mankind's most noble companions. It makes a great meal a feast and an ordinary meal great.

In spite of the widespread notion that it takes a connoisseur to determine the proper wine to be served with certain foods, there is really no hard and fast rule about which wine must accompany which food. You can really let your own taste be your guide. Basically, though, there are five different kinds of wine.

Appetizer Wines

Appetizer wines, for particular flavor, aroma and bouquet, lend themselves to before meal or cordial use. A good example of this kind of wine would be the various sherries.

Red Table Wines

These are dry mealtime wines which harmonize with main course foods and cheeses, such as a St. Julien Medoc like Chateau Beychevelle, vintage 1958, bottled by Achille Fould.

White Table Wines

These wines range in taste from dry to semi-sweet to sweet. Normally, the dry wines are served with the entrees and the sweet wines with desserts. Once again, your own taste is your best guide, but as a rule of thumb, the richer the main course the drier the wine. A fine French white table wine is Domaine de Gaillat, a graves superioures, vintage 1964—a clean, fresh taste.

Dessert Wines

Sweet, full-bodied wines—perfect with every dessert, nuts, fruit and cheeses. These include Ports, Muscatels, Oro Fino and Cream Sherries.

Sparkling Wines

Festive bubbly, wines. Champagnes are white. Crackling Rose is pink and Sparkling Burgundy is red. These are gala wines suitable for all occasions when there is something to celebrate. An excellent choice is Paul Masson Crackling Rose—delicately pink, filled with frothy bubbles and presented in a beautiful package.

Dry Wines

We've talked about dry wines. What does dry really mean? It means not sweet. Occasionally some French wines will use the word "sec"— it's just French for dry. Champagnes use "Brut", which again means not sweet. A marvelous dry wine is Chablis Grand Cru, an estate bottled wine, vintage 1963.

The Wines to Chill

Champagnes and all sparkling wines, roses and white wines are at their most flavorful when served chilled—but not too cold. Champagne—about 3 hours in your refrigerator; roses and white wines take about an hour. Red wines release the bouquet and test best at room temperature. Dessert wines—chill them or not, whichever way you like them best. A wine that you will want chilled—Paul Masson Sparkling Burgundy—bubbly and brisk, naturally fermented in the bottle—a gala wine for gala occasions.

Rose Wines

White wines and red wines and what's rose? Rose—pronounced ROZAY or just plain rose, is a white wine that has had just a hint of contact with the grape skins which impart a pink color to it. It is just about an all purpose wine that can be served anytime—before, after or during meals. One of the great ones is Rosegalant, from France's d'Anjou region.

Learn From The Labels

You can tell a lot about a bottle of wine just by looking at it. If the bottle is clear, you can see that it is a white wine, a rose or a red. If the bottle is green, it is usually a white wine. Very dark bottles usually contain red wines. You can tell by holding it up to the light. And look at the label—there's a world of information here. This label tells you that it is a German wine, from the Rhine region; that the type is Liebfraumilch; that it is a vintage wine, 1963; and, the label design usually gives you a hint of the wine's character.

Selecting Wines

How about wine selections? A sure guide to wine satisfaction—the finest is Frank Schoonmaker. Each and every bottle tasted and chosen by Mr. Schoonmaker personally—right in the French vineyards. I guarantee that you'll be pleased with the quality of all Schoonmaker selections. Here are some: Saumur-Champigny, 1964; Beaujolais, vintage 1964; and, Pouilly-Fuisse, 1964, a delicate white wine.

Serving Wines

Serving wine is simple. Wine glasses are set to the right of the water glasses. The host opens the bottle at the table, pours a little into his own glass first (just to be sure that any bits of cork are not served to a guest), then fills other glasses about 2/3 full. This is done so the delicate aroma of the wine will stay in the glass and the wine's bouquet (aroma) can be inhaled. He finishes filling his glass last. A Butterfly Corkscrew makes an easy job of opening wine and never, never breaks a cork.

The Glass

How about wine glasses? Forget the idea that you have to have special glasses for every type of wine. Sure, it adds a little fun, but you can get by very nicely with just three—a long stemmed white wine glass, a short stemmed glass for red wines, and the familiar stemmed saucer for champagnes and sparkling wines.

How far will the average bottle of wine go? The average size bottle of imported wine is about 3/4 of a quart and will serve 6 to 7 glasses. American wines are usually fifths and you can expect 8 servings. Leftover wines are no problem. Put back the cork and the wine will keep almost indefinitely in your refrigerator. Experiment a little with leftover wines in your cooking and before you know it, you'll be a gourmet cook. Just replace some of the liquids in your recipes with wine. Oh, what it does for food!

The Sauce-Making Gourmet

I have always enjoyed sauces for the sake of sauces, but I am opposed to using sauces to cover up the natural flavors of many select fishes and meats. My sauce combinations are those I feel will be of a value to the average cook who not only entertains but is interested in delighting their own family.

The French have a long established taste for sauces. Sauce-making is the basic ingredient of haute cuisine and ranks foremost among the gourmet talents that any French cook worthy of the name must learn and master.

For the amateur sauce-making is a pleasant culinary pastime. Casually approached, the at-home cook can master them one by one. Only one sauce is usually required for one meal—two at most—so there is time to learn one, then add another to your repertoire of fine sauces. The satisfaction of praise from family and guests for your sauce efforts is a goal to strive for, and keep on striving for. There are many dishes whose success depends on the sauce.

There are literally hundreds of sauces in the French cooking catalogue. They range all the way from French Dressing to White (Bechamel) Sauce to Tomato Sauce. There are sauces for salads, for marinades, for meats, for fish, for chicken, for vegetables, and for desserts.

Let us begin our sauce lesson with a cautious recommendation. The quality of your ingredients is of utmost importance. The greatest chef in the world cannot produce a great sauce with inferior ingredients. It is not possible. When you make your own stock always use fresh poultry, fish, or bones; use the best butter and eggs, use good tomatoes, mushrooms, and if the ingredients are canned, choose the best brand available.

I am going to give you three sauce recipes. First, Cucumber Sauce for fish, and the second is Raisin Sauce especially designed for ham; and lastly, a Melba sauce for dessert. This variety should expand your kitchen capability in the sauce department. None of them are difficult if you follow directions.

Cucumber Sauce For Fish

1 cup finely chopped, peeled cucumbers

1/8 teaspoon ground white pepper

1 teaspoon dry minced onion

1/2 teaspoon salt

1 tablespoon sugar

1 tablespoon vinegar

1/2 cup heavy cream

Paprika, optional

Mix cucumbers, salt, sugar, vinegar, pepper and minced onion together. Chill in refrigerator for about 30 minutes. Before serving, fold the chilled cucumber mixture into the heavy cream that has been whipped, and serve over broiled swordfish, salmon, or haddock that has been marinated with a little lemon juice prior to cooking. This sauce can also double as a spread to be used over fish prior to broiling. When this method is used, dash on a suspicion of paprika for color.

Raisin Sauce For Ham

1/4 cup sugar

1 1/2 teaspoons dry mustard

1 1/2 tablespoons cornstarch

1/4 teaspoon salt

1 1/2 cups water

1/2 cup molasses

1/4 cup orange marmalade

1/2 cup raisins

1/4 cup cider vinegar

1 tablespoon butter

Combine sugar, mustard, cornstarch and salt in saucepan. Gradually stir in water, molasses, marmalade and raisins. Cook over medium heat until mixture thickens and comes to a boil. Remove from heat, stir in vinegar and butter. Recipe makes two cups.

Melba Sauce

1 cup thawed frozen raspberries and juice

1 teaspoon sugar

1 teaspoon cornstarch

1/2 cup red currant jelly

Combine raspberries and juice, sugar and cornstarch and cook over very low heat until mixture looks clear. Strain through a fine sieve. Cool. Blend in red currant jelly. Makes one cup. Especially for Peach Melba, but this sauce is excellent for cake, ice cream, or various fruits.

Ugnstekt Fish Och Makaroni

(Baked Fish and Macaroni)

The American citizen visiting Scandinavia this summer for the first time, will be astonished by the abundance and richness of the cuisine discovered in the gay, superbly-operated restaurants and hotels of the principal cities. If he extends his visit beyond the cities and is invited into country homes, he will continue to be impressed by the variety of intrinsic-flavored foods that are occasioned in the immaculate family kitchens. The trenchant gourmet will find much to appreciate in the quality, inspiration and imagination which has long distinguished the food fare of the Northland. He will recognize that here is a great cuisine. Scandinavians reflect a traditional allegiance to the ancient French and German Court cookery from which much of their kitchen sorcery has been derived. Viking ships have long distributed their precious cargos of opulent produce, grain, fruits, and dairy products, the elaborate creations of Scandinavia's farmsteads and gardens. The compendium of wild game and seafood is of the finest on our planet.

The vacationer, at home again will recall with a special pleasure the characteristic dishes of Scandinavia, those which are different and native, least resembling his own black-eyed peas and southern-fried chicken. He remembers the assortment of appetizers which spell out smorgasbord elegance and economy. These pre-luncheon or dinner favorites are much the same in the four countries that comprise Scandinavia but are tagged with different nomenclatures; Smorgasbord in Sweden, Smorrebrod in Denmark, Voileipapoyta in Finland, and Koldt Bord in Norway. The hungry moments of the discriminating gourmet will be haunted for days to come when he thinks of the soups, the compelling flavor of the sauces which so smoothly embraces the fish dishes, add staccato to meats and game, and embellishes the already rich vegetables and desserts. Time will pass before the optimum flavor of almond, the leitmotif which laces the pastries, puddings and every kind of sweet, vanishes from the tastemosphere.

The American long an aficionado of good coffee, will remember the fragrant Scandinavian brew, together with the numerous special coffee cakes and breads which companion this beverage in the morning and again halfway to noon. The sweet tooth comes alive again during the afternoon and at dinner with a smaller and sweeter presentation of this hallmark coffee cake.

The dedicated traveller will thrill at the pleasant atmosphere of the Scandinavian luncheon and dinner tables. These people enjoy their food with gusto, and search for an excuse to get together, chat and chew. To these gregarious souls a little Aquavit or beer, coffee and wines, with bright music to dance to, makes for good living.

While the table habits of the four Scandinavian countries contrast considerably, the dishes are much the same. The names are slightly different in their Finnish, Danish, Norwegian and Swedish spellings.

RECIPE

1 1/4 cups macaroni, broken
    in small pieces
1 3/4 pounds bass or other fish
   2 small carrots
   2 small onions
Salt

SAUCE

  2 tablespoons butter
  3 tablespoons flour
1/2 teaspoon salt
1/2 teaspoon white pepper
1 1/2 cups fish stock
1/2 cup heavy cream
  1 egg yolk
  3 tablespoons white wine

TOPPING

3 tablespoons grated
  cheese
3 tablespoons bread
  crumbs
3 tablespoons butter
Paprika

Cook the macaroni in salted boiling water until tender, then drain. Clean the fish thoroughly discarding the heads, tails, and the viscera. Cook the fish and vegetables in salted, boiling water (just enough to cover), until tender. Drain, reserving the cooking stock for the sauce. Skin the fish and fillet into small pieces. Using a large saucepan, melt the butter, then stir the flour in until smooth. Add salt and pepper. Gradually add the fish stock and cream, stirring until slightly thickened. Beat the egg yolk, then add to the sauce and stir. Add the wine a few drops at a time and stir. Remove the sauce from the heat. Using a large buttered baking dish, arrange a layer of cooked macaroni then sprinkle with the cheese. Add a layer of fish, then cover with sauce. Repeat these layers reserving the top layer for macaroni. Sprinkle crumbs over the top layer and any remaining cheese. Dot with butter and sprinkle some paprika on for color. Place into a 450 degree oven and bake until the top browns and the recipe is thoroughly heated through. Recipe serves 6.

Venetian Rice and Peas

Do you know that over half the world's population depends on rice as the mainstay of their diet? Rice is a highly nutritious and easily digested food. In contrast to most other cereals, almost all of it is completely assimilated.

Perhaps you have been amazed on seeing TV shots of Orientals eating raw rice and wondered at the strength of their jaws. The answer is that their rice has not gone through the extensive milling and drying process that our familiar hard white rice has. Only the hard outer husk is removed, leaving "whole" or "brown" rice, which is a good deal more nutritious than the (admittedly more beautiful) white product.

There are even more varieties of rice than there are ways of cooking it—and there are a lot of ways to cook it! Of the two basic types of rice, long grain and short grain, both are good but each has its own best use. In general, you can assume rice is short grain unless the label specifically states long grain.

"American" or "Indian" rice, considered quite a culinary delicacy, is really not a rice but an aquatic grass. It has been cultivated by the Indians for centures but since it has never been domesticated for cultivation on a large scale, you won't find much of it on your grocer's shelves.

Actually there are hundreds of rices; among them the narrow Patna rice from India and the short plump Paella from Spain. There is Japanese rice and Chinese rice and Risioto from Italy.

Most of the rice grown in the United States comes from swampy, high-humidity sections of Louisiana and Texas. That rice is long grained and fluffy, best for use as a vegetable side dish. The rice from other parts of the United States, where it is cultivated differently, is called hill rice. It is short grained, softer and more tender and is good for desserts and soups. Some stores, especially health food stores, do carry the lightly-milled brown rice. It is high in the B vitamins, has a nut-like flavor, and requires a comparatively long cooking time.

Good cooks have argued and still argue about the proper way to cook rice. Almost a hundred years ago a celebrated gourmet wrote that rice must be cooked in an iron pot and that "rice must come out solid, retaining the exact shape of the pot, with a golden brown crust about its' top and sides".

The fight goes on as to whether rice should be cooked covered or uncovered, stirred or unstirred and on and on. One thing all agree on is that rice should be tender yet not gummy, that each grain must stand proudly apart, reluctant to merge with its fellows.

A trick taught me a long time ago by an old German cook, to coat each grain of rice with butter or oil before starting the cooking process, is an important part of the following recipe.

RECIPE

4 bacon slices, diced

3 tablespoons butter or margarine

1 small onion, minced

1 10 oz. pkg. frozen peas

3/4 cup uncooked regular white rice

2 cups canned chicken broth

1 teaspoon salt

Dash pepper

1/4 cup shredded Parmesan cheese

In heavy skillet, saute diced bacon until crisp. Remove bacon; pour off fat. In butter, in same skillet, cook onion with peas, 5 minutes, stirring frequently. Then add rice and cook until well coated with butter. Now stir in broth, salt, pepper. Simmer, covered, stirring occasionally, about 20 minutes or until rice absorbs all liquid and is tender. Toss with cheese and crisp bacon. Makes 3 or 4 servings.

Venison Steak El Paso Style

Do you know that in all the world there are only eight basic recipes? It's true. Master these eight basic arts—baking, roasting, braising, broiling, steaming, frying, sauteing and stewing—and you will never have trouble with any of the variations, whether you are preparing a simple supper or the hautiest of the haute cuisine.

Take frying, for example. Everyone knows how to fry an egg! The most reluctant husband can be coaxed into preparing his own breakfast occasionally and as soon as a child is old enough to be trusted near the stove, he is likely to be serving Mom breakfast in bed at least once a year. But oh! the abominations that are served in the name of the egg. Some vie for durability with the latest in tire vulcanizing materials.

The really sad part is that with just a little basic instruction, even the child could serve a delightfully fried egg. What's more, he would have mastered a skill to be practiced in many kitchen operations to come.

I believe it is the very simplicity of the eight basic arts which allows them to be so often overlooked. Experienced cooks have forgotten the rules (though they practice them by rote) and new cooks assume that no rules exist because they have never heard them expressed.

It only **seemed** that grandma had no recipe and followed no rules. Actually, she had simply mastered the fine arts to such a degree that her work seemed effortless (as well as failureless!).

To go back to that fried egg. The first mistake is immediately obvious. Anyone who assumes that a fried egg is actually fried, that is cooked by the heat of hot fat, will ruin every egg he fries.

Eggs are a delicate protein and proteins will shrink and toughen when exposed to excessive heat. A properly "fried" egg is not really fried but rather sauteed; which is by dictionary definition, "to cook lightly and quickly in a small amount of fat".

Sauteeing is actually quite a delicate process as compared to the more vigorous deep fat frying. Usually only the more tender meats or vegetables are sauteed as the cooking time is short and the heat moderate. Rather close attention is required, because of the short cooking time and to assure even cooking and/or browning by stirring or turning often as the recipe requires.

RECIPE

4 venison round steaks (8 to 9 ounces)

2 shallots, chopped

2 carrots, sliced

1 clove garlic, chopped

1/8 teaspoon thyme

2 bay leaves

1/3 teaspoon freshly ground black pepper

Small pinch of ground cloves

2 cups dry white wine

1 cup mild vinegar (3/4 cup cider vinegar of 5% acidity mixed with 1/4 cup water)

1/2 cup olive oil

Place the steaks in an enamel, glass or earthenware bowl. Add the ingredients and let stand in the refrigerator twenty-four hours. Turn the meat several times. Remove the steaks and dry, reserving the marinade.

Saute the steaks in shallow, hot fat until brown on both sides and done to your own taste requirements. Serve on a hot platter with Sauce Poivrade.

Sauce Poivrade

8 peppercorns, crushed

1/2 cup vinegar

1 tablespoon David Wade Worcestershire Powder

1 cup brown sauce or leftover thickened gravy

2 tablespoons red currant jelly

Mix together peppercorns, Worcestershire Powder, and vinegar and simmer, uncovered until reduced to 1/4 cup.

Add brown sauce and simmer 1/2 hour. Add jelly. Strain and serve with venison.

Viennese Upside-Down Cake

First among the fine arts of the kitchen is la patisserie, and possibly the most ancient of them, dating back as it does to the centuries before Christ, when angry Pagan gods could be propitiated by sacrifices of sweet cakes. From rude beginnings, pastry cooks have evolved confections that represent the apex of refinement and imagination. The ephemeral torten of Vienna, the fabulous gateaux of Paris, the flaky, juicy fruit pies of New England, are all fit for any man and his gods.

Good pastry cooks never lack ingenuity, know no poverty of invention. A good pastry cook must first possess a fertile imagination; then learn to command a handful of basic doughs, batters and pastes. From these basics, a creative cook can work endless variations upon variations.

I learned years ago that when preparing a special meal for honored guests that required laborious hours in the kitchen that very often the simplest concoction was received as the piece de resistance. Several years ago, I hosted a special dinner party for Jock Mahoney, who, at that time, was the Tarzan of the movies, along with other selected guests. I imported select filets of cobra from India that was presented in the form of hors d'oeuvres, and Kobe beef from Japan at $6.25 per pound, which was served as the entree. There were numerous other creations that I spent hours in the kitchen negotiating for this special party. As I was staging this meal, I suddenly realized that my preparation time was almost over and I had not as yet accomplished a dessert. Using the limited remaining time, I went to my pantry and withdrew a can of tart red sour cherries and a box of devil's food cake mix. Adding several other items to these pre-packaged convenience foods, I turned out a Viennese Upside-Down cake. To my great surprise, all of the guests insisted that this dessert was a work of the gods.

I suggest that you add this recipe to your files of pastry making and I am sure you will find, as I have, that simple recipes sometimes are more popular with your family and guests than the more elaborate ones.

RECIPE

4 tablespoons (1/2 stick)
   butter or margarine

3/4 cup firmly packed light
   brown sugar

1/8 teaspoon salt

1 can (1 lb., 4 ozs.)
   unsweetened pitted
   red tart cherries

1 package devil's food
   cake mix

Melt butter or margarine in baking pan, 9x9x2; stir in brown sugar and salt. Heat slowly, stirring constantly, just until bubbly; remove from heat.

Drain cherries, saving liquid for cake. Spoon cherries over sugar mixture in pan.

Prepare devil's food cake mix, following label directions, and using liquid from cherries as part of liquid called for on package. Pour over cherries in pan.

Bake in moderate oven (350 degrees) 1 hour, or until top springs back when lightly pressed with fingertip.

Cook on wire rack 5 minutes; cover pan with serving plate; quickly turn upside down, then carefully lift off baking pan.

Cut into squares; serve warm, plain or with milk, cream or ice cream. Makes 9 servings.

The Festive Cup

Through the years, hundreds of homemakers and gentlemen from all over America have requested that I prepare a collection of my favorite seasonal beverages. So many persons who entertain without serving alcoholic beverages are at a loss to present imaginative refreshments. While alcohol can be added to these favorite liquid refreshments of mine, they have been developed for use without it.

Celebration

2 bottles (8 oz.) maraschino cherries and juice

2/3 cup lime juice

1 quart raspberry beverage, chilled

2 1/2 quarts lemon-lime beverage, chilled

1 lime, sliced

sweetheart roses

Chop cherries finely and combine in a punch bowl with cherry and lime juice. Add raspberry beverage and lemon-lime beverage which have been chilled. Fill glasses and float sweetheart roses on top of lime slice for garnish. Serves about 12 (medium to large servings.)

Cranberry Sparkle

2 1/2 cups white corn syrup

3 pints cranberry juice

1 1/2 cups strained lemon juice

3 cups strained orange juice

3 cups carbonated water

Lemon slices

Combine fruit juices and syrup in a bowl. Mix well and chill. When ready to serve add carbonated water and pour into serving bowl over ice. Dip into cups or small glasses and garnish with a lemon slice. Makes about one gallon.

Dr Pepper Punch

1 cup sugar

6 lemons

6 limes

1/2 cup grenadine

6 bottles Dr Pepper

2 quarts chilled soda

2 trays Dr Pepper Ice Cubes

1 cup cherries (with stems)

Boil sugar in one cup of water over low flame until sugar is completely dissolved. Cool and add to strained juice of lemons and limes, pouring mixture into chilled punch bowl. Stir in grenadine, Dr Pepper and chilled soda. Add Dr Pepper ice cubes (made by simply pouring Dr Pepper into ice trays, instead of water.) Float cherries on the surface or freeze one in each Dr Pepper ice cube.

English Frost

1 cup water (for each glass)

1 teaspoon, heaping, instant tea (for each glass)

Mint, crushed

1 can frozen lemonade concentrate

1 can cold water

1 tablespoon grated lemon rind

Combine frozen lemonade concentrate and cold water. Add lemon rind and put in freezing tray. Freeze to ice crystal point. Mix water, tea and pour mint which has been crushed in glasses. Add two large scoops lemon ice crystals and a little extra crushed ice. Stir vigorously and serve at once. Garnish with mint spray which has been dusted in powdered sugar. A little extra powdered sugar may be sprinkled on top for added sweetness and decoration, if desired.

French Coffee

1 rounded teaspoon instant
coffee

1 rounded teaspoon sugar

1 cup cold water

Coffee ice cubes

Whipping cream

Cinnamon-Sugar

Combine instant coffee, sugar and cold water. Pour over coffee ice cubes (made by simply freezing coffee in refrigerator tray.) Float whipping cream which has been whipped stiff on top of coffee drink. Sprinkle cinnamon-sugar on top of cream.

Hunter's Punch

1 cup sugar

1 cup strawberries, fresh

1 cup strawberry juice

1 banana, sliced

3 lemons, juiced

2 oranges, juiced

1/2 can crushed pineapple

1 quart water

Combine sugar and water; boil until syrup is formed. Cool. Add strawberry, lemon and orange juice, and crushed pineapple. Chill thoroughly and let stand for 4 hours. Before serving mix water and fruit mixture. Then add whole fresh strawberries and banana, sliced, to punch. Serve with ice.

Kentucky Julep

6 cups cranberry juice   1 1/2 cups pineapple juice

3 tablespoons lemon juice   1 cup weak tea, chilled

Grated rind of 1/2 lemon   2 cups cold water

3/4 cup frozen orange juice   Orange sherbet

Grated rind of 1/2 orange

Mix juices and lemon and orange rind. Let stand for one-half hour. Strain and pour into glasses or punch bowl over ice. In a punch bowl float dips of orange sherbet on top. If served in glasses top each drink with one generous scoop of orange sherbet. This punch has a tangy, fruit flavor, but if a sweeter punch is desired sugar may be added to taste.

Ocean Spray

1 cup warm water   Green food color

1 cup white corn syrup   1 large bottle ginger ale

1/2 cup fresh lemon juice   Minted ice cubes

1/2 teaspoon mint extract

Mix together water, corn syrup, lemon juice, mint extract and small amount of green food color (for very delicate green tint) and chill. When ready to serve add ginger ale. Into tall glasses put minted ice cubes and pour Ocean Spray punch over cubes. Makes about 6 servings.

Poor Man's Ale

1/2 cup sugar

1/2 cup water

1/2 cup fresh, frozen or bottled grape juice

1/4 cup orange juice

1 tablespoon lime juice

1 pint ginger ale, chilled

Orange slices

Cherries

Mix all juices and set aside. Boil sugar and water 5 minutes. Cool, and add to fruit juice. Chill for 2 hours at least. When ready to serve add ginger ale. Insert cherries in center of orange slices. Stack orange-cherry slice and ice cubes, alternating to top of glass. Pour beverage into glasses and serve.

Roman Coffee

2 1/2 cups strong, cold coffee

5 tablespoons chocolate syrup

1 pint coffee flavored ice cream

Combine all ingredients in a mixing bowl and beat with rotary beater or blender until smooth. Pour into tall glasses and serve. Makes 4 servings.

San Franciscan

1 quart orange sherbet

1 quart vanilla ice cream

2 tablespoons grated orange rind

1 quart orange juice

1 quart ginger ale

Orange slices

Combine orange juice with orange sherbet and vanilla ice cream; add orange rind. Mix with rotary beater or electric mixer. Lastly, add ginger ale. Mix again quickly and pour this smooth and frosty mixture into chilled glasses. Top with orange slices and serve immediately. Or if you choose to serve from a punch bowl, put a little ice in the bowl and be sure the bowl itself is chilled. Float orange slices on top.

South Seas

1/2 cup fresh lemon juice
2 1/2 cups pineapple juice
3/4 cup lime juice

1/2 cup confectioner's sugar
Ginger ale
Pineapple rings

Mix lemon, pineapple, and lime juice with sugar. Pour in even amounts into six ice-filled glasses. Fill with ginger ale and float a pineapple slice on top of each. Insert straws through pineapple ring and serve.

Texas Cooler

1 1/2 cups orange juice
1 cup grapefruit juice
2 tablespoons lemon juice

2 tablespoons light corn syrup
1 pint ginger ale
Mint and cherries

Blend orange, grapefruit and lemon juice. Add syrup and mix thoroughly. Make ice cubes with pieces of mint and cherries. Place ice cubes in glasses. Add ginger ale to fruit juices and pour mixture over ice. Serve immediately.

The Berry Patch

2 cups boiling water

1/4 cup loose tea

1 cup plain corn syrup

3 cups cold water

1 1/2 cups orange juice

3/4 cup lemon juice

1 1/2 cups sliced and sweetened
strawberries

1 (28 oz.) bottle ginger ale

Pour boiling water over tea leaves, and brew about 5 minutes. Stir, strain, and pour into corn syrup. When cool, add remaining ingredients. Pour into glasses which have been chilled, and filled with ice cubes. Strawberry ice cubes enhance this drink, or orange slices may be used for garnish.

Makes 3 quarts.

The Floridian

2 cups carbonated cola
beverage

4 bottles carbonated cola
beverage

2 limes

1 1/2 cups sugar

1 cup water

2 tablespoons white corn
syrup

1/4 teaspoon mint extract

1 tablespoon lime juice

Sprigs of mint

Pour two cups of cola beverage into a refrigerator tray. Remove when cola ice crystals are formed.

Mix together in saucepan with lid 1 1/2 cups sugar, 1 cup water and two tablespoons white corn syrup. Heat over medium flame for about 4 minutes, covered. Take cover off and boil 4 additional minutes. Set aside to cool; then add 1/4 teaspoon mint extract and lime juice. (This mint syrup may be refrigerated for long periods.) To mix The Floridian put 1/4 cup of cola ice crystals into four large glasses. Add about 3 tablespoons (more or less according to your own liking) of the mint syrup to each glass. Now fill with bottled cola beverage and juice of 1/2 lime. Stir thoroughly. Serve at once with large sprig of mint. Glasses may be frosted, or rims frosted by dipping into lime juice (about 1/4 inch), then in delicately tinted (green) granulated sugar. Refrigerate glasses to let decoration set. When mixing drinks pour and stir carefully.

Serves four.

The Menehune

1/2 cup sugar

2/3 cup water

2/3 cup unsweetened pineapple juice

2/3 cup fresh lemon juice

2 tablespoons fresh lime juice

2 unbeaten egg whites

4 cups finely crushed ice

Combine sugar with water and heat for ten minutes. Remove from heat and chill. Mix pineapple juice, lemon and lime juice together and add to syrup. Pour into shaker or blender. Last, add egg whites and ice. Shake or blend until smooth and creamy. Pour into frosted glasses and serve immediately. Garnish with mint sprigs threaded through pineapple chunks.

The Southern Colonel

2 cups raspberry jam

1 cup hot water

1/2 cup lemon juice

1 tablespoon lime juice

4 cups water

Lemon and lime slices

Raspberries, fresh or canned

Combine raspberry jam and hot water. Heat and stir for 10 minutes. Add lemon and lime juice, then water. If any lumps remain of unmelted raspberry jam, strain. Chill. Pour over ice into large glasses. Make a kabob of toothpicks with a lemon slice, a raspberry, a lime slice, another raspberry.

The Trader

2 cups diced ripe cantaloupe

1/4 cup sugar

2 tablespoons lime juice

1 tablespoon lemon juice

Few grains salt

1 12 oz. can pineapple-grapefruit drink, chilled

Combine cantaloupe, sugar, lime juice, lemon juice and salt in a blender. After blending thoroughly, chill. Then stir in the chilled fruit drink and pour over crushed ice in frosted glasses.

Serves 3.

The Wisconsin

2 cups milk, cold

8 oz. crushed pineapple

1 tablespoon pineapple preserves

1 scoop vanilla ice cream

2 tablespoons shredded coconut

Dash nutmeg

Whipping cream

Combine cold milk, pineapple and pineapple preserves with vanilla ice cream and shredded coconut. Blend in a blender or with a rotary beater until very smooth. Pour into chilled glasses. Top with whipping cream and dash of nutmeg. Serve at once.

Windsor Punch

2 sticks cinnamon

12 whole cloves

3 tablespoons loose tea

2 cups boiling water

1/2 cup sugar

2 cups grape juice

1/3 cup lemon juice

1 teaspoon grated lemon rind

1 teaspoon grated orange rind

1 quart ginger ale

Combine spices and tea in large pitcher and add boiling water. Brew uncovered about 10 minutes. Stir, strain and add sugar. Cool at room temperature. Add juices and grated rind. When ready to serve add ginger ale. Pour over block ice into a punch bowl.

Serves 8.

Tropic Pleasure

1/2 cup shredded coconut

1/2 cup water

1 3/4 cup milk, cold

1/2 cup cream, cold

6 oz. can frozen concentrated orange juice

1 tablespoon shredded coconut

Cherries

Combine orange juice, water and coconut in container (may be blended or whipped with rotary beater). Mix for several miutes until smooth. Add milk and cream. (May be strained if taste of coconut pieces is not desired). Mix thoroughly and pour into chilled glasses. Top with shredded coconut and two or three cherries.

The Christmas Cup

THE CHRISTMAS CUP

Apple cider	Cloves
Maple syrup	Cinnamon
Lemon	Butter

Place apple cider in a kettle or chafing dish and for each cup of cider add one teaspoon maple syrup, three drops of lemon juice, powdered cloves and cinnamon to taste. Allow mixture to boil and serve hot in mugs. Garnish each cup with thin slice of lemon and a small pat of butter. If stick cloves are used, two per cup is desirable.

California Steamer

1 cup water	1 1/2 cups apricot nectar
2 tablespoons sugar	2 tablespoons lemon juice
4 whole cloves	2 tablespoons orange juice
1 stick cinnamon	2 teaspoons crushed mint
1 tablespoon brown sugar	

Cook water and sugar over low flame until sugar is dissolved. Add spices and simmer about 10 minutes. Combine apricot nectar, brown sugar, lemon juice and orange juice and add to syrup. Blend thoroughly and heat thoroughly. Pour over mint and let stand about 3 minutes. Strain into cups or mugs and serve hot. Punch may be reheated, but do not boil.

German Mocha

1 1/2 teaspoons instant coffee
dissolved in 1 cup warm
water, or extra-strength
brewed coffee

Rich milk

Whipping Cream

Add rich milk to extra-strong coffee. Stir and add whipping cream drifts to float on top. Serve from cups or mugs. Serves one.

Good Friend's Cup of Cheer

3 cups cranberry juice

1 cup water

1/2 cup grapefruit juice

1/2 cup sugar

1 stick cinnamon

8 whole cloves

3/4 teaspoon nutmeg

Orange peel, cut in thin strips
and twisted

Lemon peel, cut in thin strips
and twisted

Combine all ingredients in a kettle and simmer about 30 minutes. Strain and pour into mugs or cups. Replace orange and lemon peel for garnish.

Good Neighbor Punch

1 quart cider (apple)

1 cup dried apricots

Juice of one lemon

1/4 teaspoon nutmeg

Pinch of salt

6 whole cloves for garnish

1 cup prunes

2 tablespoons sugar

1/4 teaspoon cinnamon

Dash cloves

6 lemon slices

Wash apricots and prunes and dry. Combine fruit with cider in a kettle and heat to boiling. Lower heat and simmer for 30 minutes or until fruit is tender. Add sugar, lemon juice, spices and salt. With lemon slice and a whole clove for garnish, serve hot. If punch is too thick a little more heated cider may be added.

Hot 'n Hearty

1/2 cup grape juice   **Ginger**

1/2 cup orange juice   **1 egg white**

Cinnamon

Combine juices and heat in saucepan. Add dash of cinnamon and ginger to taste. Beat egg white until stiff and top heated juice. Serve in mugs or cups, which have been warmed.

1/2 cup pineapple juice   **Nutmeg**

1/2 cup peach juice   **1 egg white**

 1 drop almond flavoring

Combine juices and heat in sauce pan. Add almond flavoring and nutmeg to taste. Beat egg white until stiff and top heated juice. Serve in cups or mugs which have been warmed.

Hot Jungle Punch

2 cups grapefruit juice   1/4 cup lemon juice

1 cup orange juice   1 tablespoon light corn syrup

Combine fruit juices and corn syrup in a saucepan. Heat to just below boiling point. Serve steaming with a cinnamon stick.

Hot Spiced Cider

1 teaspoon cinnamon	2/3 cup brown sugar
12 whole cloves	Nutmeg
1 teaspoon allspice	Apples quartered
2 quarts cider	Swizzle sticks, or toothpicks

Tie spices in cheesecloth to make spice bag. Combine cider, brown sugar in a saucepan and heat. Place spice bag in cider and cook over medium to low flame 10 minutes (longer if a spicier taste is wanted). Remove spice bag and serve very hot in cups or mugs. Dash nutmeg on small pieces of apples on a swizzle stick or toothpick, and float on top of Hot Spiced Cider.

Nocturnal Cup

1 pot hot coffee	Whipping cream
1 pot hot chocolate	Shaved French Chocolate

Combine equal portions of hot coffee and hot chocolate in warmed mugs. Top with whipping cream which has been sweetened. Use shaved French chocolate pieces for garnish.

Skier's Warm Up

1 cup brown sugar

1 1/4 cups water

1/4 teaspoon salt

1/4 teaspoon nutmeg

1/2 teaspoon cinnamon

1/4 teaspoon allspice

1/2 teaspoon cloves

1/4 cup raisins

1 quart pineapple juice

2 cups jellied cranberry sauce

3 tablespoons lemon juice

3 cups water

Cinnamon sticks

Pineapple chunks

Mix brown sugar and spices, salt and one cup water. Heat to boiling point. With a fork or rotary beater mash cranberry sauce to smooth consistency. Mix pineapple juice, water, lemon juice and add to cranberry sauce. Add raisins and mix with spiced syrup. Heat again and serve very hot in cups garnished with a cinnamon stick stuck through a pineapple chunk.

Spiced Hot Chocolate

3/4 cup sugar

2/3 cup cocoa

1 cup water

1/4 teaspoon cinnamon

1/4 teaspoon salt

2 quarts milk, heated

1 quart cream, heated

1 teaspoon vanilla

Marshmallows

Mix first five ingredients. Add to heated milk and cream. Stir thoroughly. Place over medium flame and cook until mixture comes to a boil. Remove from flame and add vanilla. With a rotary beater, whip Spiced Hot Chocolate until frothy. Pour immediately into warmed mugs. Top each serving with large marshmallows.

Serves 16.

Spicy & Hot

1 quart water	1 stick cinnamon
1/2 cup sugar	1/2 cup orange juice
8 cloves	1 cup lemon juice

Mix water and sugar, heat to boiling, stirring until sugar is dissolved. Cover saucepan and boil 2 minutes. Add cinnamon and cloves and continue to cook for about 6 additional minutes. Add juices to this spiced syrup. Let stand few minutes, then remove cloves and cinnamon. Serve warm. This mixture can be reheated, but do not boil again.

Thoughts of Health

I have frequently mentioned on television that "We are what we eat". We are also what we drink.

The Atlas Drink

1 fully ripe banana	3 tablespoons vanilla ice cream
1 cup COLD milk	1/4 teaspoon vanilla

Peel banana. Mash in a bowl. Beat with rotary egg beater, electric mixer or blender until smooth and creamy. Add milk, ice cream and vanilla; mix well. Pour into glasses. Sprinkle nutmeg and cinnamon on top and serve immediately. Makes 1 or 2 medium-size drinks.

*For a delicious Banana-Nut drink, add 2 tablespoons chopped pecans to above recipe.

Bright Night

1 ripe banana mashed

Juice of one small orange

Scoop vanilla ice cream

1 cup cranberry juice (bottled)

Dash of nutmeg

Combine orange juice and cranberry juice and beat with mashed banana. Add ice cream and beat until creamy and smooth. Pour into tall, chilled glass and add a dash of nutmeg.

Dairy Treat

2 eggs

2 cups cold milk

Dash of Salt

4 teaspoons molasses

Nutmeg

Beat egg yolks, add molasses and mix until smooth and thick. Add milk and nutmeg to taste. Beat egg whites stiff; fold in. Sprinkle top with nutmeg for added color. Serve immediately in chilled glasses.

Two servings.

New Orleans Evening

2 cups milk

8 oz. pineapple tidbits

1 scoop vanilla ice cream

2 egg whites, beaten stiff

1/4 teaspoon vanilla

2 teaspoons sugar

Combine milk, pineapple tidbits and vanilla ice cream in a blender or beat with rotary beater until smooth. Beat egg whites until stiff and combine with vanilla and sugar. Beat to form peaks. Pour pineapple-ice cream mix in chilled glass and top with egg whites making large peaks.

Spiced Heaven

1 pint orange juice

1/2 pound sugar

4 eggs, beaten

1 tablespoon nutmeg

1 pint milk

1 teaspoon soda

1/2 tablespoon grated orange rind

Dash salt

Mix juice and sugar. Cook over low heat. Add orange rind and salt, soda and nutmeg to milk, then beaten eggs. Combine two mixtures. Serve in chilled glasses with a little ice. Scoop of vanilla ice cream or orange sherbet may be added if desired.

Sis's Toddy

2 heaping teaspoons brown sugar

1/4 cup orange juice, chilled

1 cup buttermilk, cold (no butter flakes)

1 scoop orange sherbet

Mix all ingredients together until smooth. Pour into chilled glasses. Makes one large or two medium servings.

Taste & See

2 eggs

1/2 cup cold water

6 tablespoons fresh lemon juice

1/2 cup granulated sugar

2 teaspoons grated lemon rind

3 cups cold milk

Beat eggs. Add water, lemon juice, sugar, and lemon rind. Mix well. Add milk, a cup at a time, to lemon mixture. Beat vigorously.

Serves four.

Why Not?

1/3 cup chilled orange juice

6 oz. cooked, strained prunes

1 cup cold milk

Dash salt

1 teaspoon fresh lemon juice

1 teaspoon sugar

1 teaspoon brown sugar, light

1 scoop vanilla ice cream

Mix first three items, then add salt, lemon juice and sugars. Blend with egg beater and add ice cream. Serve in cool glasses (four servings) and top with a cherry or a twist of lemon peel.

For Weight Watchers

Drink and Smile

1 cup water

1 tablespoon Sucaryl solution

1/4 cup chopped mint leaves

1/2 cup lemon juice

1/2 cup unsweetened pineapple tidbits

1 cup orange juice

1 quart orange beverage (artificially sweetened)

Crushed ice

Mint sprigs

Mix water, sweetener and mint leaves in a saucepan. Bring to boil, strain and cool. Add lemon juice, pineapple tidbits, and orange juice. Mix well and add orange beverage. Place crushed ice in tall glasses and pour Drink And Smile over ice. Serve with sprig of mint dusted in powdered sugar. 8 servings.

Fat Man's Favorite

Juice of one lemon

Water, cold

Grape juice, chilled

1 egg white

1 teaspoon sugar

1/4 teaspoon vanilla

Place juice of lemon in glass. Add enough water to fill 2/3 full. Fill with grape juice. Beat egg white, adding sugar and vanilla. Whip into Fat Man's Favorite and serve immediately.

Dieter's Delight

2 cups ice water

1/3 cup nonfat dry milk powder

2 tablespoons strawberry gelatin powder

1/2 cup fresh, washed and hulled strawberries (if you are not using a blender, slice strawberries thinly).

Combine all ingredients in a blender or bowl. Beat vigorously until smooth. Pour into chilled glass. Garnish with two or three fresh strawberries.

No-Cal Tonic

1 cup instant nonfat dry milk

1 scoop lemon sherbet

1/8 teaspoon lemon rind, or 2 drops lemon extract

2 drops artificial sweetener

Cherries, drained

Follow brand directions for mixing one cup milk from nonfat dry milk. Add lemon sherbet, lemon rind or extract and artficial sweetener Whip in blender or with egg beater. Serve immediately. Add two or three cherries for garnish.

Sunny Day

1 cup apple cider

Juice of 1/2 lemon

3 drops artificial sweetener

1/4 teaspoon cinnamon

3 tablespoons water

Mix all ingredients and place in refrigerator tray. Freeze to mushy consistency. Remove, place in bowl and beat until smooth. Serve immediately. Garnish with mint.

Festive Bowls

(For Large Groups)

Thirsty 65

4 cups water

8 cups sugar

7 cups lemon juice

4 cups crushed pineapple

1 cup orange juice

1 cup weak tea

3 gallons water

Crushed ice

Orange slices

Lemon slices

Green and red Maraschino cherries

Boil 4 cups water and 8 cups sugar for 10 minutes and cool. Add lemon juice, pineapple, orange juice and weak tea. Mix and add remaining water. Pour into punch bowl over crushed ice. Make kabobs of one slice orange, a green cherry, a lemon slice and a red cherry on top threaded on small swizzle sticks or toothpicks. Decorate punch bowl with ivy or garden greens arranged around sides, and daisies or gardenias placed in front and back of serving bowl. Dip lemonade into cups or glasses, topping each one with a kabob from the punch bowl. Have an extra supply to replenish decoration.

(This lemonade is a little strong to allow for melting ice during time of serving. More water may be added in the beginning if necessary.) Serves about 65 .

The Wedding Party

1/2 cup sugar

1 cup water

6 oz. can frozen lemon juice

6 oz. can frozen orange-
pineapple juice

1 quart white grape juice

1 quart ginger ale

Small jar Maraschino cherries
and juice

1 pint lemon sherbet

1 pint pineapple sherbet

Orange slices

Cherries

Heat sugar and water until dissolved into a syrup. Cool. Add fruit juices, ginger ale, grape juice, and jar of cherries (and juice) to syrup. Mix well and pour into punch bowl. Add ice cubes. Top orange slices with lemon and lime sherbet dips, then top sherbet with a cherry. Add remaining sherbet to punch mixture. Float orange slices with sherbet on surface of punch. Serves about 25.

When The Crowd Gathers

1 pound all-purpose coffee grind

6 to 8 quarts water (depending
on strength desired)

Cheesecloth bag

Wrap coffee in a cheesecloth bag almost twice the size of coffee grind to allow for expansion. Have a large kettle filled with boiling water. Let coffee bag down into water, moving up and down several times to be sure of full flavor. Leave coffee this way for about 10 to 15 minutes in a warm place. Before serving time, remove coffee bag and cover kettle to keep hot until serving. Serve as soon as possible. Makes about 35 to 45 cups of coffee.

Household Helps

You can make fancy little butter, or margarine swirls, dots, or edging for muffins, toast or patty shells with a pastry tube. Just fill the pastry tube with butter, hold the cylinder in your hand for a minute or two to soften butter a little and design away. Especially pretty for entertaining.

A little vinegar will soften glue that's hardened in the bottle.

Remove stains from plastic dishes by soaking them in a dishpan of water containing 2 tablespoons of household bleach. Soak them in your plastic dishpan and get it spotless too.

You can seal cellophane freezer bags with an old fashioned curling iron.

Clean combs and brushes in a solution of 1 teaspoon of ammonia to a tall glass of water. Let soak a while, then rinse. They are sparkling clean.

Here are two ways to make boiled icing that will stand the lunchbox test. After icing is stiff, beat in two tablespoons of any flavored gelatin powder while the icing is still warm. Plain gelatin can be used, but first dissolve it in a little liquid before adding to the frosting.
Second way: After icing is stiff, add two or more tablespoons of powdered sugar.

A little cayenne pepper sprinkled on objects you don't want your dog to bother will discourage him . . . for good!

Easy fire starter is a candle stub. If you have a fireplace, then save all candle stubs for this use. Place it so that the candlewax drips over the kindling. Usually, one stub will start a fire and this works even if the kindling is damp.

A little olive oil will remove a piece of paper that stubbornly sticks to a polished table top. Rub it on and remove the stuck paper.

Use shampoo for stubborn collar dirt, apply and rub prior to washing. Shampoo is, of course, especially compounded to dissolve body oils from hair, and works equally as well on clothes. Good also for perspiration spots.

To frost grapes, dip clusters in egg white, then in granulated sugar and chill. Delicious as appetizers and decorative too.

If you want to frost window glass, you can do it this way: Mix epsom salts with varnish. Form a thin paste and apply to the glass surface.

Small frozen juice cans or small soup cans are excellent for storing refrigerator cookie dough. The ends may be saved to push the dough out.

For a teething baby, try actually freezing the teething ring. The cold ring is soothing to irritated gums. One of the special teething rings which are full of liquid can be purchased and frozen before use.

Kitchen check-up. Keep ready to eat foods like crackers, cereals, jellies, cookies in the cabinet nearest the dining area. Make use of trays. A few place settings of flatware and dishes to save time in setting the table — especially useful for the breakfast rush. Do you have an outlet near the cabinet where you store your mixer? An outlet near where you keep your toaster? Do you have clean dish towels in a drawer next to the sink so you won't have to dash across the kitchen with dripping hands? Same idea for paper towels. All of these little details give you efficiency and convenience which saves work time in the kitchen.

To keep white collar and cuffs or other white trim on girls' and women's dresses really white, dip a small toothbrush in bleach solution (diluted, of course) and brush-rub over the white parts just before laundering dresses, blouses or jackets. Takes only a few extra minutes, but the fresh, new look is worth it. They'll also stay pretty much longer.

If you have floor-length curtains or drapes, vacuuming and cleaning around them is hard to accomplish without lifting them up. Try sewing a snap at the bottom of each corner and a snap-mate about halfway up (on back of the curtain). Then when you are cleaning, simply snap them up and out of the way of your vacuum or mop.

For the small fry: A child can handle a small sponge better than a wash cloth for bath or hands and face clean-up detail. For the child who is not really interested in eating, experiment with outlining **his own initials** on the food you serve him — puddings, cereal, bread, etc. Makes the food "especially for him."

Use flea powder to get rid of ants. It works well and flea powder won't harm your pets. Might help them!

Getting in a rut? Serving the same old breakfast juices to your family? Try some mix and match combinations such as these: Grapefruit and cranberry juice, half and half; pineapple and apricot juice (half and half); to orange juice add snipped mint leaves and a tablespoon of crushed pineapple; a small scoop of vanilla ice cream in a glass of Shurfine grape juice offers them an intriguing treat for the taste buds.

If you have a key that is stubborn about working smoothly, rub its edges with a soft lead pencil.

A little talcum powder sprinkled on shelves prevents sticking.

Pour a little cold water over egg yolks to preserve them. Refrigerate. They stay fresh a long time, sealed with water.

The easiest way to make an aluminum foil liner for a baking dish or pan is to shape the foil over the outside of the inverted pan and then fit the foil inside.

An apple corer makes a good garden tool for small weeds. Digs down deep enough to get to roots and will not disturb roots of valuable plants. Also good for planting small plants or transplanting young sprouts.

Short on eggs? Right in the middle of a recipe, or at breakfast-time? One tablespoon of very cold water added to one egg white makes about twice the volume — taking the place of an extra egg white. A little water can be added to scrambled eggs instead of milk. Whip until frothy. Eggs will be light and tender and volume is also increased by the same method.

Paint the handles of your garden tools to prevent slivers of wood from sticking in your hands. Paint is a protection for the tool handles too. If you use bright colors, tools are easily spotted in the garden or store-room.

For a sick child, make a bed table by taking a cardboard box and cutting it out to fit over the knees. Makes a good work table to use in bed.

EASY MEAT LOAF: 1 pound ground beef, 1 cup corn flakes, 1 can of chicken soup with rice. Mix together. Bake in a greased casserole for 45 minutes.

Planning a cookout? Rub a cake of soap over the bottom of your pots and pans before you use them in an open fire. After cooking, when water is applied at clean-up time the soot and stains wash away in the soapy suds.

Since there is a wide difference in individual preference for salt, many recipes state simply: "salt to taste" — but if you prefer more specific instructions, here is a chart for general salting portions:

Fish	1/2 tsp. per pound
Meat with bone	1/2 tsp. per pound
Meat without bone	1 tsp. per pound
Potatoes	1 tsp. per qt. of water
Spaghetti, macaroni, noodles	1 tsp. per qt. of water
Fresh vegetables	1/4 tsp. per cup of water
Frozen vegetables	follow directions on package
Canned vegetables	already salted, adjust to taste
Salad vegetables	need no salting as salt is in the dressing

For economy's sake, you can use bacon, sausage, or ham fat from left-over grease can in the place of shortening when you make biscuits or breads. It will work, and you'll get some interesting different flavors.

To store dishes easily, which you don't use often, stack them with paper plates in between. This keeps them free of dust and protects them from scratches.

Put a little liquid wax in your woodwork cleaning water. The wax will protect the walls twice as long and make them shine bright.

Think ahead. Try emptying your vacuum cleaner bag before you start to vacuum. If any of the dirt and fuzz is spilled, you're right on the spot ready to clean it up.

Extra easy, extra quick dessert. Freeze a can of Shurfine applesauce. Open both ends of can and slide out. Slice frozen applesauce and serve. Good plain, or can be topped with sour cream, ice cream or whipping cream and a cherry on top!

Another troubling household problem are casters which won't roll . . . Lubricate them with castor oil. Castor oil will preserve the rubber while other solutions will often rot the rubber.

Use adhesive tape to wrap around the screws inside drawers to keep them from tearing dainty underclothing and nylon hose when they are taken from the drawer.

To save paint mess-up, glue a paper plate to the bottom of your paint can. keeps from dripping on the floor and is an additional help of providing a place to lay the paint brush.

How to frost glasses for appealing cold drinks. Place glasses in very hot water and leave them until they have absorbed quite a bit of heat. Then, without drying, place them in the refrigerator and leave them for 3 or 4 hours or overnight if possible. They will have a pretty frost which will enhance your cold drinks.

Give the dresses and blouses hanging in your closet a dress-up treat — make padded dress hangers by using straight wooden hangers, paper toweling and bright silk, velvet, or satin ribbon. Fold the paper toweling into 1-inch strips and cover by wrapping tightly with several layers of the toweling. Overlap the edges so there will be no spaces between the strips. Then secure the paper padding to the wooden hanger by wrapping rather tightly with gay ribbon. Fasten the ends of the ribbon by sewing it to the toweling and tucking the edges under so they won't ravel.

About storing cheese. Cream cheese cannot be frozen with good results. It gets lumpy and sometimes grainy. Exception would be when mixed with certain other ingredients, but this cannot be counted on. Grated cheese loses its flavor fast, so grate cheese as needed. If you have left-over cheese which has been grated, place it in an air-tight container and store in the refrigerator as soon as possible.

Tempt the kiddies to drink their milk. Tint it pink with a few drops of red food coloring.

To peel peaches quickly. Dip them in simmering water. Hold them there for about one minute. Then dip into cold water and the skins will slip off easily.

To get the whole meat out of pecans, put them in boiling water for a few minutes. Remove from heat and let stand for about 10 minutes. Crack each end of the nut and the meat will slide out without breaking.

To remove discoloration on china. Add a little soap to the dishrag and then dip it in baking soda. Rub over the spots and they will vanish.

Choosing oranges. For beauty, sections, slices, etc., buy the thick-skinned oranges. (They are light for their size. If you want oranges for juice, buy the thin-skinned oranges. (They are heavy for their size.)

If you are growing plants in water, try putting a piece of charcoal in the water. Keeps water from becoming stagnant.

What causes egg whites not to beat up properly? One of two reasons: Yolk in the whites, or grease in the bowl or on the beaters. Eggs will beat up better and more quickly if they are at room temperature when beaten.

Hate to chop up an onion just to get the 1 tablespoon your recipe calls for? Why not do it all at one time. Chop several onions in a chopper, grinder, or the old-fashioned chop by knife method. Measure by tablespoons into individual plastic bags, label the amount inside each bag and freeze them. Then when you need a tablespoon or two or three, they are ready for use. All the mess is over with.

An attractive centerpiece can be made in a hurry from items you already have around your house. Take three or five (odd numbers are the easiest to arrange) sherbet glasses, goblets, or parfait glasses and fill them with celery or carrot sticks, olives, pickles, salted peanuts or popcorn. Place them on a colorful place mat or napkin. Cut the stems from three or four artificial flowers and scatter the flowers between the glasses. You have a pretty center piece which looks like it was planned without hurry and make-dos.

Shaping croquettes is easy if you'll use a lightly greased one-half cup measuring utensil.

Make yourself a nice belt hanger. Take a wooden hanger and screw cup hooks into both sides. Be sure to leave enough space in between the hooks for the belts.

It may come as a surprise to you that bones are not nutrition for dogs. The only food value they have is a little calcium. What bones do for a dog is develop his jaw power, his bite, and clean his teeth and breath. Always give your dogs a large bone to chew whether he is large or small, because small bones splinter and may cause stomach damage. Never feed him chicken, fish, or rabbit bones, either.

Index

A

B

281

R

S

300

T

U

V

Vegetables: